Constant

Constant playing the guitar in his studio,
surrounded by his Space Sculptures, 1958
photo: Aart Klein

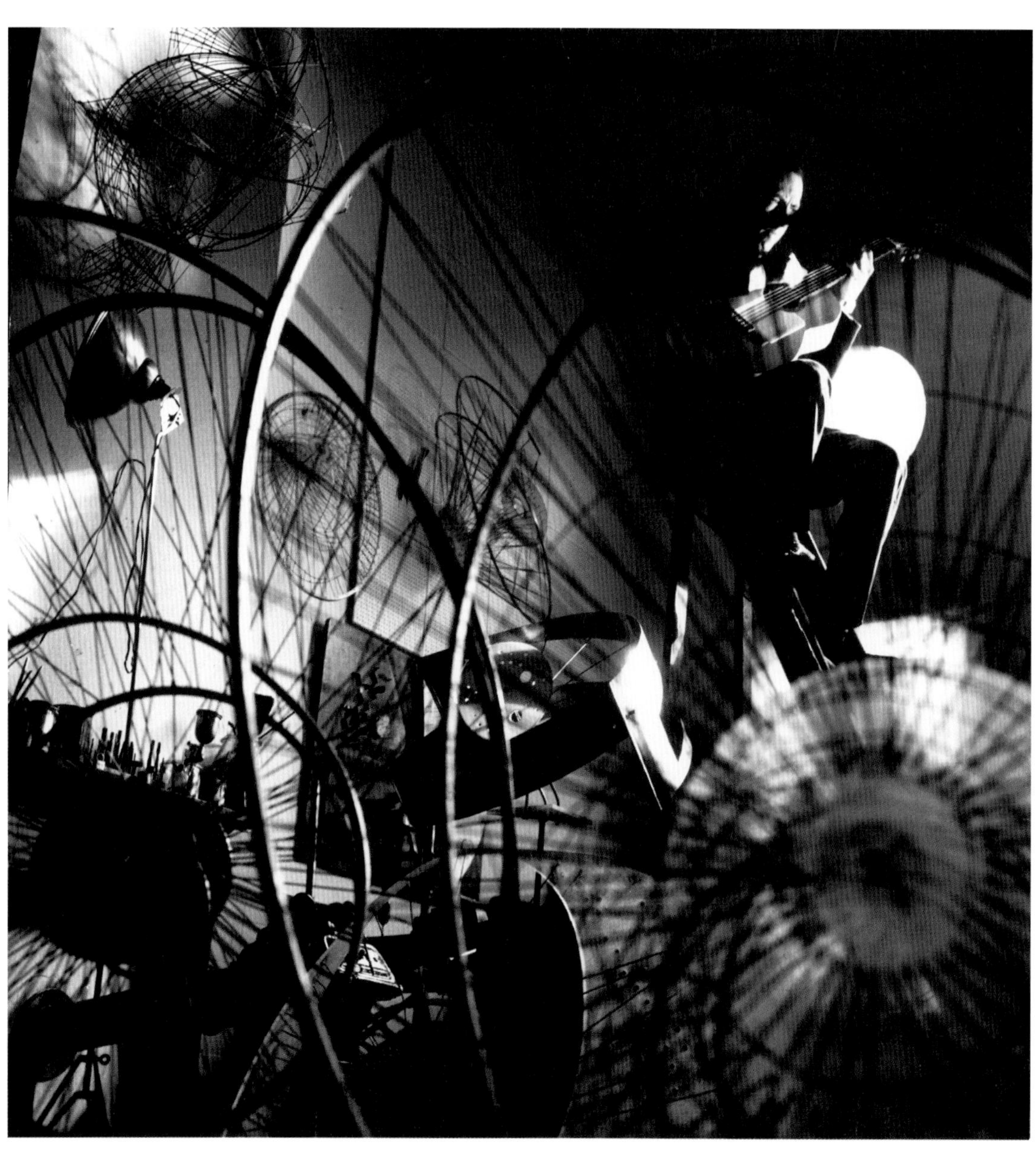

from Cobra to New Babylon

CONSTANT

SPACE × COLOUR

Cobra Museum nai010 publishers

Constant in his studio, c. 1957
collection Fondation Constant

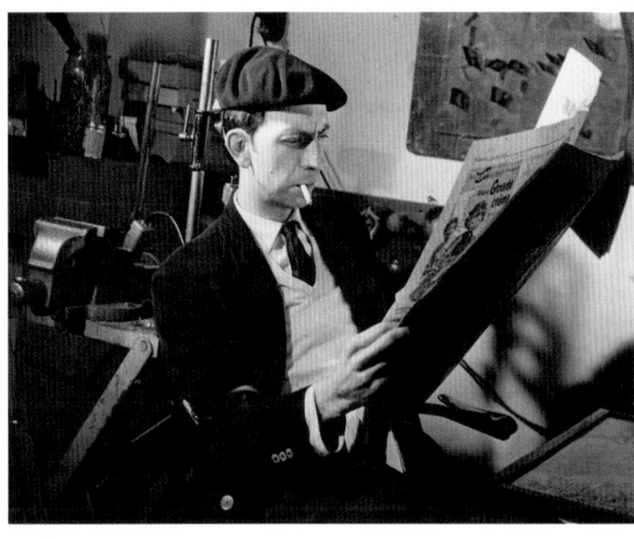

Contents

After Us, Liberty

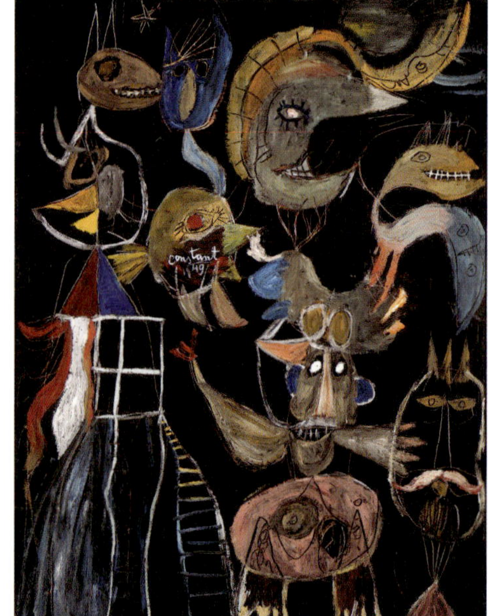

Après nous la liberté (After Us, Liberty), 1949
oil on linen, 139.5 x 107 cm
collection Tate Modern. London

Constant Nieuwenhuys (1920-2005) is known as the co-founder of the international Cobra group and as the initiator and maker of the *New Babylon* project. This publication and the eponymous exhibition add a third influential chapter to Constant's artistic practice: the 1950s. At this time, Constant's work underwent a radical transformation. The path he followed from Cobra to *New Babylon* was crucial to his development as a visual artist, yet this evolution has never before been the main subject of a museum presentation.

One of the highlights of the collection of London's Tate Modern is Constant's painting *Après nous la liberté* (After Us, Liberty), in which a playful grouping of fantastical creatures is set against a black background. The painting is dominated by the blue-white-red of the *tricolore*, the French flag: a reference to the values of liberty, equality and fraternity. Constant connected the experimental spirit of Cobra to the liberation of human creativity and the flourishing of a new people's art. It is significant that he altered the title of the painting after the dissolution of Cobra in late 1951. Of the various titles under which the work had been presented over the course of 1949 – *Hoera, de bourgeoisie, À nous la liberté, Après nous la liberté* – Constant chose the last. The pugnacity emanating from this title is characteristic of his work and ideas during this period, according to Marcel Hummelink in his book *Constant en de artistieke avant-garde in de jaren 1946-1960* (Constant and the artistic avant-garde from 1946 to 1960).

The title *Après nous la Liberté* is of significance in explaining Constant's work and ideas from a present-day perspective. His legacy is a source of inspiration and reference for an international community of art historians, curators, collectors, artists and architects. Constant always demanded liberty in order to provide, as a visual artist, a radical and visionary interpretation of the reconstruction of post-war Europe. He sought liberty by pushing – and transgressing – the boundaries of society. As a result of this attitude he was constantly expanding the boundaries of his own artistic practice. The fantasy figures of Cobra were followed by abstract painting, an exploration of a 'synthesis of the arts', a study into the effects of space and colour, a transition from the two-dimensional to the three-dimensional plane, the *New Babylon* project, and ultimately a return to the essence of the art of painting with the 'colorist experiments', from 1969 until his death in 2005. This evolution is chronicled in Trudy van der Horst's outstanding biography.

During the 1950s, Constant explored new domains of work as well as new media. In his illuminating essay, Ludo van Halem sketches a portrait of an artist trying to redefine his position by forging practical and theoretical alliances with a series of different artists. For instance, Constant collaborated with the architect Aldo van Eyck (1918-1999) on *een ruimte in kleur* (A Space in Colour) for the exhibition 'Mens en Huis' (Man and home) at the Stedelijk Museum in Amsterdam in 1952. He joined Gerrit Rietveld (1888-1964) in producing a model interior for the 'Kleurenharmonie in uw woning' (Colour harmony in your home) event at the Bijenkorf department store in 1954. And he made the film *Gyromorphosis* (1958) with the American filmmaker Hy Hirsch (1911-1961), shown at his first solo exhibition of constructions and models at the Stedelijk Museum in 1959. *Constant. Space+Colour* contains a treasure trove of hitherto unpublished material connected with these experiments and alliances. Reconstructions of the collaboration with both architects and of his first solo exhibition have been produced especially for the exhibition at the Cobra Museum. The contribution by Ludo van Halem and Laura Stamps, contemporary art curator at the Gemeentemuseum Den Haag in The Hague, deals with the art history research that formed the basis for the reconstructions.

The voice of the artist himself resonates through this publication in the form of a selection of texts he wrote during this specific period. They provide a glimpse into the radical transformation he was undergoing.

The idea to designate the years between the end of Cobra and the beginning of *New Babylon* as a decisive period in Constant's development arose in 2010, in a dialogue between the Cobra Museum and Trudy Nieuwenhuys-van der Horst. The museum considers it part of its remit to cast a critical eye over the recording of art history and, where necessary, to offer a broader perspective.

As an expert in Dutch modern art and in Constant's work in particular, Ludo van Halem, twentieth-century art curator at the Rijksmuseum in Amsterdam, was the ideal guest curator. Since the early 1990s he had been exchanging ideas with Marcel Hummelink on an exhibition devoted to the 1950s. Trudy Nieuwenhuys-van der Horst, as co-curator and head of research at the Fondation Constant, has been of immeasurable value to the success of this project. Hilde de Bruijn, curator at the Cobra Museum, and Kim van der Horst, manager of the Fondation Constant, provided vital support in creating the exhibition.

In the spirit of Constant, the Gemeentemuseum Den Haag, which manages the largest museum collection of *New Babylon* works, the Cobra Museum and the Fondation Constant worked in collaboration. Two concurrent exhibitions have created a unique momentum around this multifaceted visual artist.

Renowned architect and kindred spirit Ben van Berkel, with his UNStudio team, produced a contemporary exhibition design for the Cobra Museum, which does perfect justice to Constant's body of thought.

The Cobra Museum is honoured to be able, in cooperation with these partners, to shed new light on the current significance of the legacy of one of the most important artists of the twentieth century. This ambitious project was made possible through the support of the Municipality of Amstelveen, BankGiro Loterij, Business Club Cobra Museum, Mondriaan Fonds, Prowinko Nederland BV and Forbo Flooring. Finally, our thanks go to designer Lex Reitsma and Barbera van Kooij of nai010 publishers without whose efforts this publication would not have seen the light of day.

Katja Weitering
Artistic director

Els Ottenhof
Executive director

Constant. Space + Colour

From Cobra to New Babylon

Ludo van Halem

It must have been a unique experience for an artist used to oil paints, gouache and chalk to suddenly have in his hands something that did not resemble those familiar, proven artist's materials in any way whatsoever. Acrylic, or more formally polymethylmethacrylate, could be sawn or drilled through, it could be reshaped when heated and it could be glued, but there was not much more you could do to this artificial glass. The material was developed in 1928 and marketed by the American chemicals company Rohm and Haas under the brand name Plexiglas.[1] In the post-war Netherlands, where shortages were still the rule in many areas, it must initially have been a relatively rare material, difficult to obtain.

In 1954 Constant used this unusual material to create a number of sculptures.[2] Each consists of metal frames into which clear or coloured acrylic panels have been inserted. These panels are flat or curved, sawn into various geometric forms, sometimes perforated, and secured to the frame by metal spokes and nuts. The edges of the material seem to light up, and if one walks around one of these structures, one sees a series of different compositions of clear or coloured planes and light and dark lines that move across and through one another. Analogous to the common term 'composition' for non-representational paintings, Constant used the building term 'construction' for these pieces. Only a few of these first constructions from 1954 are known [fig. 1]. Several ended up in the collections of international museums,[3] others were destroyed or later reused as part of a different construction.[4]

In the years before 1954 the painter Constant had only rarely produced three-dimensional work, yet now he was suddenly creating various abstract three-dimensional compositions of geometric forms, and in a new material that was still highly unusual in sculpture.[5] Prior to the Second World War, only a few pioneers had worked with acrylic or other transparent plastics, among them Naum Gabo and László Moholy-Nagy. In the Dutch sculpture of the early 1950s, in any event, acrylic as a material was an unprecedented novelty. The retrospective book *Nederlandse beeldhouwers van deze tijd* (Contemporary Dutch sculptors), published by Theo van Reijn in 1949, contains not a single exception to the use of such traditional materials as plaster, clay, bronze, stone and wood, while innovative members of Constant's generation such as his friends Carel Visser and Shinkichi Tajiri were mainly working with iron at the time.

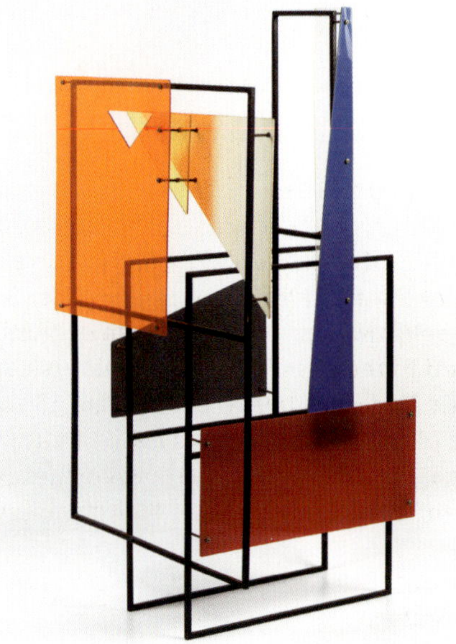

[1] *Constructie met gekleurde vlakken* (Construction with Coloured Planes), 1954
Plexiglas and black steel, 119.5 x 62 x 57.2 cm
collection Fondation Constant, long-term loan to the Stedelijk Museum Schiedam

Misery

Constant's use of materials in 1954 was indeed exceptional, and probably even unique, for the Netherlands. This held true not only for his three-dimensional work but also for his graphics. He may have been the first, in 1953, to produce graphics using silk-screen in the Netherlands, using equipment handed down by his friend, Schiedam printer Goos Verweij.[6] But there was also a radically new choice of a visual idiom that seemed to contradict the primitivist figuration he had so fiercely championed a short time before, the art which, under the banner of the Experimental Group in Holland and Cobra, had ignited quite a few controversies and of which he was one of the most talented and prominent practitioners. After all, had Constant, in his defence of this art, not explicitly turned against geometric abstraction? Had he not written, 'We must soil the virginal purity of Mondrian, be it merely with our misery', a bold statement that would later be quoted multiple times?[7]

Initially Constant himself seemed to abide by his words. Whereas at the first exhibition of the Cobra movement in 1949 at the Stedelijk Museum in Amsterdam he had shown paintings full of fantasy, populated by anthropomorphized animals and zoomorphized humans, at the movement's second and last exhibition at the Palais des Beaux Arts in Liège in 1951 he showed a series of five paintings all bearing the title *La guerre* (War).[8] And indeed these paintings showed nothing but misery: scorched landscapes, buildings on fire, twisted wheels, bodies ripped apart, people screaming with terror, their hands outstretched in desperation.

So incisive and direct a representation of fear, pain and the sufferings of war was anything but common in Dutch art in the first five years following the end of the Second World War. At the first major exhibition, 'Kunst in vrijheid' (Art in liberty), held after the Liberation at the Rijksmuseum in 1945, hardly any paintings or sculptures took the just-ended war as a subject. The art produced in 'liberty' – by artists who had not given in to the requirement to register with the German occupier's Chamber of Culture – consisted mainly of more or less traditional still-lifes, landscapes, portraits and figure studies. No attempt was yet being made, so soon after the Liberation, to represent the unimaginable human tragedies precipitated by the war.[9] The explanation offered by the art critic Jan Engelman was that 'mature works, in which the most profound things are said, are not usually created in the midst of crisis'.[10]

One work of art in the Netherlands, however, generated a different perception. Shortly before the Experimental Group in Holland was founded and held its first collective exhibition at the Bijenkorf department store in Amsterdam, the Stedelijk Museum organized an exhibition devoted to the popular French-Belarussian artist Ossip Zadkine (1890-1967). Of the 56 sculptures, one plaster statue of a figure, its mouth stretched open, raising its arms to the heavens, caught the attention of Gerrit van der Wal, the Bijenkorf's

1 See en.wikipedia.org/wiki/Poly(methyl_methacrylate). Plexiglas is now sold by Altuglas International (subsidiary of Arkema). Plexiglas (ICI) and Lucite (DuPont) are also commonly used brand names.

2 It is not know which brand(s) Constant used. He obtained the material from Van Buseck Kunststoffen on the Windroosplein in Amsterdam (information provided by Trudy Nieuwenhuys-van der Horst based on interviews with Constant). This firm was founded in 1952.

3 There are two different *Constructies met doorzichtige vlakken* (Constructions with Transparent Planes) from 1954, in the Kaiser Wilhelm Museum in Krefeld (*Untitled*) and in the Museu d'Art Contemporani de Barcelona (*Construction aux plans transparents*), as well as a *Constructie met gebogen vlakken* (Construction with Curved Planes) at the FRAC Centre in Orléans. *Constructie met gekleurde vlakken* (Construction with Coloured Planes) (also known as *Constructie met rechthoekige vlakken* [Construction with Rectangular Planes]) is on long-term loan from the Constant Foundation at the Stedelijk Museum Schiedam.

4 See Marcel Hummelink, *Après nous la liberté. Constant en de artistieke avant-garde in de jaren 1946-1960*, Amsterdam 2002, figs. 98-100. An example of a modified early construction is 1959's *Klein Labyr* in the collection of the Gemeentemuseum Den Haag.

5 The current location of two of Constant's early sculptures is known: 1947's *Mannetje* (Little Man) (collection of the Gemeentemuseum Den Haag) and 1948's *Verstrikte vogel* (Strangled Bird) (collection of Jan and Ellen Nieuwenhuizen Segaar). Trudy Nieuwenhuys-van der Horst also found a three-dimensional work of steel wire and latticework, dated 1948, and a construction consisting of painted wooden blocks with rope, dated 1948, in his archive. It is unclear which collections now hold these works.

6 The portfolio *Voor een spatiaal colorisme*, Amsterdam 1953, contains three silk-screen prints made by Constant using Verweij's equipment. Aside from these three silk-screen prints, a silk-screen print by Constant's friend Stephen Gilbert is also known to exist, very probably produced with this equipment (private collection), as well as a picture postcard by Constant and two by Gilbert. Correspondence about these between Constant and Goos Verweij is held by the Stedelijk Museum Schiedam. On this, see Ludo van Halem (ed.), *CoBrA: The Colour of Freedom: The Schiedam Collection*, Rotterdam/Schiedam 2006, 116-123, 207.

7 Constant, 'It is Our Desire That Makes Revolution', 1949. This text is included in the chapter 'Constant's Writings'.

8 See the catalogue lists included in *Cobra. Organe du front international des artistes experimentaux d'avant-garde* 4 (1949) and *Cobra. Revue international de l'art experimental* 2 (1951) 10. For the first exhibition, see also Peter Shield, 'The 1949 Cobra Exhibition at the Stedelijk Museum Amsterdam. A Substantive Reconstruction', *Jong Holland* 22 (2006) 1, 8-18 and Peter Shield, 'The 1949 Cobra Exhibition. A Substantive Reconstruction, Part Two', *Jong Holland* 23 (2007) 1, 43-46.

9 See exh. cat. *Kunst in vrijheid*, Amsterdam (Rijksmuseum) 1945. One exception is the Amsterdam painter Melle, who alludes to the German occupation with titles such as *Germanendom* and *Winter '44-'45*, cat. nos. 465 and 468.

10 Jan Engelman, 'Hedendaagsche schilderkunst in het Rijksmuseum geeft talrijke manieren te zien', *De Tijd*, 13 October 1945.

managing director and an aficionado of modern art.[11] At his request, Zadkine had a bronze cast from the plaster model, and this was subsequently shown under the title *Design for a Destroyed City* in the Zadkine exhibition at the Museum Boymans in Rotterdam, which opened on 1 December 1949 [fig. 2]. The same day, the newspaper *Het Vrije Volk* announced that an anonymous Amsterdam enterprise – the Bijenkorf would not reveal its role until 1978 – wished to donate this sculpture, in a monumental format, to the city of Rotterdam in commemoration of the devastation of its city centre during the German bombardment of 14 May 1940.

In the exhibition catalogue, art critic and director of the Rijksmuseum Kröller-Müller, A.M. Hammacher, described how radically Zadkine's visual idiom deviated from the iconography common to war monuments: 'It is no mourning, silent figure of repentance. It is not the fallen warrior, not the classical hero, not victory, not discontent or peace. It is Desperation itself; it is humanity screaming to the heavens, utterly appalling distress. No heroics, no lamentations. It is ignominy and it is destruction, profoundly moving.'[12] In the years that followed, until its installation in 1953, the statue was the focus of a great deal of attention in the media – even on television, still in its infancy. The appreciation it elicited demonstrated that there was a definite need for an expressive realism as a counterpoint to the many forms of symbolic representation of the heroism and tenacity of those who had died for their country.[13]

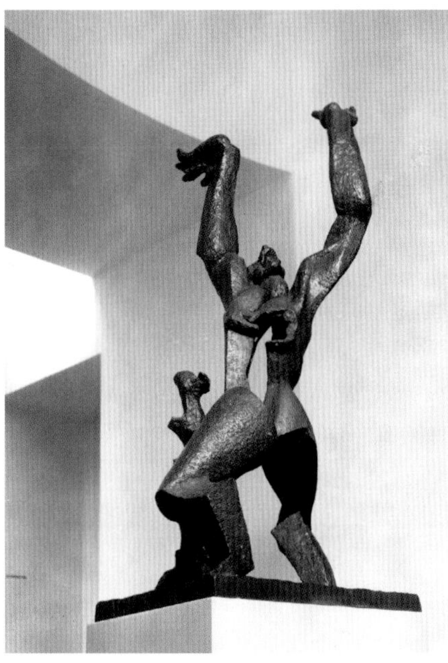

[2] Ossip Zadkine, *Design for a Destroyed City*, 1947, on display as part of the exhibition 'Ossip Zadkine', Museum Boymans, Rotterdam, 1 December 1949 - 12 February 1950
bronze, 120 x 75 x 60 cm
private collection

In the Dutch artistic landscape of the time, both Zadkine's *The Destroyed City* and the group of paintings, drawings and graphics Constant produced about the war were exceptional works of art. Both drew from the iconography of Picasso's *Guernica* from 1937 and the various art works associated with it.[14] Distended mouths and outstretched arms in particular expressed pain, suffering and despair – two motifs explicitly isolated by the artist Alberto Giacometti, whom Constant admired, in his sculptures *La main* (Hand) and *Tête sur tige* (Head of a Man on a Rod), both from 1947.[15] In Constant's compositions too, the chaos of the devastation displayed in his war paintings would gradually make way for an emphasis on a single motif, which acquired all the more evocative power as a result, such as in 1952's *De hand* (Hand, p. 45).

Colour

The war paintings and drawings mark the beginning of a decade in which the 'dialectic of the experiment' predominated, as Constant himself observed in a reflective text about this period in 1965.[16] Between his involvement with Cobra and the moment he came out with the visionary project for a new society, *New Babylon*, his work underwent a turbulent evolution. While most of the artists from the Cobra circles more or less stuck to their visual idiom and their craft, Constant was continually breaking with every established precept imaginable. The very choice of a material like acrylic, shortly after Cobra, was '[a] dramatic departure from everything that you had done, and I don't think that any other Cobra artist ever did anything like this', concluded German art historian Benjamin Buchloh in a conversation with Constant in 1999.[17]

While this remarkable artistic evolution has been discussed regularly in various studies – among which historian Marcel Hummelink's 2002 dissertation provides the most detailed picture – it has hitherto never been accorded a cohesive museum presentation.[18] Many of the works of art from this period, especially paintings produced from 1952 to 1954, were kept by Constant in his studio and seldom exhibited. In recent years *New Babylon* has drawn particular international attention, in part spurred by studies by American architecture historian Mark Wigley.[19] The true significance of the 1950s for Constant, however, emerges from the aforementioned conversation with Buchloh.

Constant was primarily a painter, and he remained one, as he emphasized repeatedly in this conversation. The discovery of space, which would come to occupy such a major place in his work, initially occurred by way of the realm of colour, the work domain of the painter par excellence.

The simplification of motifs from the war paintings, already visible in *De hand* or *De vlam* (Flame, p. 46), would expand between 1951 and 1953 into a series of paintings composed of highly simplified colour forms slotted into one another somewhat like puzzle pieces. Through conversations with British painter Stephen Gilbert (1910-2007), Constant became convinced that the abstract art he had rejected only a short time before did, in this new form, present possibilities after all [fig. 3].[20] A portfolio of graphics by 12 exponents of this tendency, including Serge Poliakoff (1906-1969), a prominent representative of the Nouvelle École de Paris, and Roger Hilton (1911-1975), one of the pioneers of British abstract art with whom Constant had become friends during a study trip to England in 1952, was to have served as a visual manifesto [figs. 4 and 5]. But by the time the portfolio was ultimately presented in January 1954, Constant had already left this phase behind.[21]

The woodcuts Constant produced to illustrate the long poem *Het uitzicht van de duif* (View of the Dove) by his friend Jan Elburg (1919-1992) seem to have played an important role in this process, not only because simplification of form and limitation of colour is a given in this technique, but also because it led to a realization that had a broader significance: 'The simpler the work becomes in its execution, the more is required of the maker to maintain the excitement of the initial impulse. This is, in short, the meaning and the problem of modern art as a whole, in which all the effort is directed at a limitation of means, and a greater purity of the plastic form,' Constant wrote to Goos Verweij, who would print *Het uitzicht van de duif* in August 1952 (p. 48-49).[22]

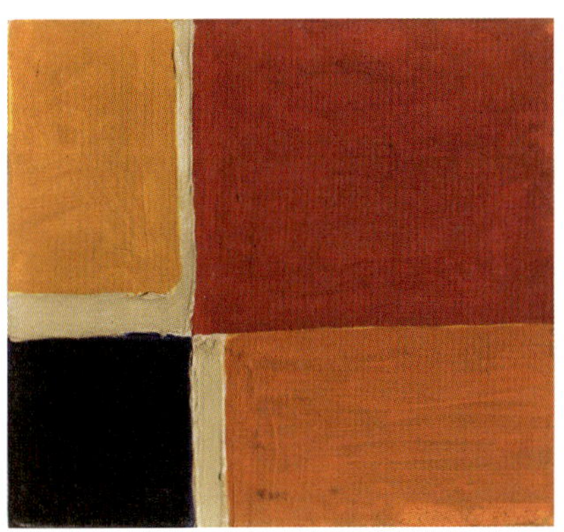

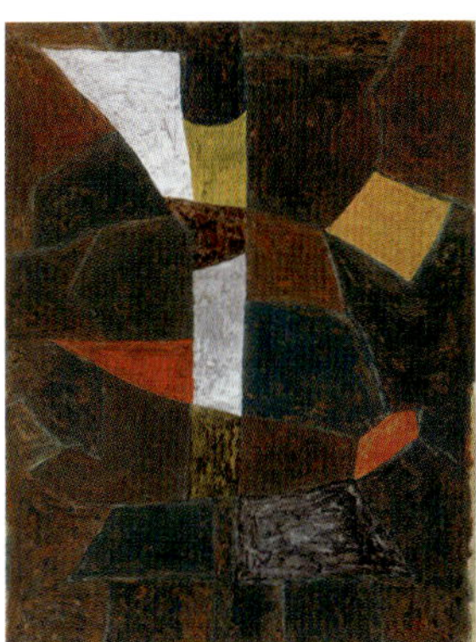

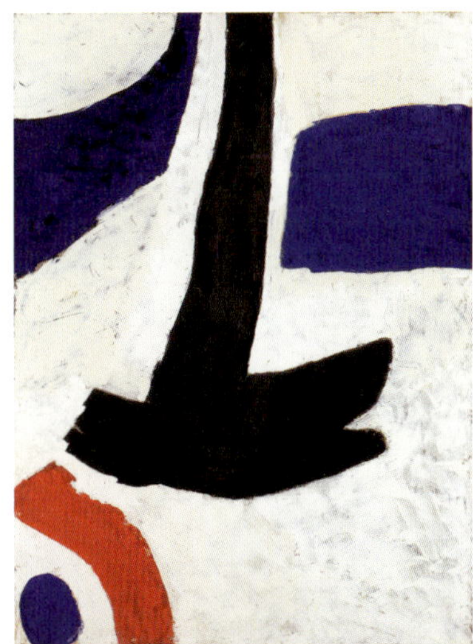

[3] Stephen Gilbert, *Untitled*, 1953
oil on linen, 20.7 x 23.2 cm
private collection, Amsterdam

[4] Serge Poliakoff, *Composition*, 1953/1954
gouache on brown paper, 62.5 x 47 cm
collection Ellen and Jan Nieuwenhuizen Segaar

[5] Roger Hilton, *July 1953*, 1953
oil on canvas, 121 x 91 cm
collection Stedelijk Museum Amsterdam

11 Exhibited under the title *Ontwerp voor een vernielde stad*, exh. cat. *Zadkine*, Amsterdam (Stedelijk Museum) [1948], cat. no. 50. I wish to thank Patricia van Ulzen for the detailed information on the history of Zadkine's sculpture (see also note 13).

12 In exh. cat. *Zadkine*, Rotterdam (Museum Boymans) 1949, n.p., cat. no. 68.

13 See Susan Hogervorst and Patricia van Ulzen, *Rotterdam en het bombardement. 75 jaar herinneren en vergeten*, Rotterdam 2015, in particular Chapter 2: '"Ik heb tranen geboetseerd." Zadkine als vertolker van het Rotterdamse oorlogsleed', 68-115. This publication refutes the myth that *The Destroyed City* was initially reviled.

14 See Graham Birtwistle, 'Constant and Picasso. The Language of War Art', *Jong Holland* 7 (1991) 2, 28-47 and Ludo van Halem, *Picasso, Klee, Miró en de moderne kunst in Nederland 1946-1958*, Rotterdam/Schiedam 2006, 74-75.

15 Constant knew Giacometti personally. On this, see Trudy van der Horst, 'Biographie de Constant', in: Maurice Fréchuret et al., *Constant, une rétrospective*, exh. cat. Antibes (Musée Picasso) 2001, 134 and Benjamin Buchloh, 'A Conversation with Constant', in: Catherine de Zegher and Mark Wigley (eds.), *The Activist Drawing: Retracing Situationist Architectures from Constant's New Babylon to Beyond*, New York 2001, 15-25.

16 Constant, 'The Dialectic of the Experiment'. This text is included in the chapter 'Constant's Writings'.

17 Buchloh, op. cit. (note 15).

18 See note 4.

19 Mark Wigley, *Constant's New Babylon. The Hyper-Architecture of Desire*, Rotterdam 1998 and De Zegher and Wigley, op. cit. (note 15). For the most recent exhibition on *New Babylon* see exh. cat. *Constant. New Babylon*, Madrid (Museo Nacional Centro de Arte Reina Sofía) 2015-2016. For a detailed bibliography and overview of exhibitions see the website of the Fondation Constant: www.stichtingconstant.nl.

20 'Almost everything you see here is the same vacuous, impersonal abstraction, and the reaction of the painter must necessarily be one of two: either bow and sacrifice his personality to the Paris "art world", or turn away more and more from abstract art', Constant wrote to Aldo van Eyck from Paris in 1950, quoted in Hummelink, op. cit. (note 4), 113.

21 Hummelink, op. cit. (note 4), 145-146. The portfolio was published under the title *Douze lithographies des peintres Calliyannis, Constant, Carrey, Dumitresco, Hilton, Serge Poliakoff, Istrati, Gilbert, Greta Sauer, Pons, Selim Turan, Wendt, presentée par R.V. Gindertael*, Paris 1953.

22 Quoted in Hummelink, op. cit. (note 4), 121.

These were statements that were more in keeping with the purist visual idiom of De Stijl than with the expressive figuration of the Experimental Group in Holland and Cobra. Constant had been familiar with Mondrian from a young age, because the father of his first wife, Matie, the composer Jacob van Domselaer, owned two of Mondrian's paintings, which Constant had restored.[23] 'I knew Mondrian very well, otherwise I couldn't have rebelled against him', he told Buchloh.

In 1951 there was an opportunity to get to know the work of other artists and architects associated with De Stijl first hand at the historic retrospective put together by the Stedelijk Museum in Amsterdam. The scope of this pre-war avant-garde was made clear to an entirely new post-war generation at this exhibition. Not only were paintings by Bart van der Leck, Piet Mondrian, Vilmos Huszár and Theo van Doesburg on display, but also a broad sampling of the furniture and architecture of Gerrit Rietveld – who was largely responsible for the exhibition – and the work of such De Stijl architects as Cornelis van Eesteren, J.J.P. Oud and Jan Wils. The impact was significant. Hans Jaffé, curator of the Stedelijk Museum, set to work on his ground-breaking dissertation on De Stijl, and various initiatives were launched through which younger artists declared themselves the movement's artistic heirs. The name of the Liga Nieuw Beelden (League for new representation), founded on 24 January 1955, was a direct reference to the Nieuwe Beelding (neoplasticism) propagated by De Stijl, and three years later the journal *Structure* was born, initially named *De Stijl Continued*, soon followed by the journal *De Nieuwe Stijl*.

Even Constant seemed unable to resist the appeal of De Stijl. Rebellion turned into assimilation. With his friend architect Aldo van Eyck, Constant published a portfolio in 1953 in which they looked back on their collaboration on *een ruimte in kleur* (A space in colour), an environment they had created for the home exhibition 'Mens en Huis' (Man and home) at the Stedelijk Museum. Van Eyck had designed the space, and at his invitation Constant had produced a large painting taking up an entire wall. The collaboration with an architect and the overwhelming effect of the colours purple, blue, crimson, vermilion and ochre in the brightly lit space inspired Constant to write the manifesto 'Spatial Colorism', on the balance between colour and space as well as the collaboration between painter and architect. Constant sent a copy of the manifesto to Gerrit Rietveld, who sent it back to him, with comments, by return post.[24] The discussion that followed led to Rietveld inviting Constant to design the spatial colour scheme for a model interior commissioned by the Bijenkorf that would be displayed in the home furnishing department of its Amsterdam store in 1954.[25]

By then Constant, with Stephen Gilbert, had conceived the idea of launching a new journal under the name *Art et Habitat*, which would deal with the relationship between architecture and painting. A large part of the discussion between Constant and Gilbert focused on the artistic legacy of De Stijl, which still seemed to hold potential for the future. 'In his treatment of the plane, by using the unity that can be repeated indefinitely in a variety of orientations, the modern architect seeks to achieve a spatial projection very similar to Mondrian's last paintings,' Gilbert wrote in an article intended for the journal, for example.[26]

In Paris Gilbert had also become acquainted with Hungarian-French sculptor Nicolas Schöffer (1912-1991), and when preparations for *Art et Habitat* foundered, the idea arose of working together, under the avant-gardist name Néovision, in the realm of spatial art and the living environment. By then Gilbert had begun producing coloured metal sculptures and subsequently architectural models [fig. 6]. Schöffer had been producing what he called *spatiodynamic* reliefs and constructions since 1949, consisting of panels of painted metal or coloured acrylic mounted in rectangular frames of iron and aluminium [fig. 7]. The play of line and colour definitely recalled 'Mondrian's last paintings' as well, with its double crossing lines and rhythmically ordered colour planes. These were the models that persuaded Constant to leave the flat plane of the painting and begin working with 'spatial colorism', Hummelink concludes in his dissertation.[27]

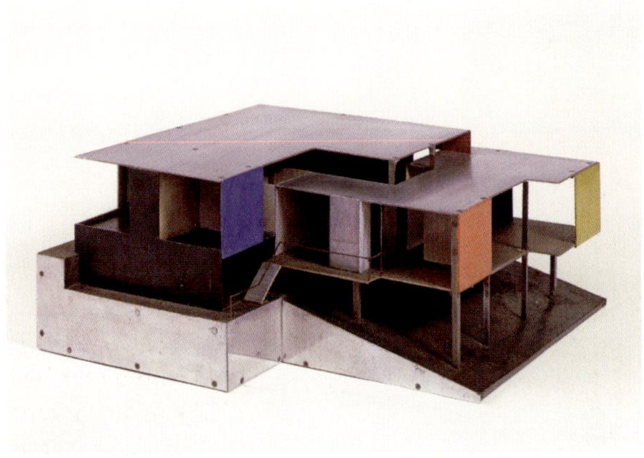

[6] Stephen Gilbert, *House Model 'Néovision'*, 1955
painted aluminium and steel, 35.5 x 35.5 x 12.7 cm
Collection of Abstract and Constructivist Art, Sainsbury Centre for Visual Arts, University of East Anglia

In Constant's work 'the soiling with misery' made way for 'a great purity of the plastic form' – the spatial organization of pure colour. This process can be traced step by step from 1954's *Constructie met gekleurde vlakken* [fig. 1]. It can be seen as a more complex three-dimensional version of the 1953 painting *Compositie met oranje driehoek* (Composition with Orange Triangle, p. 65), which looks like a (mirror) abstraction of 1952's *De vlam*. In turn, that painting is a simplification of the motif from 1950's *L'Incendie* (Fire, p. 43), one of the first paintings to incorporate Picasso's characteristic war iconography.[28]
Indeed, *Constructie met gekleurde vlakken* is a key work in the development of Constant's work, encapsulating a large part of the idiom of the years to come. The transparent colour planes would continue to play a role from the first to the last models for *New Babylon* and define the atmosphere and identity of the sectors that make up this imaginary metropolis. From the dark memories of the war slowly emerged the dream of a future world in which space and colour would form a poetic unity.

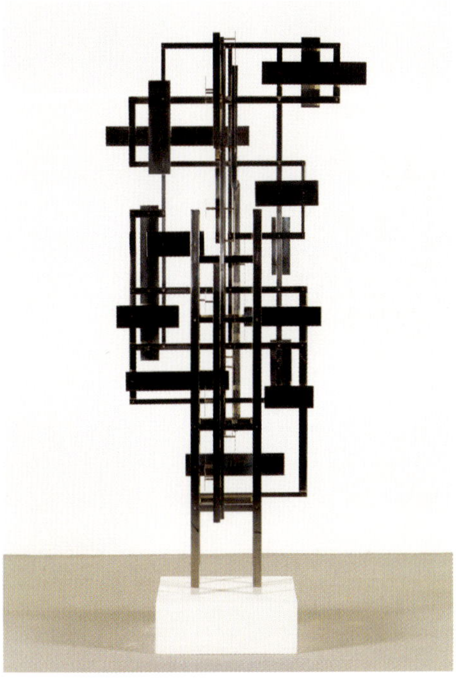

[7] Nicolas Schöffer, *Construction spatiodynamique 24*, 1955-1968
chromed steel, 199.5 x 95.5 x 68 cm
collection Royal Museums of Fine Arts of Belgium, Brussels

Space

Closely related to the *Constructie met gekleurde vlakken* was another construction, produced in monumental dimensions – 15 metres high – in 1955. Constant had been granted the honour of producing two (temporary) monumental sculptures for the reconstruction exhibition 'E55' in Rotterdam: a *Verende constructie* (Springy Construction) of rectangular and curved frames, which was installed in the 'Lunar Valley' of the Space Travel section, and the large rectangular construction of steel beams and coloured wooden panels that was installed as a Symbol of the Will and Work of the Netherlands in the midst of the provincial pavilions in The Park (p. 140).[29] Also dubbed the *Monument for the Reconstruction*, it was a temporary counterpart to *The Destroyed City*. While this monumental commission signified an acknowledgment of Constant's 'spatial colorist' sculpture, he himself did not give it much thought for very long. Indeed, he would describe his artistic exploration of the 1950s as an 'activity [of] constant building and tearing down again. My ideal is not the absolute harmonic form, but the form in motion, the form that is born and dies, the relative form. What I seek is *la forme informe*, the undetermined form, the form with a thousand faces, the form without beginning and without end, without boundaries, the formless, the invisible form, the eternally repeatable, eternally variable, yet never familiar form.'[30]

Constant's contribution to 'E55' provided new impetus to his work, whereby the concept of 'space' acquired a different meaning and a greater dimension. He had originally interpreted

23 Constant found these paintings in deplorable condition in the shed at the home of the Van Domselaers in Bergen and restored them in his studio (information provided by Trudy Nieuwenhuys-van der Horst based on interviews with Constant). They were *Composition in Brown and Gray,* 1913 (collection of the Museum of Modern Art, New York) and *Lozenge Composition with Yellow, Black, Blue, Red, and Gray*, 1921 (collection of the Art Institute of Chicago).

24 Constant, 'Spatial Colorism'. This text is included in the chapter 'Constant's Writings'.

25 On this, see the chapter 'Space and Colour in Practice'.

26 The Hague, Netherlands Institute for Art History (RKD), Constant archive, NL-HaRKD-0095 inv. no. 291.

27 Hummelink, op. cit. (note 4), 175-199.

28 Van Halem, op. cit. (note 14), 74-75.

29 Peter de Winter, *Evenementen in Rotterdam. Ahoy', E55, Floriade, C70*, Rotterdam 1988, 42-83.

30 Constant, unpublished typescript, written for audio documentation at the Stedelijk Museum, Amsterdam, Spring 1958. This text is included in the chapter 'Constant's Writings'.

space as architectonic space, but through his encounters with various architects who also took part, via the 'de 8' architects' group, in the conferences of the CIAM (Congrès Internationaux d'Architecture Moderne), he soon came to think of it as the human living environment, the 'habitat' that was the focus of the ninth conference in Aix-en-Provence, France, in mid 1953. In his discussion with Rietveld he had already quoted, approvingly, the motto of the earlier conference in Bridgwater in 1947, formulated by Sigfried Giedion, which seemed to be a precursor of the habitat discussion: 'To create an environment that will satisfy man's material and emotional needs and stimulate his spiritual growth.'[31] The way this concept of space evolves into a notion of a complete urban living space – 'unitary urbanism' – and the social space necessary for the development of human creativity can be very clearly traced in the texts Constant wrote during the 1950s. It is in this space that the *homo ludens* of *New Babylon* will move about.[32]

One aspect of Constant's concept of space has been overshadowed by the amount of attention that has been devoted to the creation of *New Babylon* in the context of the Mouvement International pour un Bauhaus Imaginiste (M.I.B.I.) and the Situationist International, two movements Constant briefly joined in 1956 and 1958, respectively. This concept of space exists from 1955 to about 1959 alongside and contemporaneously with the formation of his ideas about the urban space of *New Babylon* and is connected to the universe, the outer space whose 'conquest' in the second half of the 1950s became part of the Cold War between East and West and which was guaranteed major public interest.

Constant's *Verende constructie* was installed in the 'Lunar Valley', a rock garden that also featured a revolving crane, 60 metres high, that hoisted visitors aloft in 'world gondolas'. In the pavilions around it, the launch of a spacecraft was simulated and an impression of space travel was provided by means of light effects, electronic sounds and the suggestion of weightlessness. There were people working in spacesuits; images of a passing space station and of a landing on one of Saturn's moons were shown.[33] One absolute novelty was a model of an artificial satellite, added during the course of the exhibition.[34] Two years later the Soviet Union won the first stage in the 'conquest' of outer space by launching the artificial satellite *Sputnik 1* into orbit around the earth on 4 October 1957. It was a hitherto unprecedented futuristic and technological context for Constant's work. From 1955 onward he would produce an impressive series of works with outer space and space travel as their theme, a subject that, in Dutch art history, was as exceptional as the war had been around 1950.

Constant then discarded the building term 'construction' for his sculptures and gave them titles like *Ruimte en beweging* (Space and Motion, 1955, p. 93), *Observatorium* (1956, p. 79), *Planetarium* (1956), *Ruimtecircus* (Space Circus, 1956/1961, p. 94), *Zonneschip (*Sun Vessel, 1957), various *Nébuloses mécaniques* (1958, p. 98 and 100) and *Ruimteschip* (Space Vessel, 1959).[35] The world of energy, engineering, chemistry and space travel that was so gloriously celebrated in that extensive reconstruction exhibition, in books like Sigfried Giedion's *Mechanization Takes Command* (1948) and John Diebold's *Automation: The Advent of the Automatic Factory* (1952), but also in a film like General Electric's *This is Automation* (1955), aimed at familiarizing the public at large with this subject, nurtured the optimistic faith in progress expressed by Constant in texts

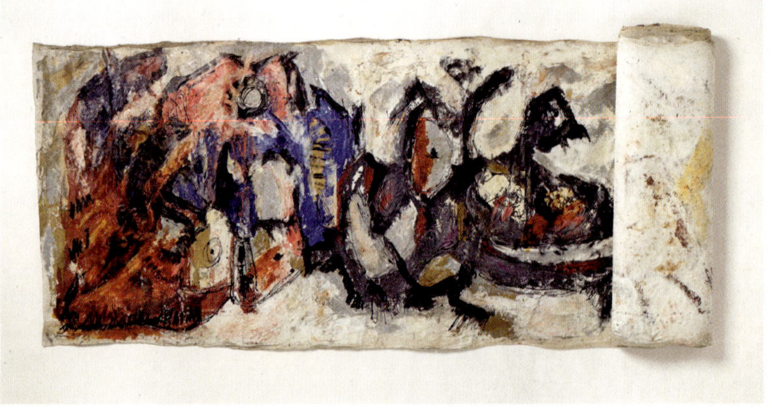

[8] Giuseppe Pinot Gallizio, *La sirena e il pirata* (The Siren And The Pirate), 1958
mixed media on canvas, 95 x 1770 cm
collection Galerie Van de Loo Projekte, Munich

such as 'Technicism' or 'Tomorrow Life Will Reside in Poetry' in 1956. In the first text (which remained unpublished) he stated explicitly that 'we adopt the realities of technological production as key to an aesthetic of form'.[36]

This makes it all the more remarkable that at the same time he embraced a way of painting that seemed to have anything but a technological character. Once more he traded in the geometric abstraction that he had tried out a mere two years before and that linked him to Mondrian and other De Stijl artists or their imitators, this time for an informal visual idiom that came into being by letting dripping, liquid paint run in various directions across the canvas and by working with various textures, by adding a variety of substances to the paint. Yet this is only an apparent contradiction. This new way of painting seemed primarily spurred by a stay in Alba in 1956, where Constant was able to get to know the *pittura industriale* of Italian painter, chemist and vintner Giuseppe Pinot Gallizio (1902-1964). In his *laboratorio sperimentale,* painting was produced 'on an assembly line', without shying away from unusual interactions with paint [fig. 8].

At the same time, Danish painter and theorist Asger Jorn (1914-1973), whom Constant had invited to Alba to contribute to the First World Congress of Free Artists, took a stand against the didactic precepts of the Swiss Max Bill, head of the Hochschule für Gestaltung in Ulm, acknowledged as the successor to the pre-war Bauhaus. There could be no greater contrast imaginable than that between Jorn's labyrinthine idiom of form, which aimed to be a 'living art' and Bill's cool, concrete art, which according to Jorn led to a dead end [figs. 9 and 10].

Constantly 'building and tearing down' is how Constant would describe his 'activity' in 1958. The new form of painting deviated radically from what he had built up in the preceding years and within which he tried to capture the sublime space of the universe, with titles like *Sterrenbeeld* (Constellation), *De zon* (The Sun), *Paysage lunaire* (Lunar Landscape) and *Grote Beer* (Ursa Major), all in 1956 (p. 101, 116, 109), and the series of four paintings *Structures dans l'espace* (Structures in Space), *Voyage dans l'espace* (Space Travel), *Kosmisch landschap* (Cosmic Landscape) and *Ruimtelandschap* (Space Landscape) in 1956-1958 (p. 102-105). Dripping and spattering paint or subtly coloured lines against an ink-black background and endlessly spinning spirals seemed more suited to expressing something of the amazement about outer space than the clear line of geometric abstraction.

Constant's space voyage culminated in a unique collaboration with American filmmaker and photographer Hy Hirsh (1911-1961). In 1957

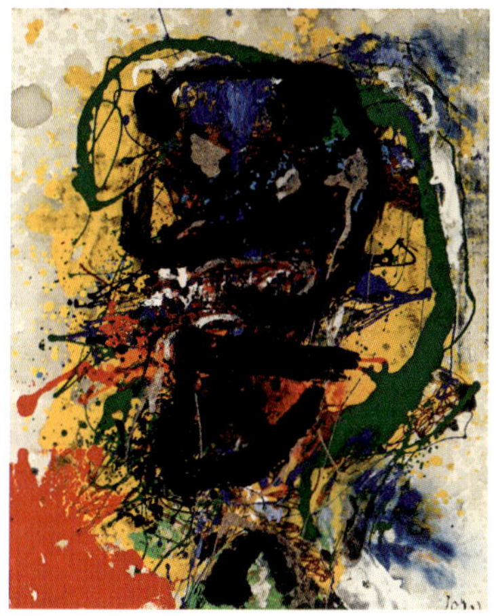

[9] Asger Jorn, *Le voyageur de Munich* (The Traveller of Munich), 1959
oil, Ripolin and sand on canvas, 79.9 x 65 cm
collection Stedelijk Museum Amsterdam

[10] Max Bill, *Champ avec un accent en vert* (Field With A Green Accent), 1946-1948
oil on canvas, 120.5 x 120.5 cm
collection Musée de Grenoble

which he – as Bill had also done – had explored the cool aesthetics of repetition, for example with the painting *Variations rythmiques* in 1953 (p. 71). And the fact that he sold it covered in spots in 1958 is significant (cf. p. 159). Once again it was time to 'soil virginal purity', but this time not in order to paint misery. Parallel to the space sculptures, Constant produced a series of paintings in

they began working together on a film about the Space Sculptures Constant had produced in recent years. Hirsh was highly skilled in technical film effects and worked in the Netherlands for Joop Geesink's animation studio Dollywood, among others. Constant's sculptures, or portions of them, were filmed as they revolved and were lit with different coloured lights. The various bits of

31 Letter from Constant to Gerrit Rietveld, 9 February 1954, The Hague, Netherlands Institute for Art History (RKD), Constant archive, NL-HaRKD-0095 inv. no. 352. The quotation is taken from Sigfried Giedion, *A Decade of New Architecture*, Zurich 1951.

32 Constant introduced *homo ludens* (playing, creative man) into his *New Babylon* project after reading Johan Huizinga's *Homo Ludens: A Study of the Play-Element in Culture*, originally published in 1938. On this, see, among others, Trudy van der Horst, 'Biography of Constant', in exh. cat. *Constant. New Babylon*, The Hague (Gemeentemuseum Den Haag) 2016, 236.

33 De Winter, op. cit. (note 29), 50-51.

34 'De E-55 heeft al een kunstmaan', *De Surinamer*, 6 August 1955. De Winter, op. cit. (note 29), 11, states that this was a model of *Sputnik 1*. No confirmation of this could be found in the Dutch newspapers consulted via Delpher.nl through 15 April 2016.

35 See exh. cat. *Constant*, The Hague (Gemeentemuseum Den Haag) 1965, unpaginated. Of the works cited, *Ruimteschip* (Space Vessel), cat. no. 153, has yet to be identified.

36 Constant, 'Technicism', unpublished text, July 1956. This text is included in the chapter 'Constant's Writings'.

footage were then laid one on top of the other, creating a colourful vortex of shapes and lines within a seemingly infinite space [figs. 11 and 12]. The film was titled *Gyromorphosis* (loosely translated as 'spinning forms') and subtitled *Space Sculptures by Constant* and took on the character of a (cosmic) ballet by being rhythmically set to the number *Django*, approximately seven minutes long, by The Modern Jazz Quartet.

Unity

Hirsh's film was premiered in Brussels during the 'Expo 58' world fair. In the Netherlands the film was probably first shown at Constant's first solo exhibition at the Stedelijk Museum, held in 1959 and titled 'Constructies en maquettes' (Constructions and models). In this exhibition Constant's

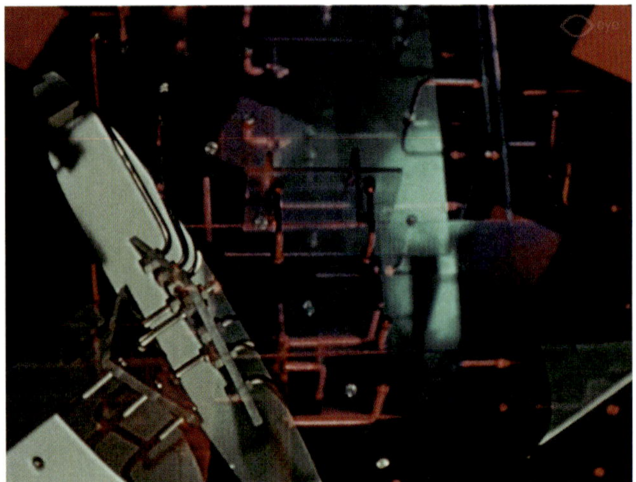

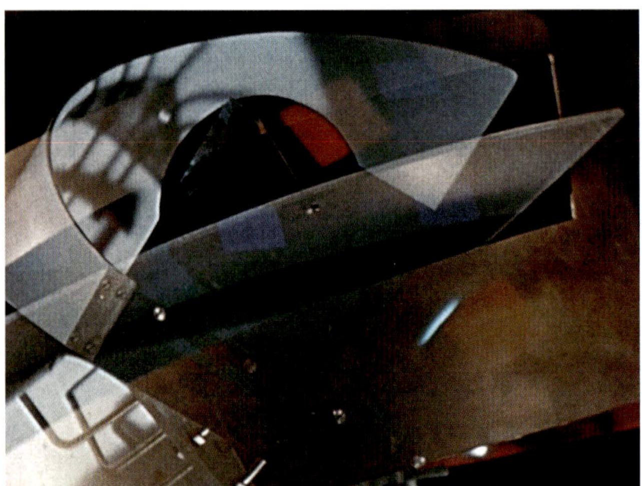

[11 and 12] Hy Hirsch, *Gyromorphosis (Space Sculptures by Constant)*, 1958 (film stills)
16 mm film, 7 min.
collection of the EYE Filmmuseum, Amsterdam

sculptures were displayed on black platforms and with coloured light projections, analogous to the images that unfolded in *Gyromorphosis*.[37]

As a presentation form, this exhibition seems to have been the precursor for the various ways in which Constant would exhibit his *New Babylon* models in the years that followed – one of the most remarkable experiments being a presentation in a completely darkened museum hall with an intense lighting from above, so that they seemed to hover like spaceships.[38] Colour and space became inextricably intertwined: *New Babylon* was defined as early as 1958 by models of sectors coloured – and titled – yellow, red or orange (p. 128). These colours would continue to recur, right up to the very last representations of the *New Babylon* spaces, such as 1967's *Ladderlabyrinth* (Ladder Labyrinth, p. 132).

Indeed, coloured spaces formed the expression of the 'absolute' unity of the arts he had been seeking during the 1950s. There was no longer any distinction between painting, sculpture, architecture and urbanism. The amazing new material with which Constant had begun to work in 1954, the acrylic that was saturated with colour and yet let light through, that defined space yet kept it transparent, had proved indispensable in this quest for the joining of colour and space.

37 Documentation on this exhibition could not be found. The exhibition file in the archives of the Stedelijk Museum in Amsterdam (Amsterdam City Archives) contains only an invitation letter and an announcement of the film showing. A few summary details about the design were gleaned from various newspaper reviews (preserved in the Constant file by the Press Documentation department of the Netherlands Institute for Art History (RKD), The Hague) and from a 1959 letter from Martin Visser to Constant, Netherlands Institute for Art History (RKD), Constant archive, NL-HaRKD-0095 inv. no. 210.

38 This installation from 1974 was reconstructed in the exhibition 'Constant. Nueva Babilonia' at the Museo Nacional Centro de Arte Reina Sofía in Madrid in 2015-2016.

Constant in his studio, surrounded by his Space Sculptures and models: one of the towers of *Verticale Stad* (Vertical City) and *Constructie in oranje* (Construction in Orange). On the wall to the left, a detail from *Variations rythmiques* (Rhythmic Variations) and a photo of *Monument van de wederopbouw* (Monument for the Reconstruction), c. 1958
collection Fondation Constant

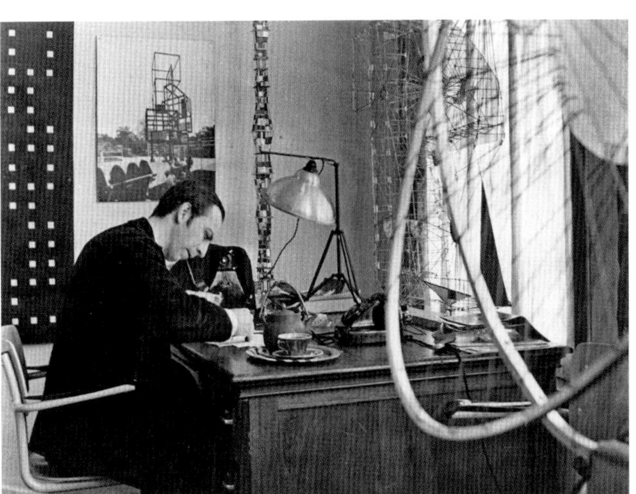

Space and Colour in Practice
On Reconstructions of Experimental Spaces

Ludo van Halem and Laura Stamps

Paintings, drawings, graphics, constructions, models and collages generally define the image of Constant's oeuvre. Less well known is that, between 1952 and 1974, he also created experimental spaces of a temporary nature, mostly as part of a larger exhibition. Of all these environments, only the documentation remains. Only a few people will have seen them in real life. As part of the exhibitions at the Cobra Museum for Modern Art in Amstelveen and the Gemeentemuseum Den Haag in The Hague, several of these temporary spaces have been reconstructed, allowing a new generation to get to know this aspect of Constant's oeuvre.[1] Thanks to these reconstructions, a much better insight emerges into his ideas about the human habitat and the relationship between space and colour, a theme that Constant developed in the 1950s and that came to full fruition in his representations of the imaginary city of the future, *New Babylon*.[2]

The Gemeentemuseum Den Haag has reconstructed the *Ludieke trap* (Playful Stairs) that Constant made for the exhibition 'Weg wezen. Recreatie vroeger, nu en straks' (Getting away: recreation in the past, present and future) in 1969 at the Amsterdams Historisch Museum [fig. 1]. Part of the *Deurenlabyrinth* (Door Labyrinth), which was shown as part of his exhibition 'New Babylon' at the Gemeentemuseum Den Haag in 1974, has also been reconstructed.[3] At the Cobra Museum, the early experimental spaces created in collaboration with others have been reconstructed: *een ruimte in kleur* (A Space in Colour), created by architect Aldo van Eyck in 1952 for the exhibition 'Mens en Huis' (Man and home) at the Stedelijk Museum in Amsterdam, for which Constant produced a painting that occupied an entire wall,[4] and the 'Suggestion for the home' designed by architect Gerrit Rietveld in 1954 for the Bijenkorf department store, with a colour scheme by Constant. Reconstructions of the way Constant presented his own work have also been produced at both museums.

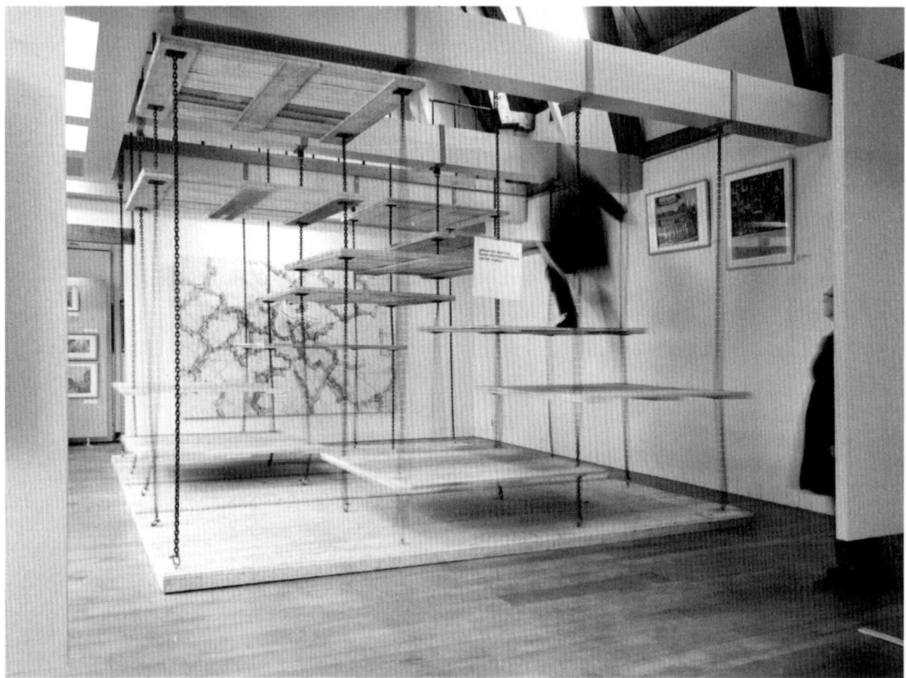

[1] *Ludieke trap* (Playful Stairs), installation at the exhibition 'Weg wezen: recreatie vroeger, nu en straks', Amsterdams Historisch Museum (20 November 1969 - 15 February 1970). In the background, *New Babylon over Amsterdam*, 1968, watercolour and ink on city map, 200 x 300 cm, collection Amsterdam Museum

A Playful Life

Constant first emphasized that his work also had an imaginary dimension in 1959, in his solo exhibition 'Constructies en maquettes' (Constructions and models) at the Stedelijk Museum in Amsterdam. The three-dimensional constructions of wire and Plexiglas were displayed on black platforms and lit with variously coloured lights, creating a pattern of swirling lines of colour in a darkened space. The atmosphere of that first solo exhibition has been recreated at the Cobra Museum. This manner of presentation had a sequel 15 years later in the exhibition 'New Babylon' in 1974, a conclusion to the project on which he had been working since 1956. The Gemeentemuseum Den Haag has now reconstructed the tables Constant designed for the models, with thin, black steel legs, at a different height for each model. The earliest models were exhibited in a completely darkened space, lit only by a single light bulb. This lighting causes them to loom out of the darkness and they almost seem to float in mid-air, strongly emphasizing the immaterial, conceptual nature of the project [fig. 2].

Constant, however, was not content with mere suggestion; he also wanted to make palpable, in practice, how playful life in *New Babylon* might be. With sculptor Nic. Tummers (b. 1928) he created the *√2-omgang* (√2 circuit) in 1965 for the exhibition 'Nieuw Beelden' (New representation) at the Stedelijk Museum in Amsterdam, a play apparatus designed to constantly surprise its user with drop-offs, a springboard and ringing telephones. In 1966 he worked with Tummers and photographer Bram Wisman (1920-2008), among others,

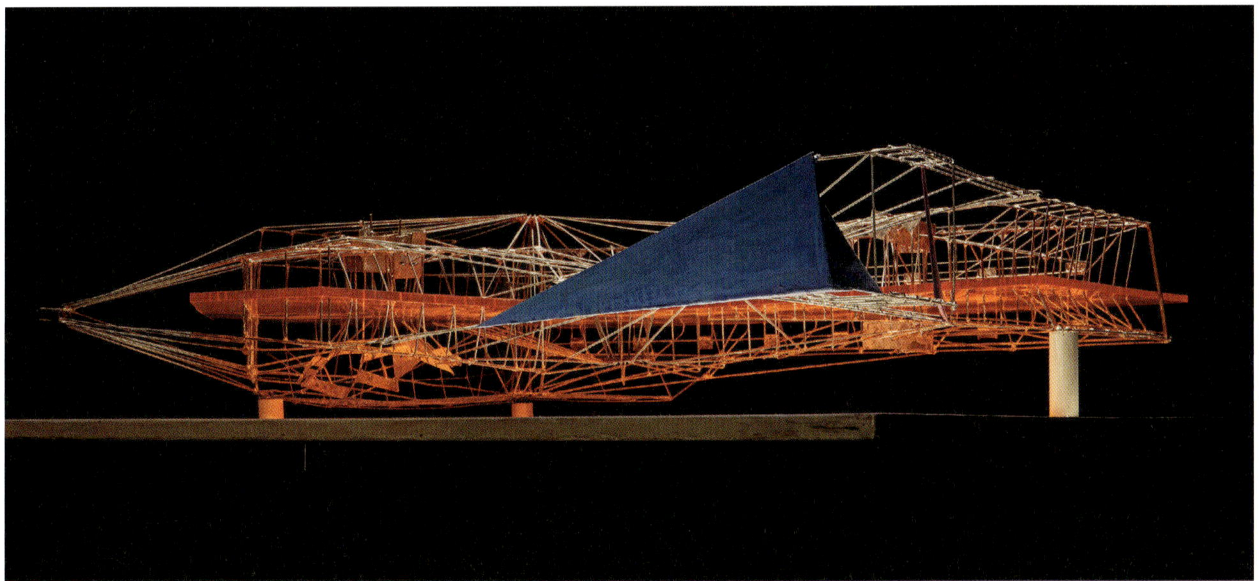

[2] *Constructie in oranje* (Construction in Orange), 1958
metal, Plexiglas and wood, 24.6 x 110.2 x 100.5 cm
collection Gemeentemuseum Den Haag
Installation at the exhibition
'Constant. Nueva Babilonia', Museo Nacional
Centro de Arte Reina Sofía, Madrid
(21 October 2015 - 29 February 2016)

on *Experiment Studio Rotterdam*, a labyrinthine series of rooms in which visitors were challenged by means of fragrance, mirrors or sound. In 1969 Constant designed the installation *Ludieke trap* at the Amsterdams Historisch Museum, made of wooden panels attached to support beams with chains. Hanging on the wall was the geographical map *New Babylon over Amsterdam*, which he had been commissioned to make by the museum a

1 'Constant: Space+Colour: From Cobra to New Babylon', Cobra Museum for Modern Art, Amstelveen, 28 May - 25 September 2016; 'Constant. New Babylon: After Us, Liberty', Gemeentemuseum Den Haag, The Hague, 28 May - 25 September 2016.

2 On this, see 'Constant's Writings' and Constant and J.L. Locher, *New Babylon*, [The Hague: s.n., 1974], published on the occasion of the exhibition 'New Babylon', Gemeentemuseum Den Haag, 15 June - 1 September 1974.

3 A reconstruction of the *Deurenlabyrinth* (Door Labyrinth) was part of the exhibition 'Constant. Nueva Babilonia' at the Museo Nacional Centro de Arte Reina Sofía, Madrid, 20 October 2015 - 29 February 2016.

4 A reconstruction of *een ruimte in kleur* (A Space in Colour) was also part of the exhibition 'Constant. Nueva Babilonia' (note 3). On this, see also Ludo van Halem and Laura Stamps, 'Experiment in paars en blauw', *Tijdschrift van de Rijksdienst voor het Cultureel Erfgoed* 8 (2016) 1, 8-9 and Céline Vermeire, 'Reconstructie van "een ruimte in kleur" van Aldo van Eyck en Constant', *kM. Materiaaltechnische informatie over kunst en vormgeving* 25 (2016) 98, 36-39.

year earlier. The structure of the *Ludieke trap*, which was anything but stable (the panels moved as one climbed it), led to the apex of the vaulted ceiling, suggesting 'going through the roof'.

In addition to the *Ludieke trap*, the Gemeentemuseum Den Haag also features a partial reconstruction of the *Deurenlabyrinth*. The labyrinth had always been an important theme within *New Babylon*, and this experimental space in fact represented the literal end of his exhibition 'New Babylon' in 1974.[5] It made palpable how one would relate to space and time in a playful society. In our modern production-oriented society, the most efficient way is considered the best way, but in *New Babylon* every way, every day, presents a labyrinth of possibilities. It was precisely this which would stimulate creativity in a positive way.[6]

With the exhibition in 1974 Constant wanted to present *New Babylon* one more time in its entirety, in order to then bring the project to a close. He felt he had said all he had to say about it. In interviews about the exhibition Constant said that he still believed in *New Babylon*, but that he did not think it would become a reality any time soon. A long, confusing and destructive period would precede the creation of this new world; the *Deurenlabyrinth* was the symbol of this confusion. Humanity will either eventually find its way out of the labyrinth of confusion, or it will continue to wander about, lost. In that sense, *New Babylon* is an open ending...

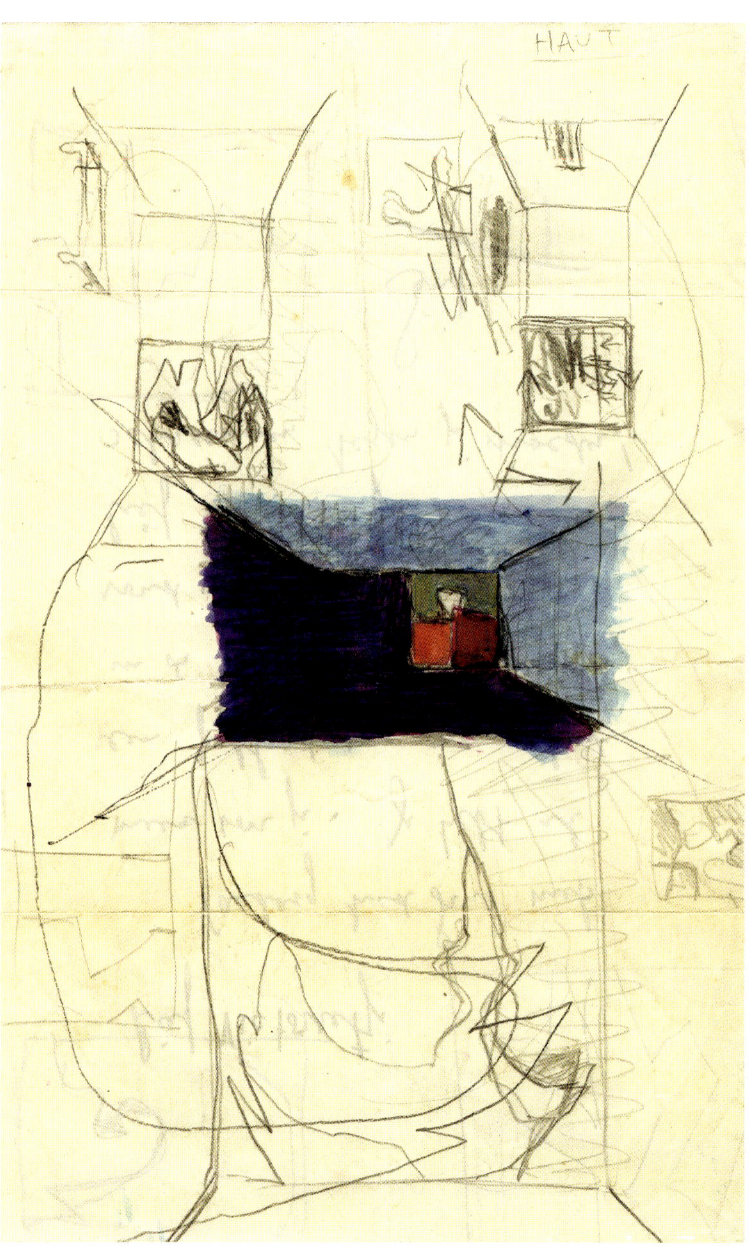

[3] Constant and/or Aldo van Eyck,
sketch for *een ruimte in kleur* (A Space in Colour), 1952
pencil and gouache on paper, 19.6 x 12.2 cm
collection Aldo and Hannie van Eyck Archives

Simple and Strong Colours

The two temporary environments Constant worked on in 1952 and 1954, with Aldo van Eyck and Gerrit Rietveld respectively, marked the earliest beginnings of a search for what colour can mean to the experience of space. In 1952 Van Eyck asked Constant to collaborate on a space he was to design for the exhibition 'Mens en Huis' at the Stedelijk Museum in Amsterdam. This exhibition was an initiative of the eponymous foundation Stichting Mens en Huis. The moralistic message of the exhibition's organizers was that a properly arranged home interior and responsibly designed home furnishings would promote well-being.[7] Constant recalled that Van Eyck wanted to make a statement against this cultural elitism: 'Aldo wanted to do something to counter to this, something that was actually not allowed within the context of the exhibition. He designed a square space, 7 metres by 7 metres, and 3.5 metres high. The floor and half of the walls were deep purple; the other half and the ceiling were deep blue. ... In actuality these were rather soft hues, applied on burlap in one of those soft wall paints of the period. On one of the walls Aldo also reserved a square, 3.5 metres by 3.5 metres, and asked me to produce a painting for it. We picked one of my ... paintings as the starting point: a composition of two reds, a light and a dark cadmium red, and a golden ochre with a big fat white splotch in it, with prison bars in front of it. ... I then painted an enlarged version there'[8] [figs. 3 and 4]. Van Eyck initially wanted to put the words 'to each his own bad taste' on the opposite wall, but of course the organization did not appreciate this. A few verses

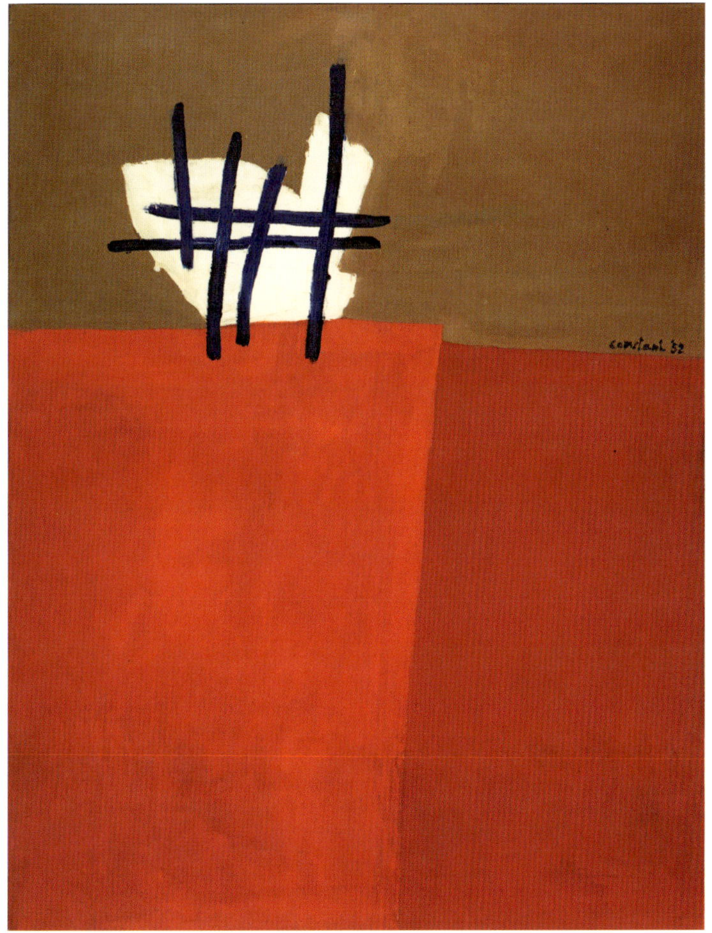

[4] *Ruimtelijk colorisme* (Spatial Colorism), 1952
oil on linen, 125 x 97 cm
collection Fondation Constant, on long-term loan to the Stedelijk Museum Schiedam

This painting was exhibited in 'Constant. New Babylon' at the Gemeentemuseum Den Haag, 2016, and served as an example of the use of colour and painting technique for the Cobra Museum's reconstruction of the wall painting in *een ruimte in kleur*

5 See Constant and Locher, op. cit. (note 2), 71.

6 In Constant's paintings from the 1970s the labyrinth is still an important element, as a backdrop for playful as well as for destructive practices.

7 See W.H. Gispen, 'Eerst de mensen hervormen, dan het meubel? Ethische boetepredikers spuien hun bombast', *Elseviers weekblad* 13 December 1952.

8 Francis Strauven, 'Constant: zou hij ontevreden zijn met zijn architectuur?', in: *Niet om het even, wel evenwaardig. Van en over Aldo van Eyck*, Amsterdam [1986], 38-40, 39.

by Lucebert (1924-1994) from his new collection *Apocrief* were used instead.[9] A 'bench of solid wood' and a 'very strong, bare light bulb', as Constant described them, completed the ensemble.

The reconstruction was produced using not only the colour silk-screen prints Constant produced after the project was over for the portfolio *Voor een spatiaal colorisme* (For A Spatial Colorism), but more especially the photographs taken by Jan Versnel (1924-2007) [figs. 6 and 7]. The original negatives of these reveal a multitude of details that could not be discerned from the halftone photographs in publications, such as the wonderfully minimalist structure of the bench designed by Van Eyck and the pattern of the floor panels.[10] In addition, it turned out that Constant's picture was not painted directly on the wall, but produced as a separate oil painting, which seems to be brought forward somewhat by a broad pine frame. This three-dimensional treatment underscores the role of the painting as the central visual element in the space. The lighting is a surprising aspect. In Versnel's photographs, the blinding effect of the strong 1000-watt light bulb is softened somewhat by his photographic lights, but in reality the bright lighting imparts an unusual intensity to the colours and creates stark shadows that turn the space into a theatrical decor, in which Lucebert's verses seem to ring out like hammer blows [fig. 8].

This radical colour experiment was followed two years later by an exercise in the use of colour in a space that had to be suitable for habitation. The Bijenkorf department store had invited Gerrit Rietveld to design a small 'Suggestion for the home' for a family with two children as part of

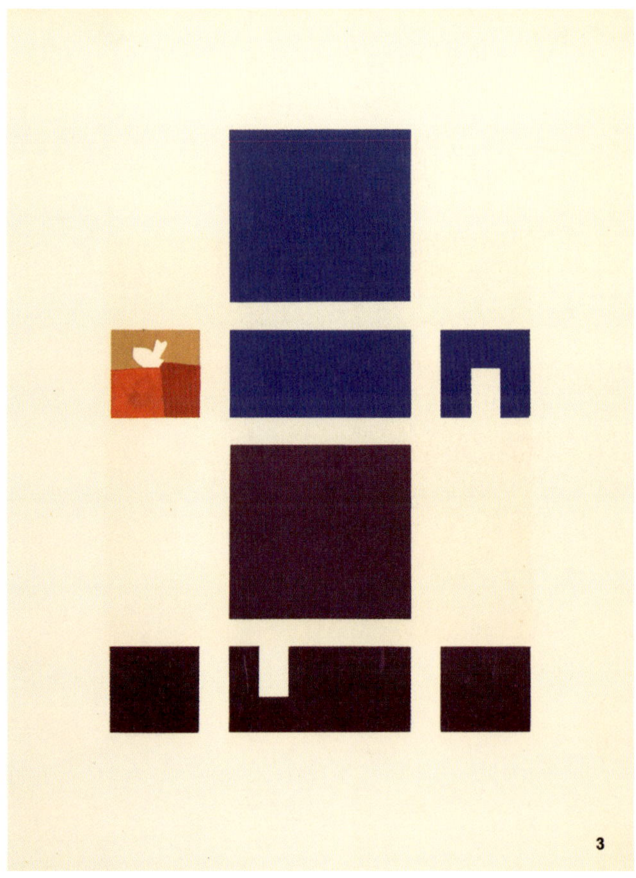

[5] Constant and Aldo van Eyck, *Voor een spatiaal colorisme* (For A Spatial Colorism), 1953 page 3 of a portfolio of 4 silk-screen prints and 4 pages of text 34.5 x 25.5 cm collection Stedelijk Museum Schiedam

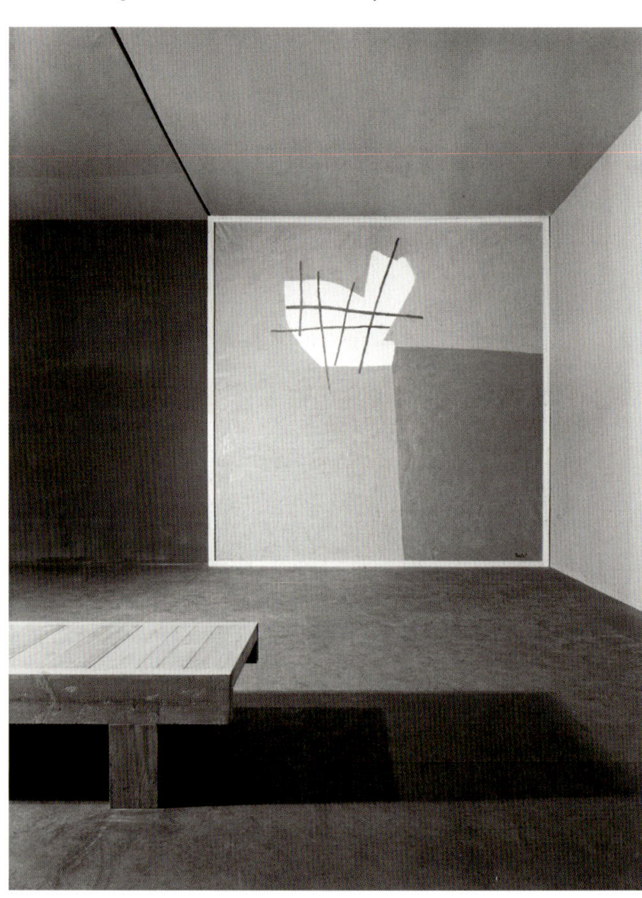

[6] *een ruimte in kleur* (A Space in Colour), at the home exhibition 'Mens en Huis', Stedelijk Museum Amsterdam, 1952 photo: Jan Versnel

9 Vincent Ligtelijn, *Aldo van Eyck. Werken*, Bussum 1999, 82.

10 The Jan Versnel archive is maintained by the Maria Austria Institute in Amsterdam.

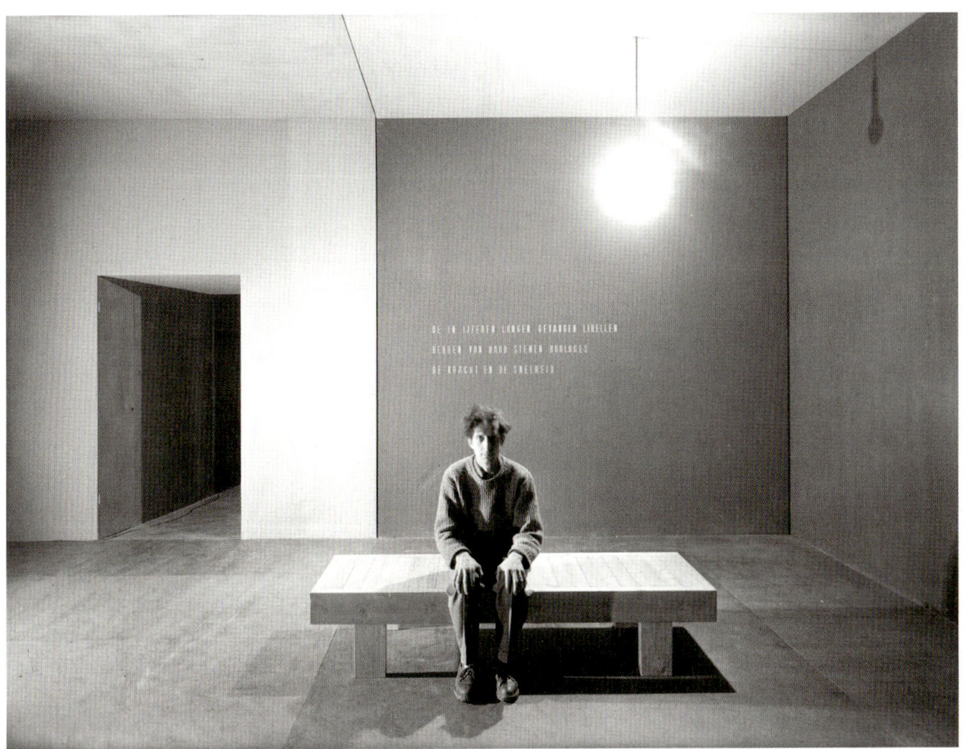

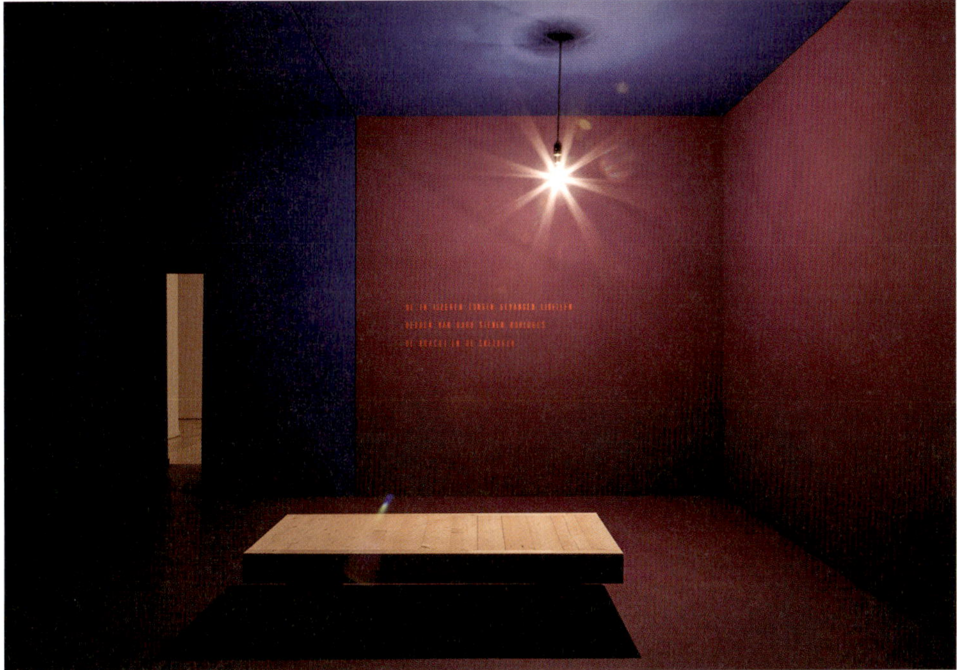

[7] *een ruimte in kleur* (A Space in Colour), with Aldo van Eyck seated on the bench he designed for this space, Stedelijk Museum, Amsterdam 1952 photo: Jan Versnel

[8] Reconstruction of *een ruimte in kleur* (A Space in Colour) in 'Constant. Nueva Babilonia', at the Museo Nacional Centro de Arte Reina Sofía, Madrid 2015-2016

the furniture show 'Ons Huis – Ons Thuis. Kleurenharmonie in uw woning' ('Our house – Our home: colour harmony in your home'). This evolved into a complete home, 52 square metres in size, with a combined living room-bedroom for the parents, a kitchen-diner, sleeping and study areas for the two children and a wet room with toilet, washbasin and shower. The many cupboards made it possible to keep the small home tidy. The long space, about 5 metres by 10 metres, was open on one side, giving visitors to the furniture show an unobstructed view of virtually all the rooms [figs. 9 and 10].

In Rietveld's first sketch, these different home functions are indicated by floor sections in primary colours, as he had done 30 years earlier in the Rietveld Schröder House [figs. 11 and 12]. After meeting Constant, he decided to give him the opportunity to put his ideas on 'spatial colorism' into practice. Constant adopted Rietveld's primary colours, but he wanted to make a bigger gesture: 'I have reduced the colour chaos ... of the multitude of household objects ... to a few strong base colours. For the living room, blue and grey; this creates space and makes the living room look deeper. ... The very limited sleeping space is made restful by having yellow flow over the floor, walls and beds and simplifying their forms. ... Finally, black serves to open up and add depth to the back wall, extending so as isolate the white toilet room and giving the kitchen its rightful place in the living room,' he wrote in an explanation for the department store [fig. 13].[11]

To Constant these were 'simple and strong colours that retain their spatial effect even in chaotic home environments and maintain a

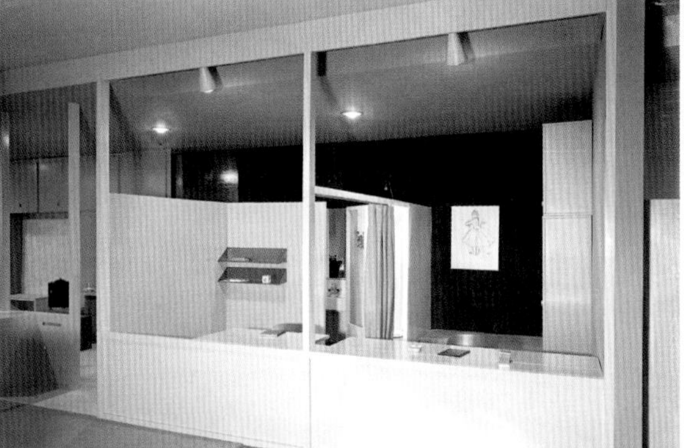

[9] Gerrit Rietveld and Constant, 'woonsuggestie' (Suggestion for the home), the Bijenkorf, Amsterdam, 1954 (view of the study and sleeping areas) photo: Jan Versnel

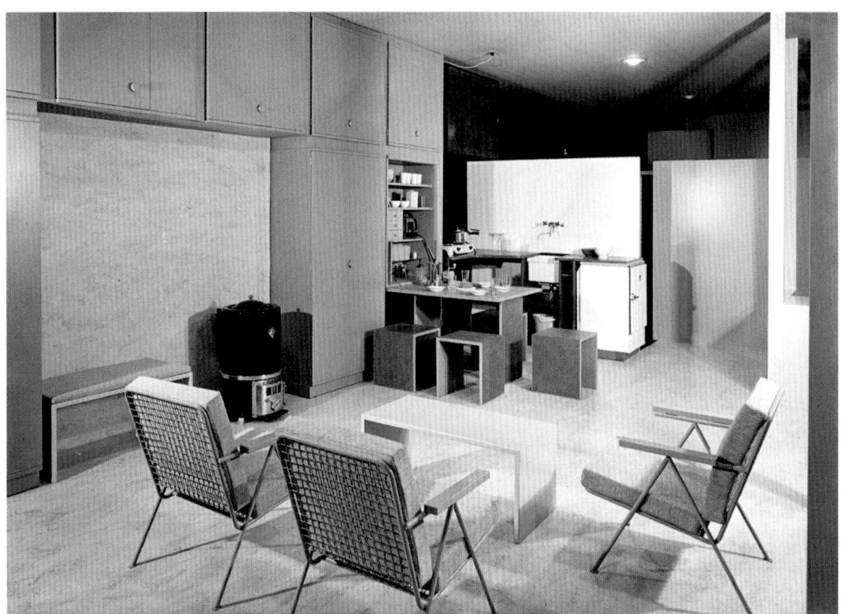

[10] Gerrit Rietveld and Constant, 'woonsuggestie' (Suggestion for the home), the Bijenkorf, Amsterdam, 1954 (view of the living area) photo: Jan Versnel

11 Letter from Constant to Mr H. Spruitenburg [the Bijenkorf], 12 February 1954, The Hague, Netherlands Institute for Art History (RKD), Constant archive, NL-HaRKD-0095 inv.no. 353.

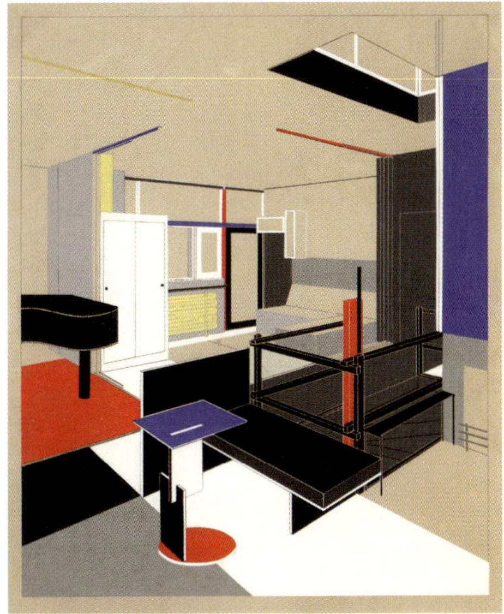

[11] Gerrit Rietveld, interior drawing of the Rietveld Schröder House, undated (1951)
gouache on paper on cardboard, 64 x 49.5 cm
collection Rietveld Schröder Archive, Centraal Museum, Utrecht

[12] Gerrit Rietveld, sketch of the 'woonsuggestie' (Suggestion for the home), the Bijenkorf, 1953
pencil, colour pencil and ink on paper, 40 x 23 cm
collection Rietveld Archive, Het Nieuwe Instituut, Rotterdam

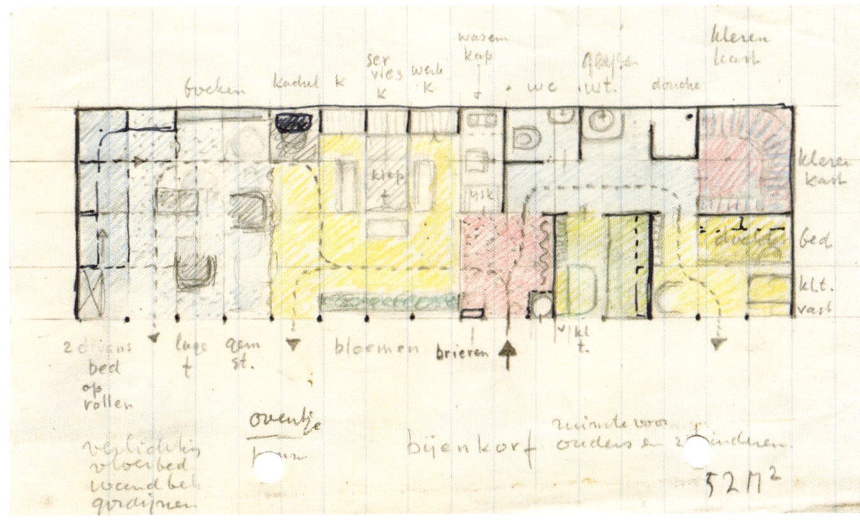

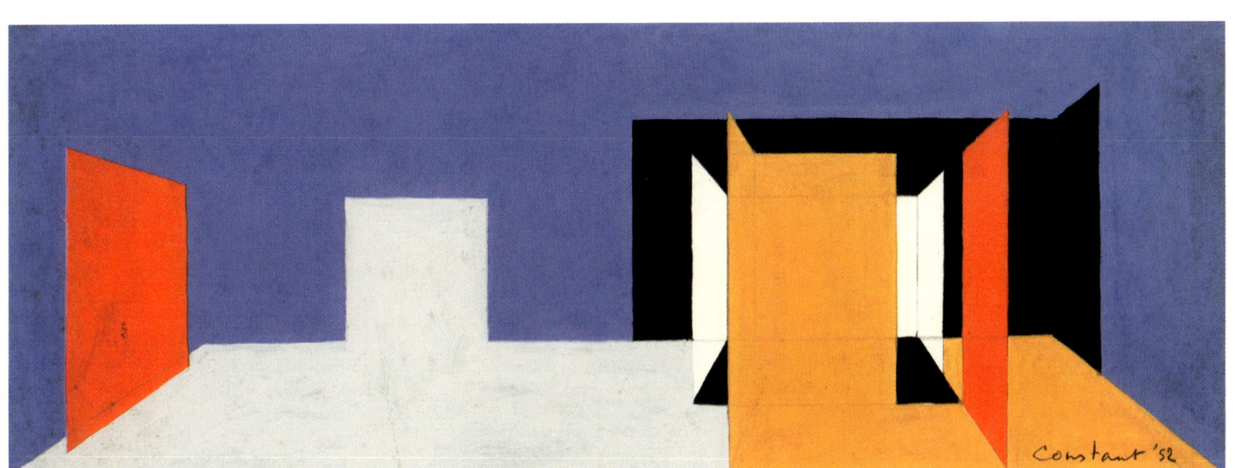

[13] Sketch of colour plan for the 'woonsuggestie' (Suggestion for the home) by Gerrit Rietveld at the Bijenkorf, 1953
(incorrectly dated 1952)
gouache on paper, 9.4 x 26 cm
Constant archive, Netherlands Institute for Art History (RKD), The Hague

sense of strict orderliness in this minimal area'.[12]

To a much greater extent than in *een ruimte in kleur*, the reconstruction shows that the colours of the available materials play a significant role. Floor coverings, upholstery and curtain fabrics, after all, are available in a limited palette and determine the final result, then and now. 'Spatial colorism is not a theory but a practice' is how Constant had concluded his manifesto, but whether this practical exercise had produced a satisfying result is far from certain, for he altered a photograph of the interior taken by Jan Versnel. Unhindered by any practical considerations, he projected his painting *Zwart, rood, groen* (Black, Red, Green, 1953) on the wall of built-in cupboards, entirely obscuring all the crockery [fig. 14]. Although Constant would continue to seek collaboration with others on many occasions in later years, this use of colour in a home setting was a one-off, and perhaps something too ordinary as well. A decade later Constant once more created space for free and radical experiments in the grand concept of *New Babylon*.

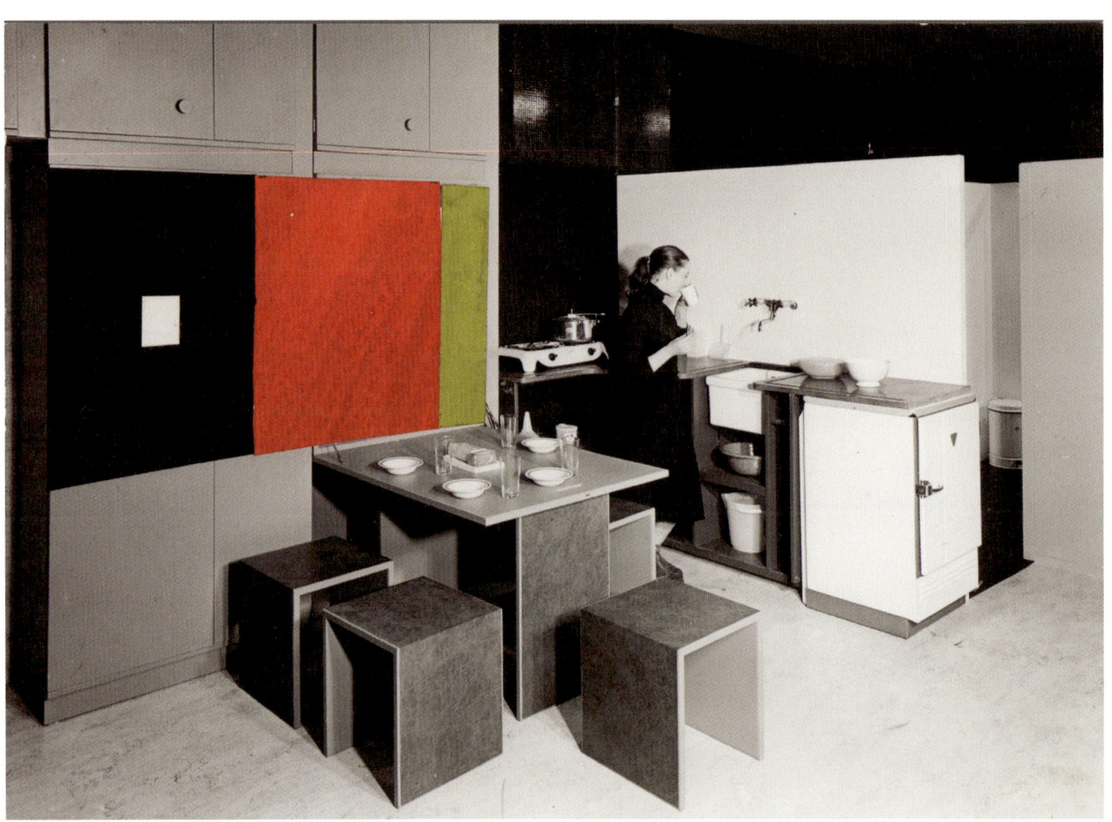

[14] Photo montage for 'woonsuggestie' (Suggestion for the home), the Bijenkorf, 1954
photo collage on silver gelatine print,
16.5 x 23 cm
collection Fondation Constant

12 Letter from Constant to Mr H. Spruitenburg [the Bijenkorf], 12 February 1954, The Hague, Netherlands Institute for Art History (RKD), Constant archive, NL-HaRKD-0095 inv.no. 353.

Constant in his studio, c. 1958. In the foreground, *La fleur mécanique* (The Mechanical Flower, 1956-1959); hanging from the ceiling *Lijn zonder einde* (Infinite Line, 1958) and *Construction dans un volume* (Wire Construction in Prism, 1957) collection Fondation Constant

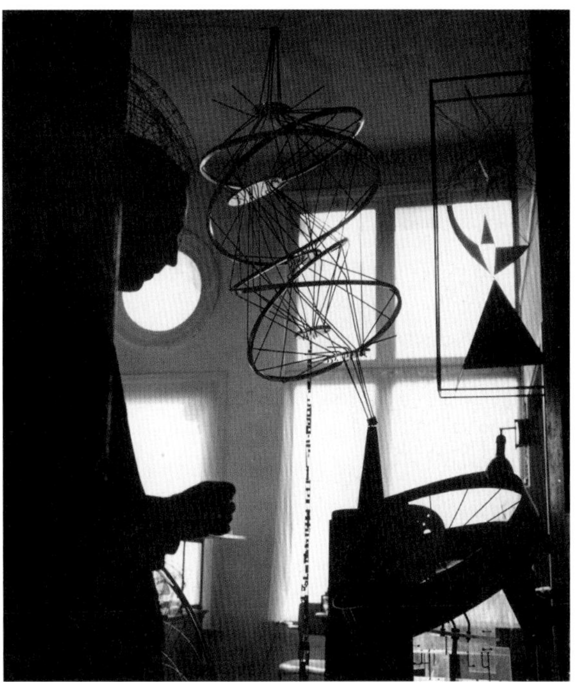

1949-1951
The War

At the 'IIe Exposition internationale d'art experimental' in 1951 at the Palais des Beaux Arts in Liège, Constant showed five paintings all bearing the title *La guerre* (War). They were part of a much larger group of works in which he portrays, in addition to the horrors of the war, the fear, suffering and desperation of war victims. It is a farewell to Cobra. Gradually the war scenes, dominated by chaos, are simplified to clear, incisive images in strong colours and lines.

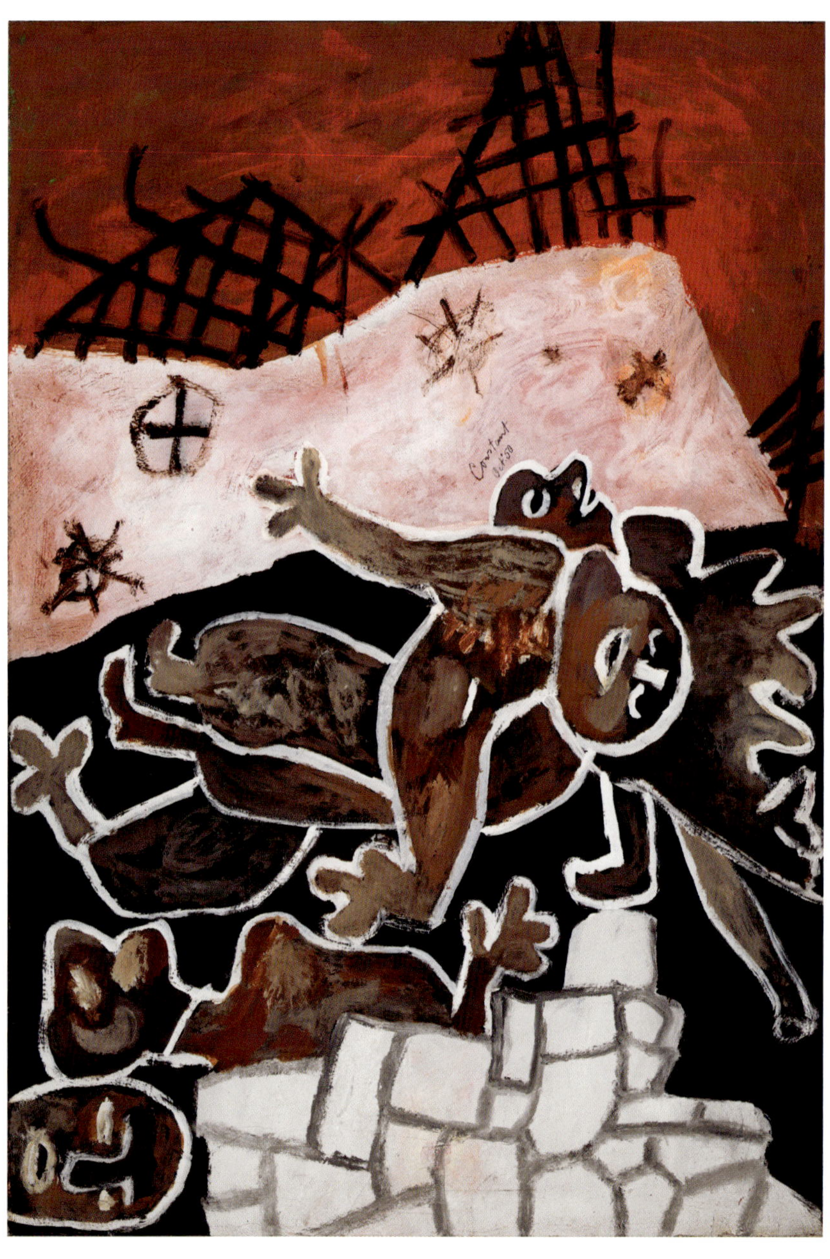

La guerre II (War II), 1950
oil on linen, 99 x 69.3 cm
collection Stedelijk Museum Amsterdam

Animaux (Animals), 1949
oil on linen, 85.2 x 70.5 cm
collection ABN AMRO, long-term loan to
the Cobra Museum of Modern Art,
Amstelveen

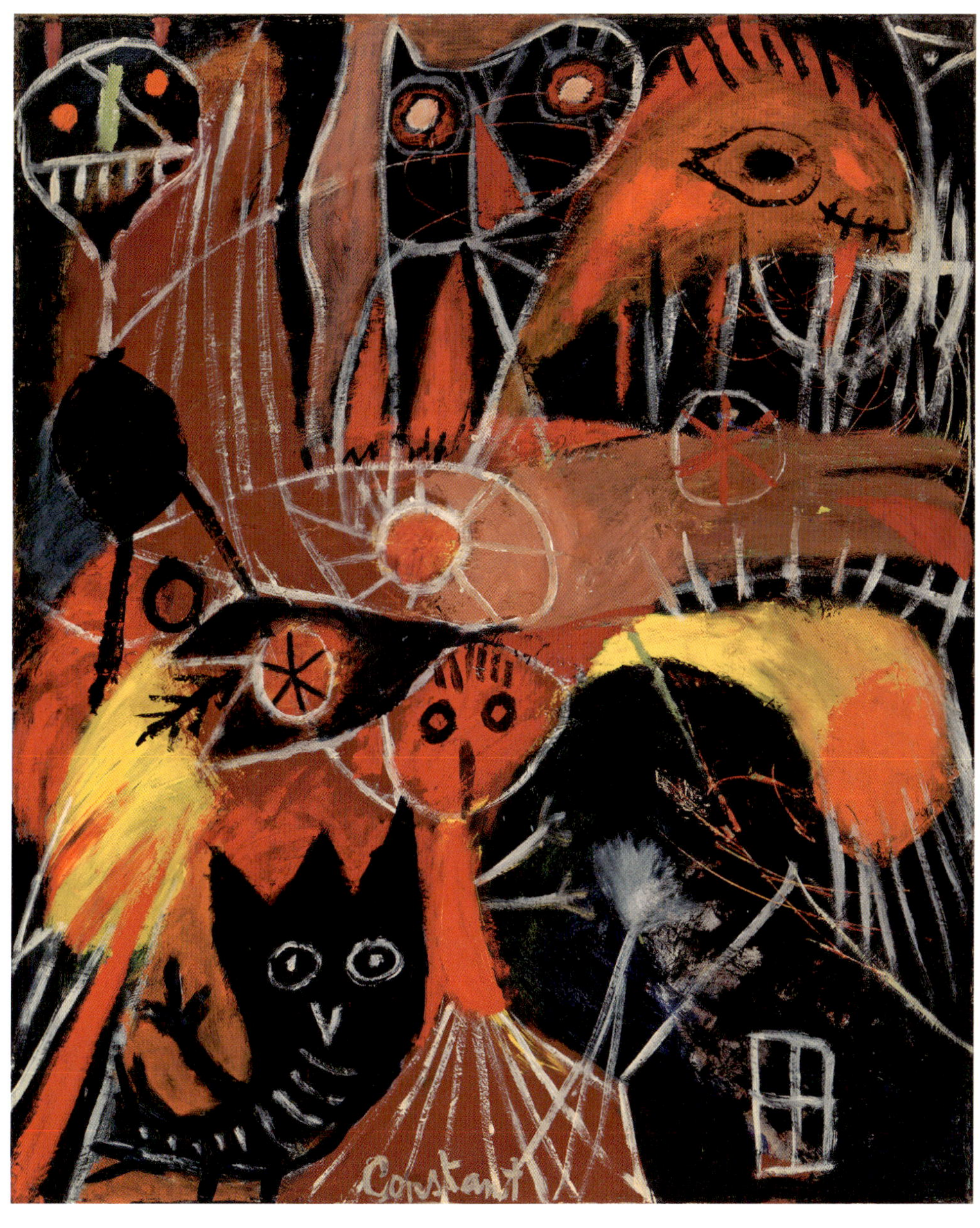

Le bouc émissaire (Scapegoat), 1949
oil on linen, 92 x 75 cm
collection Kunstmuseum Bochum

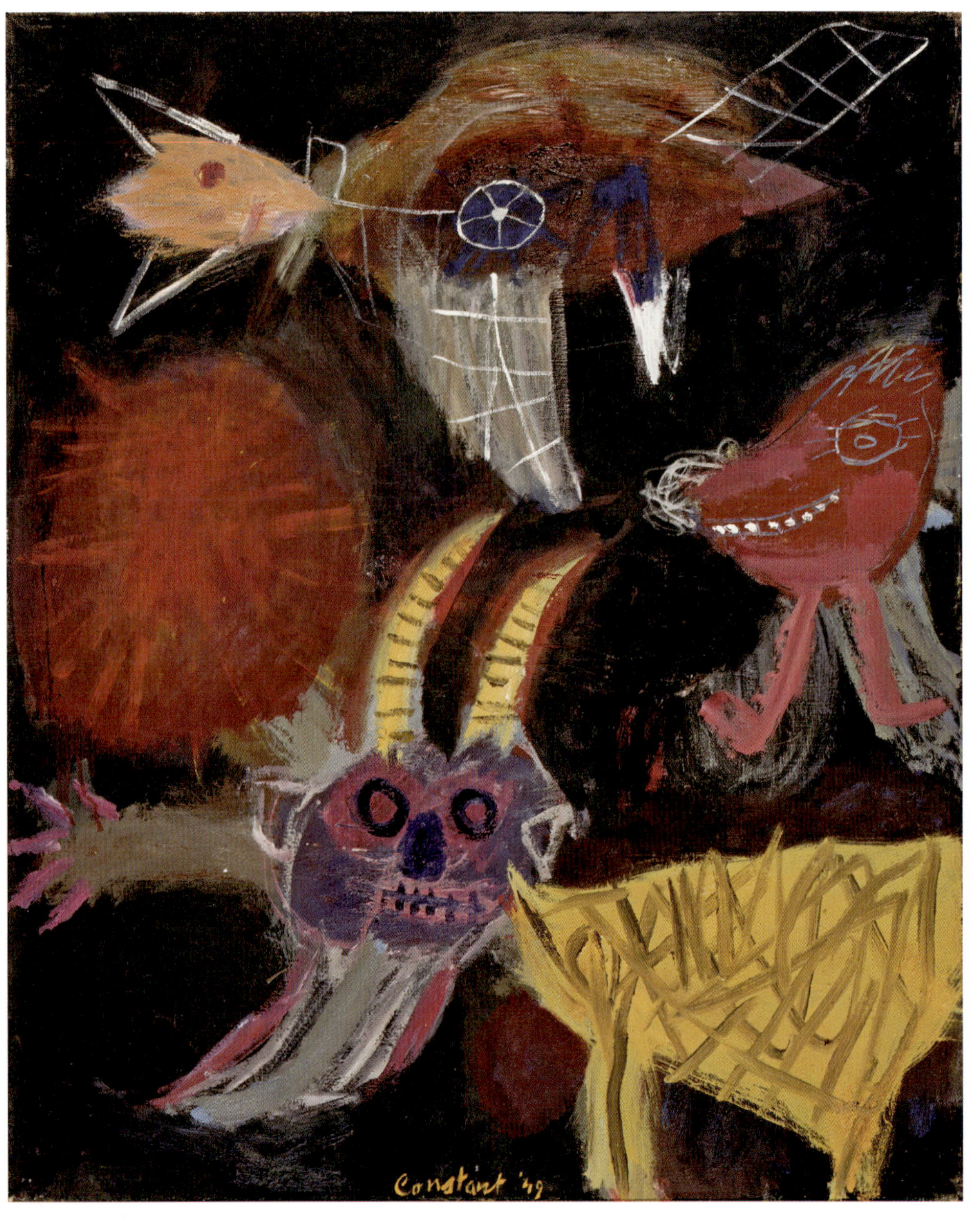

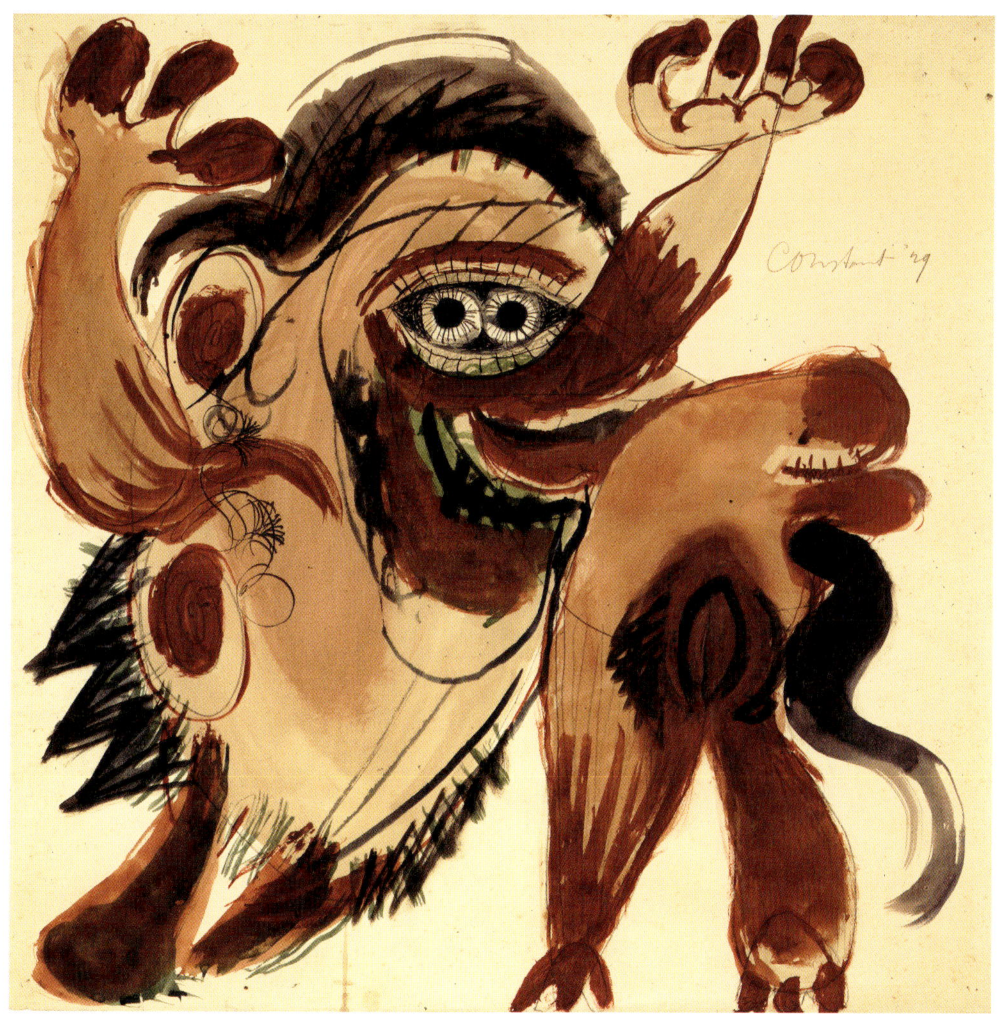

Moment érotique, 1949
watercolour on paper, 59.5 x 61.5 cm
collection René Meeuwissen, Oirschot

Zonder titel – L'Imagination effrayante 1
(Untitled – Terrifying Imagination 1), 1951
gouache and crayon on paper, 31 x 38.5 cm
private collection

Brisant bommen – L'Imagination effrayante 2
(Brisant Bombs – Terrifying Imagination 2), 1951
gouache and crayon on paper, 31 x 38.5 cm
private collection

Zonder titel – L'Imagination effrayante 3
(Untitled – Terrifying Imagination 3), 1951
gouache and crayon on paper, 31 x 38.5 cm
private collection

Slagveld – L'Imagination effrayante 4
(Battlefield – Terrifying Imagination 4), 1951
gouache and crayon on paper, 31.1 x 38.3 cm
private collection

Zonder titel – L'Imagination effrayante 5
(Untitled – Terrifying Imagination 5), 1951
gouache and crayon on paper, 30.8 x 38.4 cm
private collection

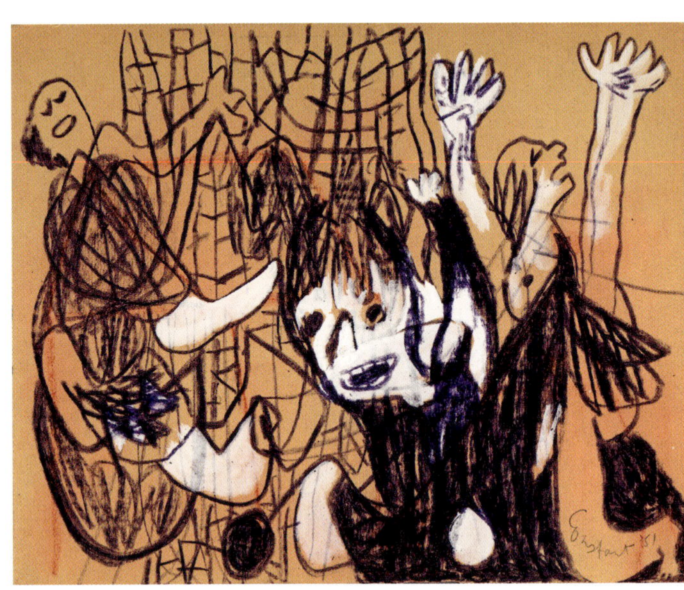

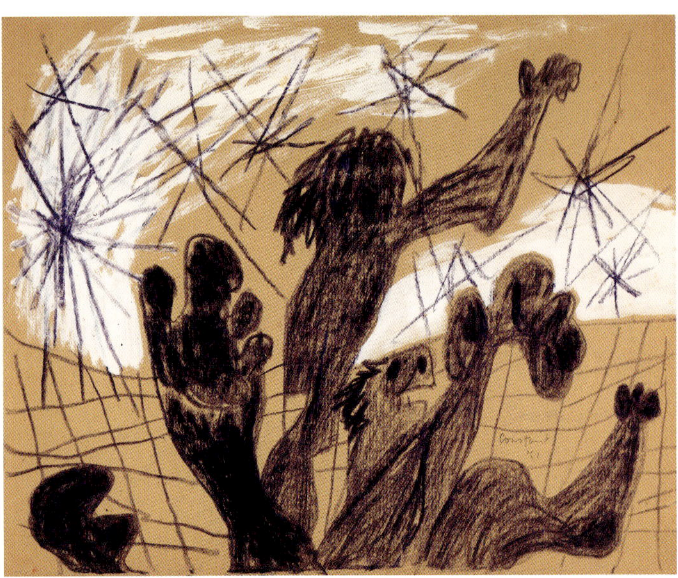

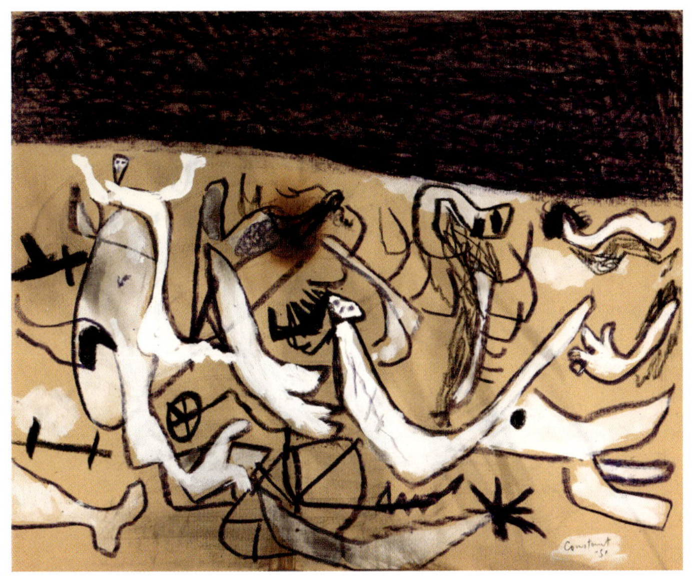

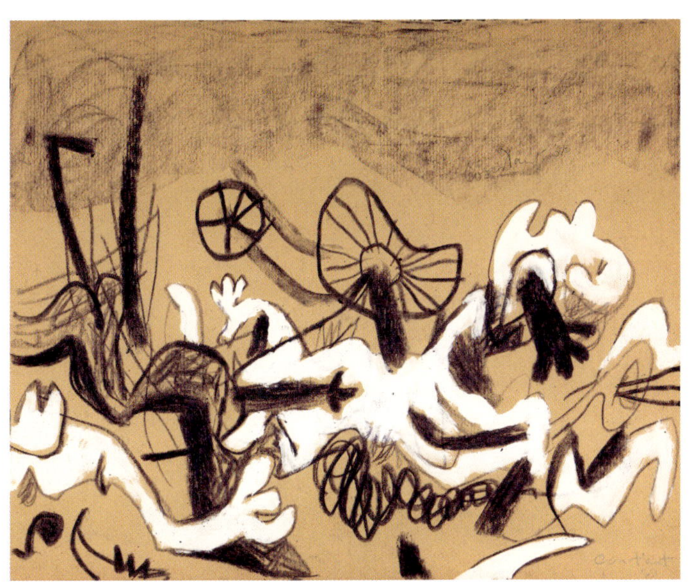

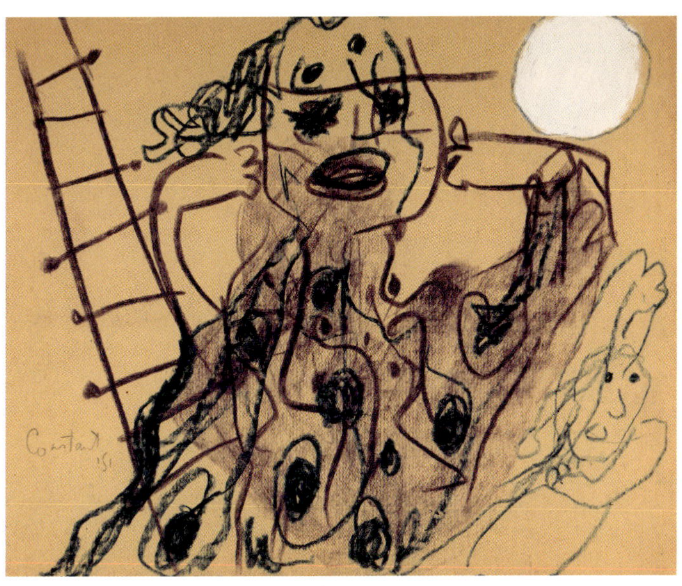

Moeder en kind (Mother and Child), 1951
coloured crayons on paper, 36.4 x 45.4 cm
collection Teylers Museum, Haarlem,
the Netherlands

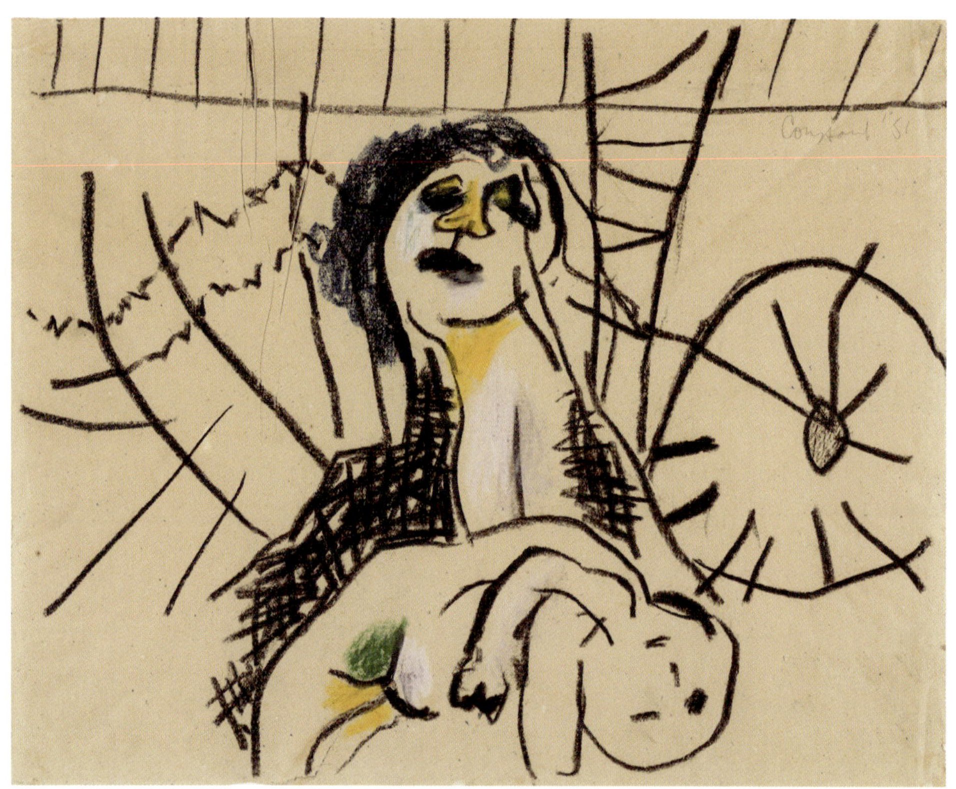

La guerre (War), 1951
charcoal and chalk on paper, 36.6 x 45.4 cm
collection Fondation Constant

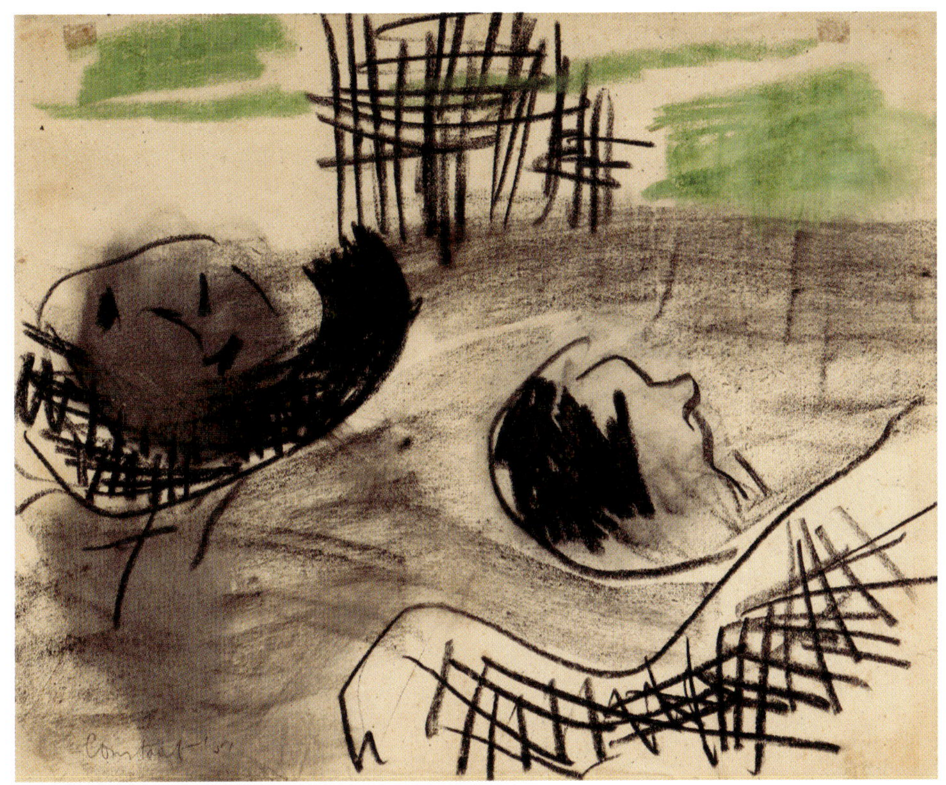

De oorlog II (War II), 1951
crayon and watercolour on paper, 36.7 x 45.7 cm
collection Stedelijk Museum Amsterdam

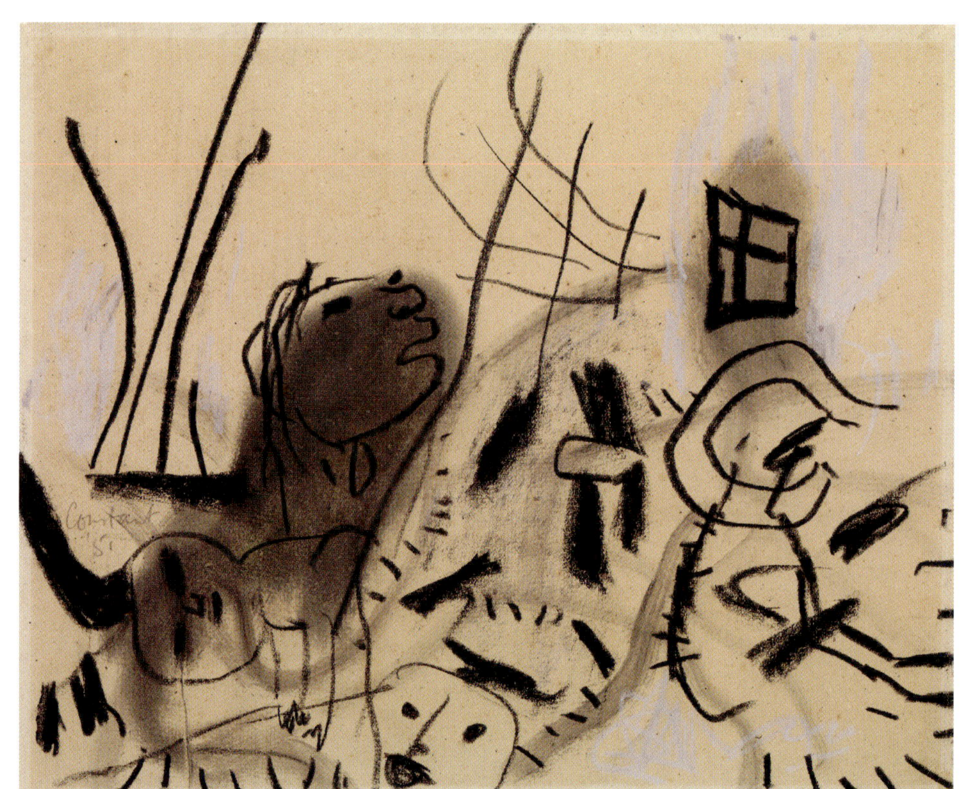

Zonder titel – Oorlog II (Untitled – War II), 1951
pastel crayons and wash on paper, 36.4 x 45.5 cm
collection Rijksmuseum, Amsterdam

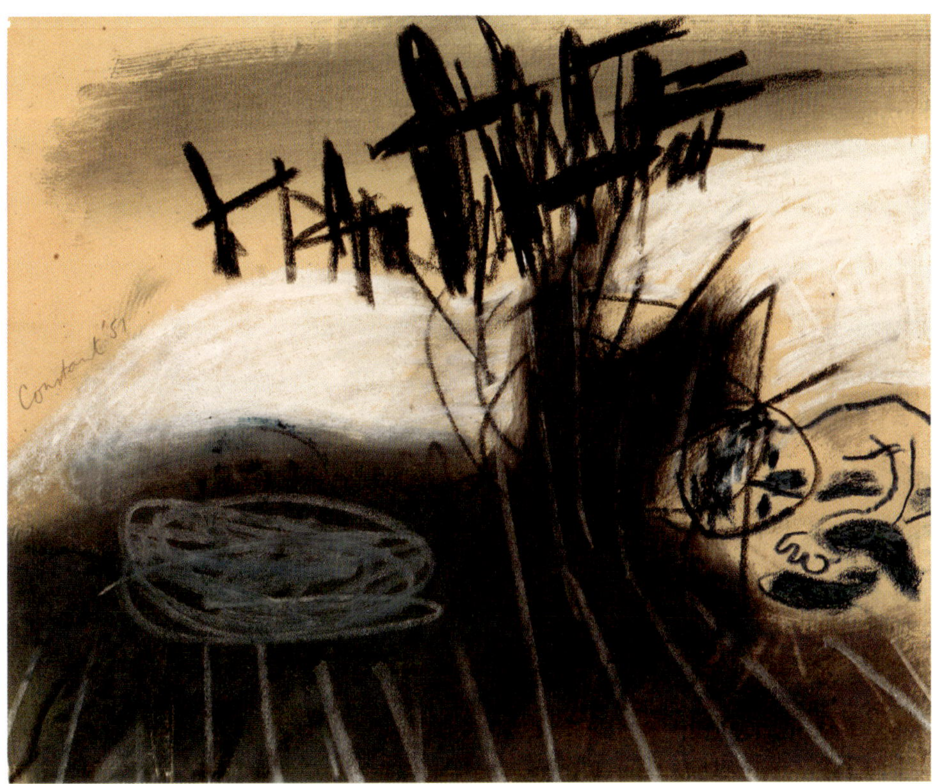

8 x La guerre (War), 1951
portfolio with 8 lithographs,
edition of 50, 40 x 30 cm each
collection Cobra Museum of Modern Art,
Amstelveen

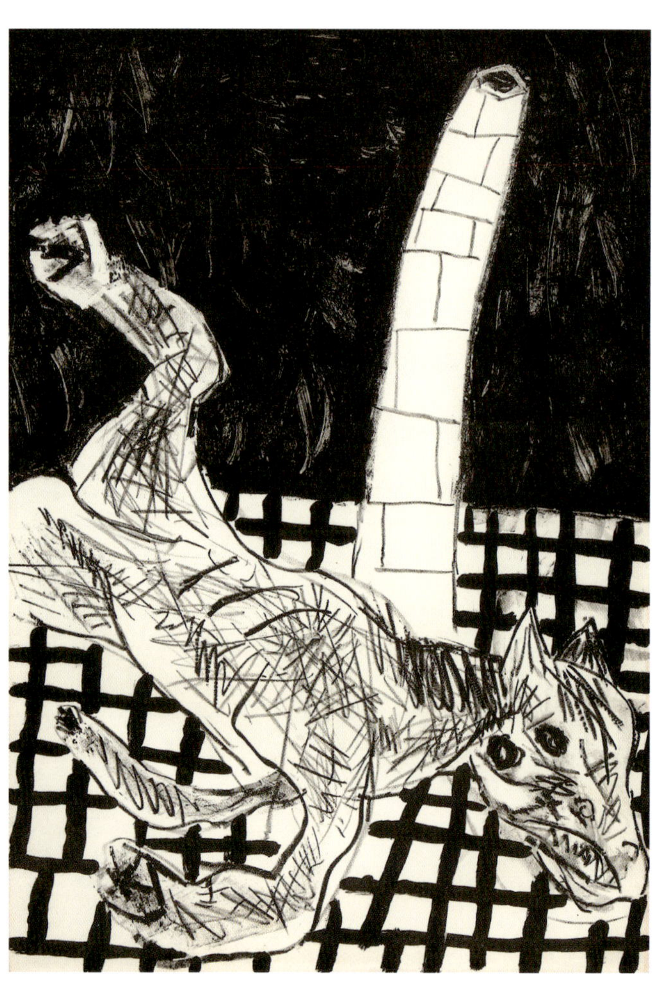

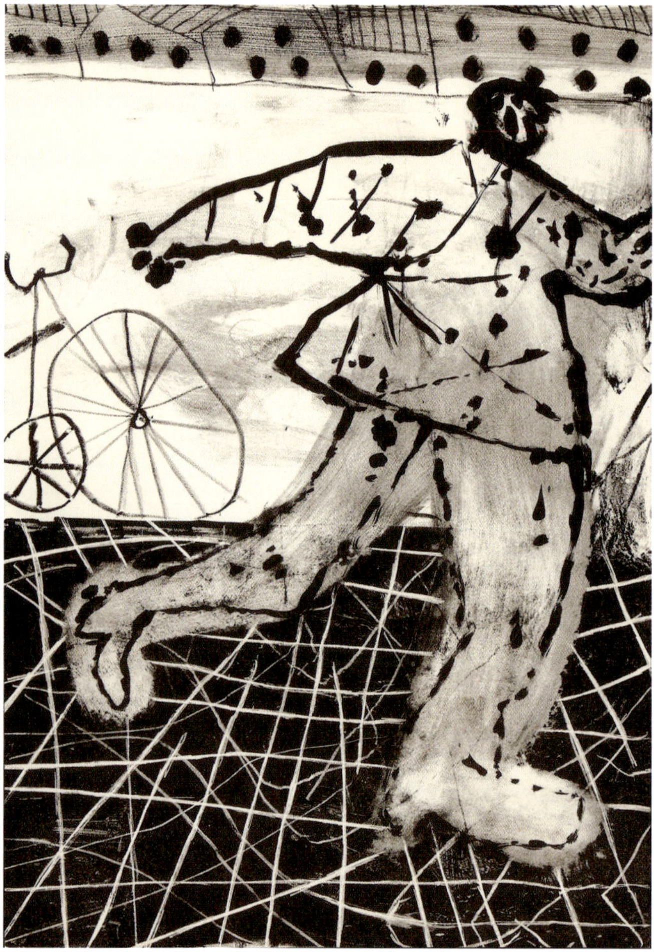

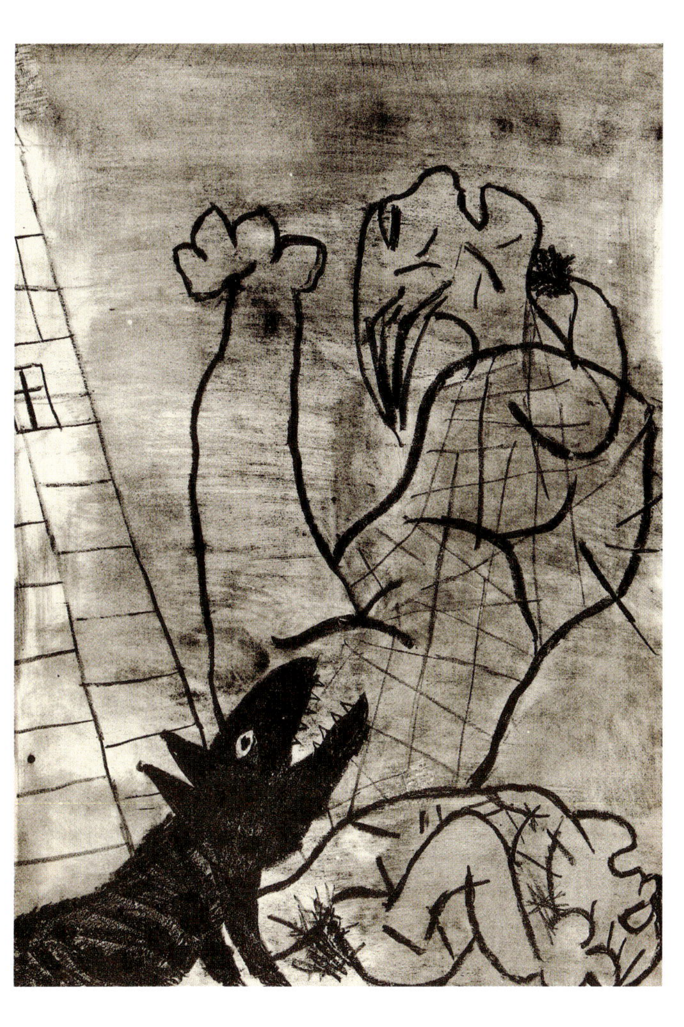

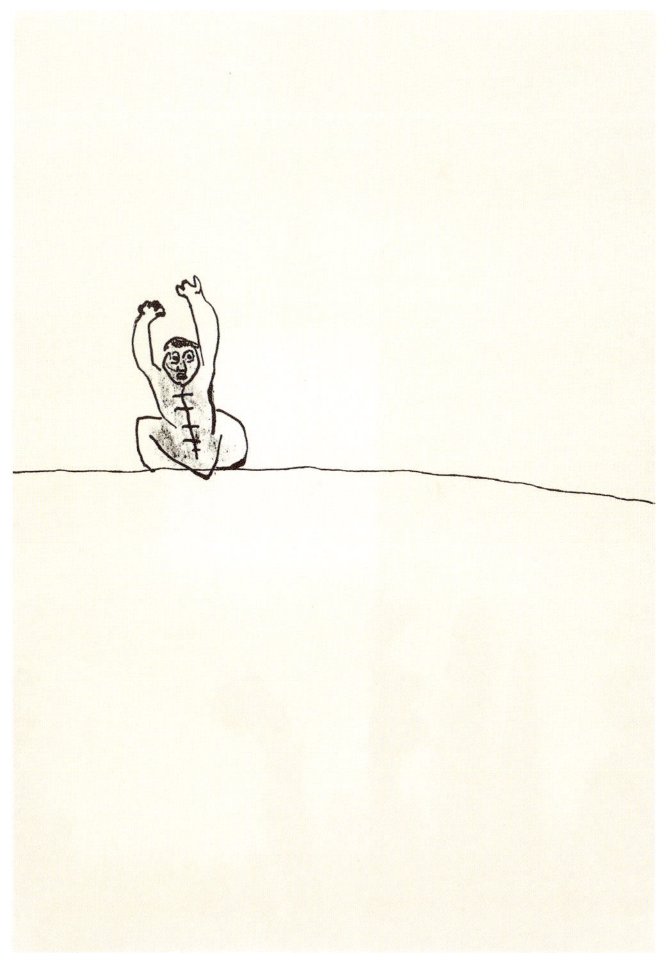

8 x La guerre (War), 1951
portfolio with 8 lithographs,
edition of 50, 40 x 30 cm each
collection Cobra Museum of Modern Art,
Amstelveen

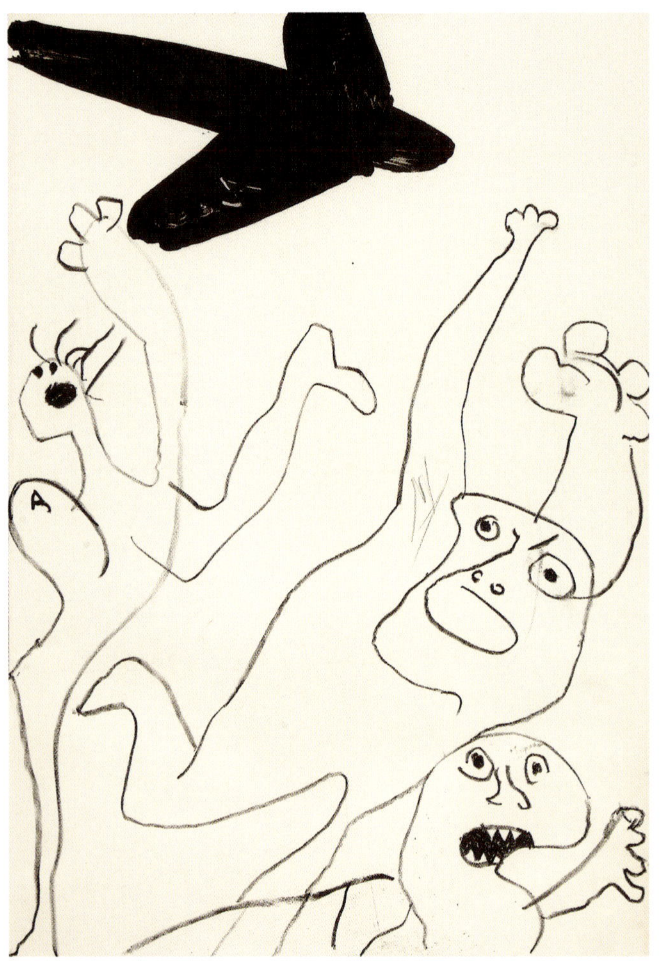

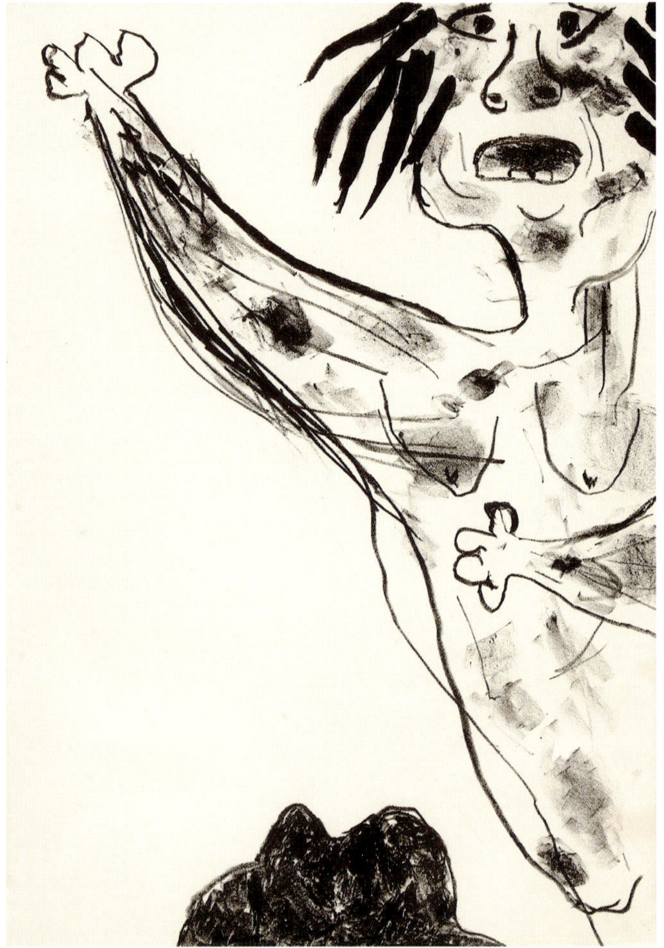

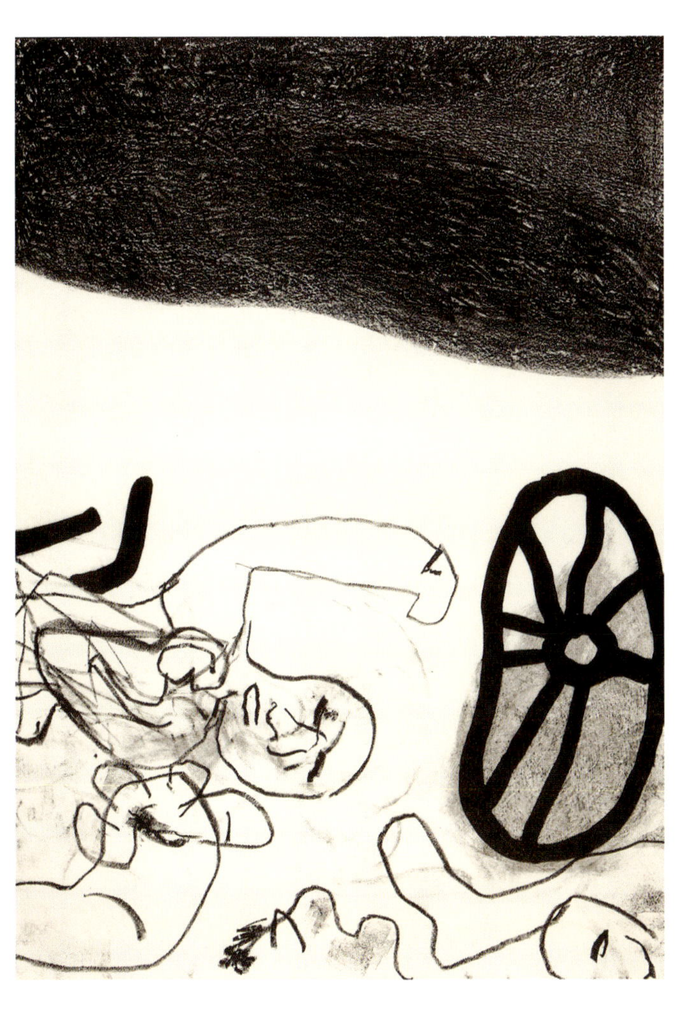

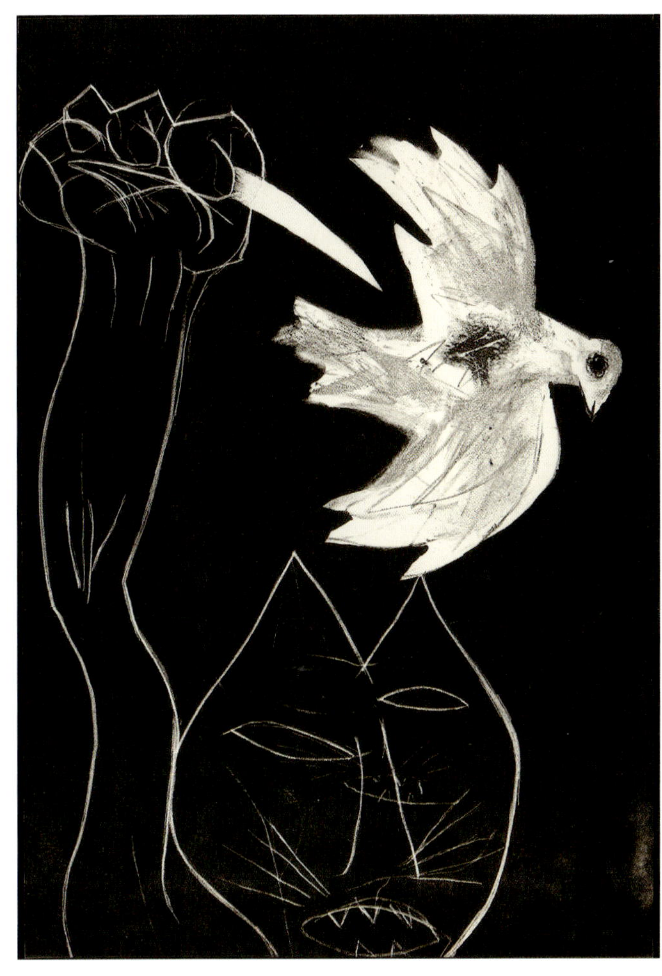

Cycliste tombé (Fallen Cyclist), 1950
oil on linen, 75 x 80 cm
collection Groninger Museum, Groningen

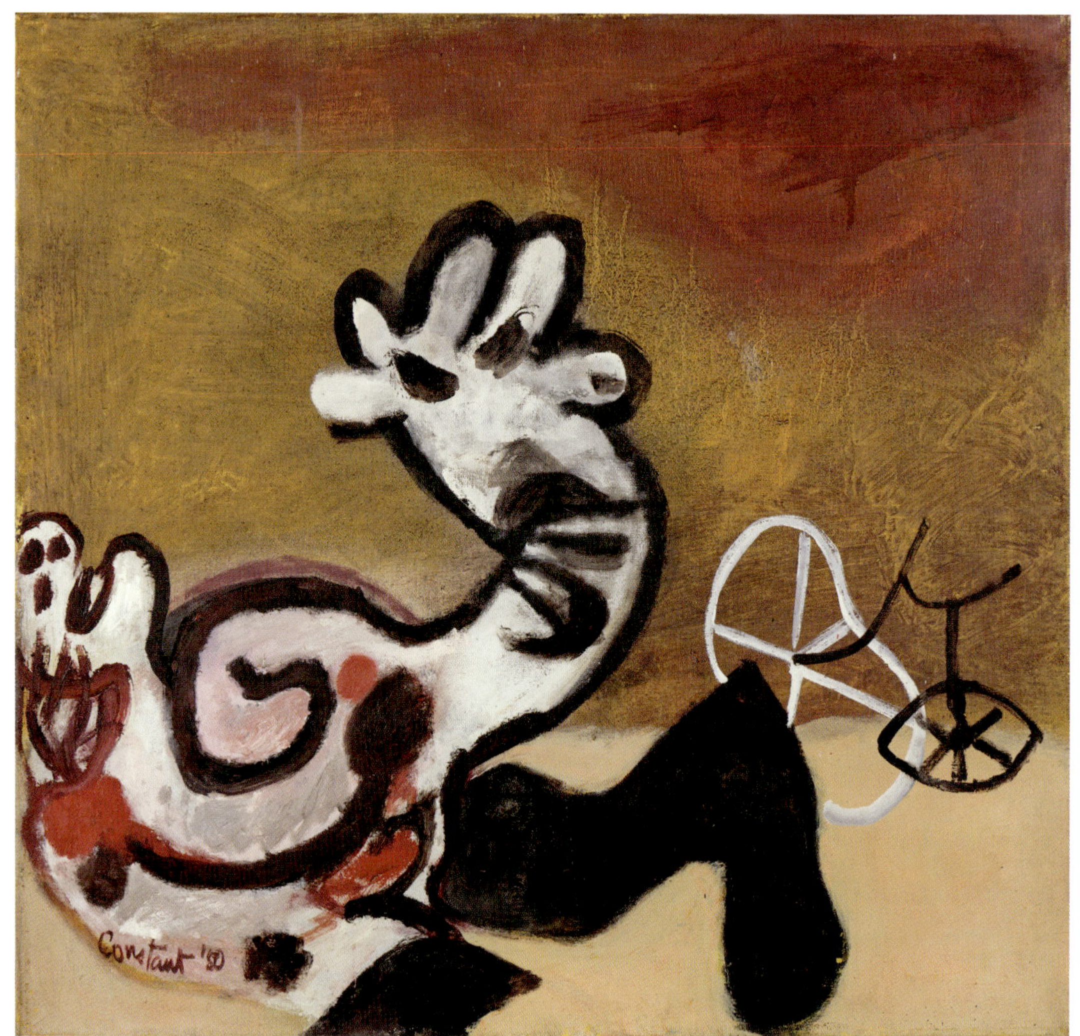

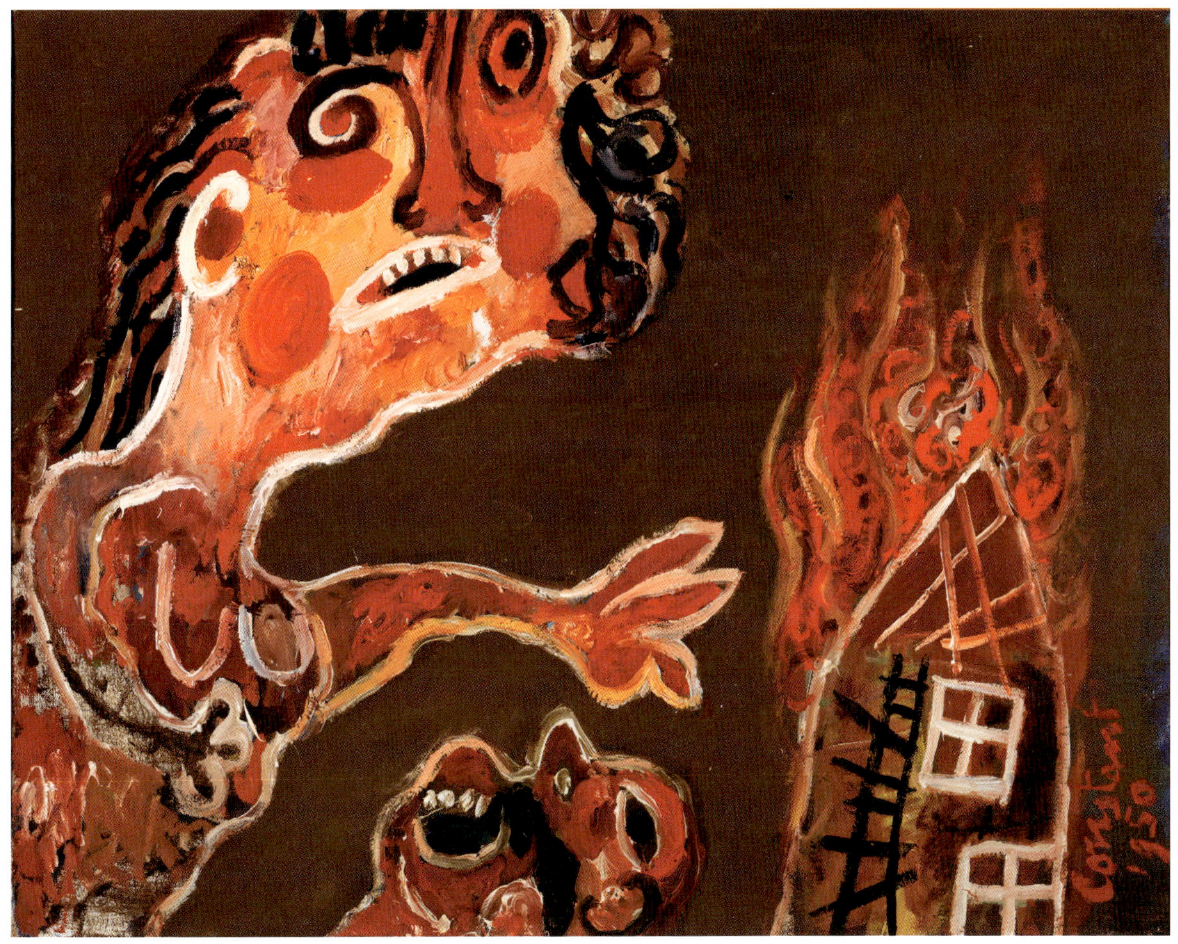

L'Incendie (Fire), 1950
oil on linen, 50 x 65 cm
collection Fondation Constant

Gevallen paard (Fallen Horse), 1950
oil on linen, 111.5 x 110 cm
collection Centraal Museum Utrecht

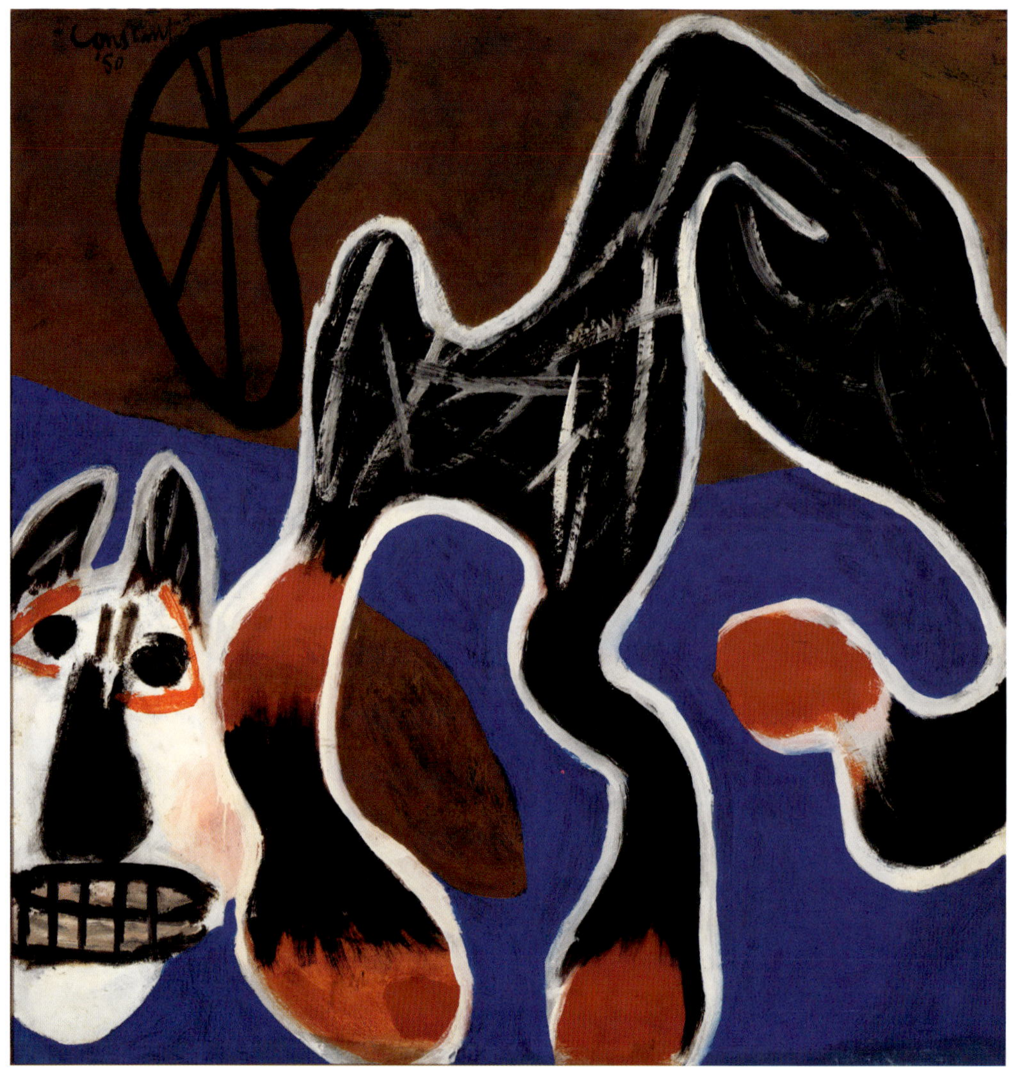

De hand (Hand), 1952
oil on linen, 115.3 x 146.9 cm
collection Cobra Museum for Modern Art, Amstelveen

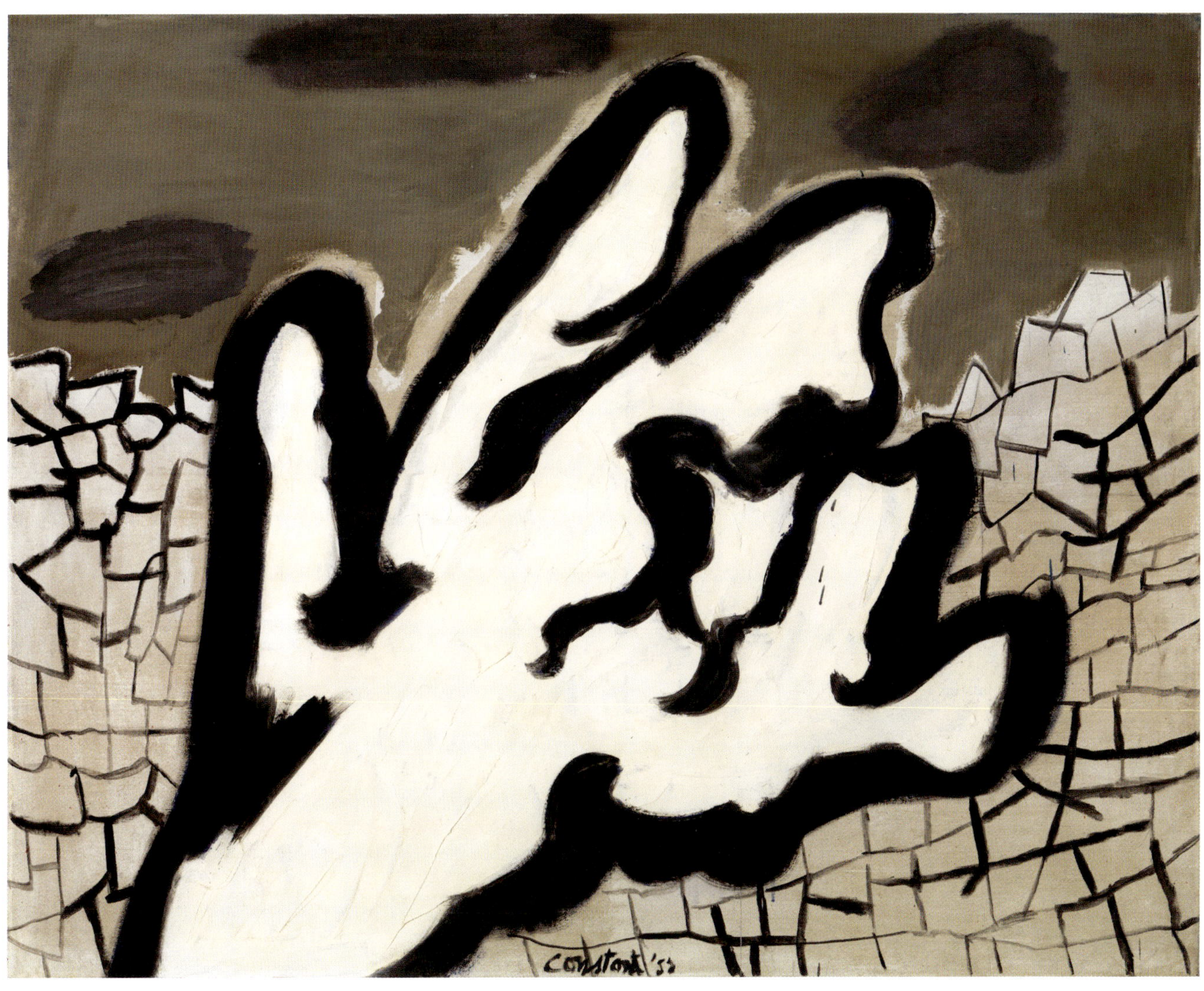

De vlam (Flame), 1952
oil on linen, 143.5 x 109.5 cm
collection Fondation Constant, long-term loan to the Stedelijk Museum Schiedam

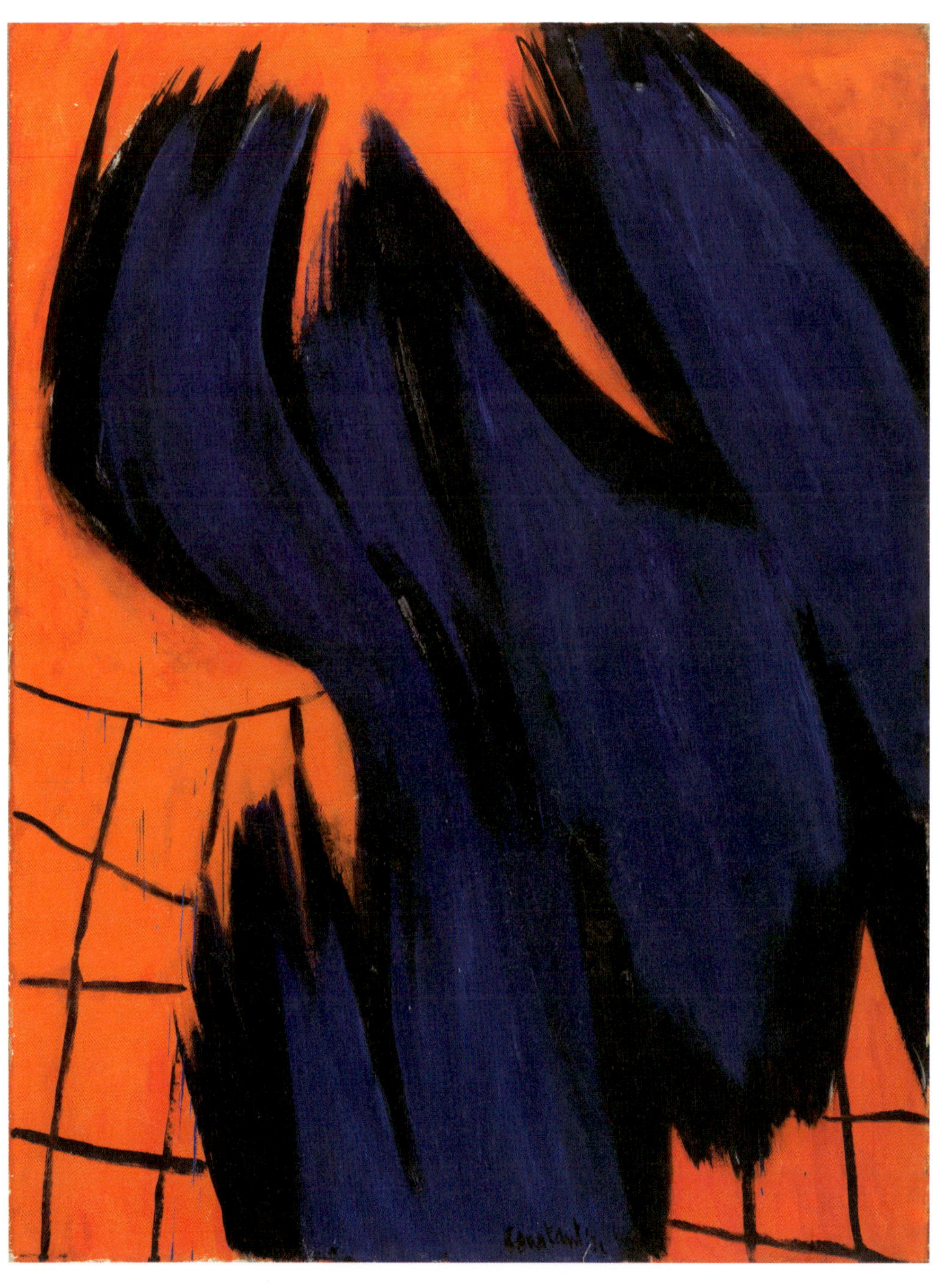

Gewonde duif (Wounded Dove), 1951
pencil on paper, 76 x 64 cm
collection Fondation Constant

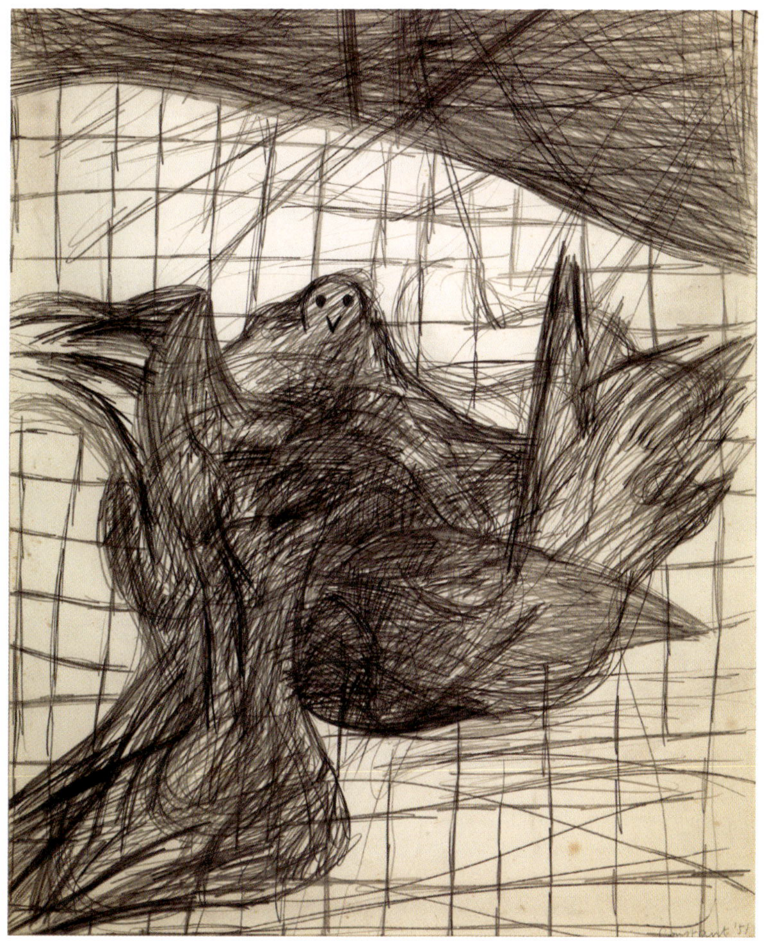

Jan Elburg and Constant, *Het uitzicht van de duif*
(View of the Dove), 1952
portfolio with 9 colour woodcuts,
edition of 125, 34 x 54 cm each
collection Cobra Museum of Modern Art,
Amstelveen

Koud als de vis, als het kijken van kruipende dieren,
als onderkoeld zonlicht onder ijs;
planten zijn stom en de dieren zwijgen.
Ik heb mijn eigen ontredderd leven
om te weten hoe het met anderen is
in dit opgepompt en geverfd paradijs.

Wat de arbeiders met de rug van hun kinderen
en met het vel van hun handen betalen,
betaal ik mee: een losgeld van onrecht
met de gehavende taal van mijn blinde
ontevredenheid, maar altijd betaal ik te weinig:
slechts met de tijdlijke tik van mijn hart;
niet met de koekoeksklok van mijn bloed.

Met het beschadigd protest om een vrijheid
van veilig te zijn tegen zonbrand en regen
en honger en hoon van de windbuilen,
betaal ik mee aan een nooit te voldoene
hypotheek die de voorouders voor is gelogen
met de prenten van helden en stadhouders,
met de rekensommen van a naar b
en de doodgewone hooghollandse taalles.

Uitsluitend aan de gedachten als kamerplanten,
bestoft in het avondlicht, gaan steden dood;
uitsluitend aan de terrassen met krokante vrouwen,
uitsluitend aan de wanhoop thuis en de gregoriaanse
schooldeun achter de geeuwende ramen
slijten fabrieken en handelshuizen.
Uitsluitend aan haat sluit het hart zich, de wenk
van de handen met lettertekens als rook;
uitsluitend aan leugens sterft het woord,
aan leuzen en lessen het goed vertrouwen
van wind en water en oevervogels.

Wij, die die wereld bekijken met een vers
op de tong als een fluittoon van hoon,
wij dragen in wangen opgeborgen
een koperen doodshoofd dat boos is:
door hamers van binnenuit nors gebeukt;
in het zoeklicht van buiten verstard tot een grijns:
de lach van het cynische incasseren.

Zo kunnen de straten en kamers ons opleveren.
Wij zijn, want de straat kan ons opleveren,
met een voet en een voet en een hand
en een handtastelijk duidelijk gelijk,
grof en verongelijkt, omdat wij zijn die wij zijn:
met handen en voeten en monden ontkomen
aan deze onmenselijke mentaliteit:
lipstick te zijn van de klassenstaat.

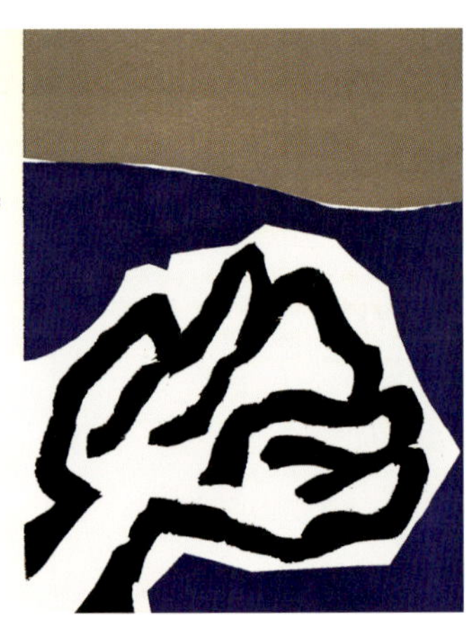

Maar de ogen gezouten door zweet en tranen,
maar het tergende ruien van de kalenders:
dat doen de dagen hem, wat doen de dagen?
Wat doen wij? Wij schuren de muren dun
met schampere krassen van kinderkrijt,
met een mes en een vijl van gewone wensen,
om eenmaal bewust de lamlendigheid
van het bukken, omkeren en bezwijken
aan de veiligheid van het onrecht en leed
van het arbeiderskind en de ongelijke
bevoorrechting ver om ons dood te weten.
Voorwaarts, en niet vergeten.

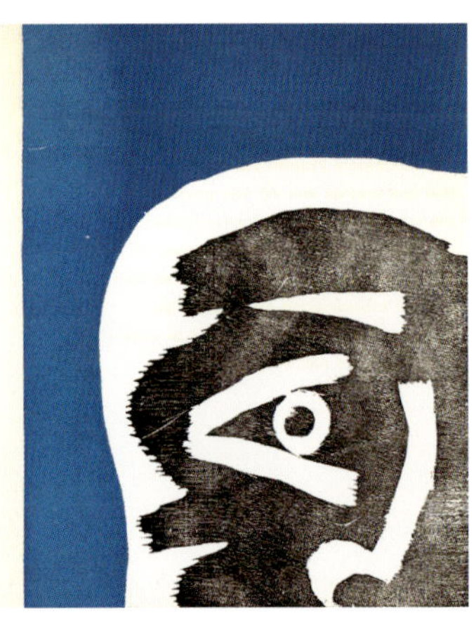

Wie biedt? Wat baat mij de stapelplaats
janmaats en machinegeweren? Wie biedt meer,
biedt mij een plaats zonder praatjes
van maan, mooie mogol of moloch of mammon,
een gewone plek zon, zonder gouden verleden?
Magnaat, magistraat, advocaat van de duivel,
wie biedt? En ik vraag geen afbraak.

Zij hebben octrooi op instortende huizen
en kleerscheuren, alleenvertoningsrecht
van mijn regen, op de rechte weg
de tol, om mijn geld te geven, te heffen,
het vruchtgebruik van gewassen:
koolzaad en graan en de zoete peen.

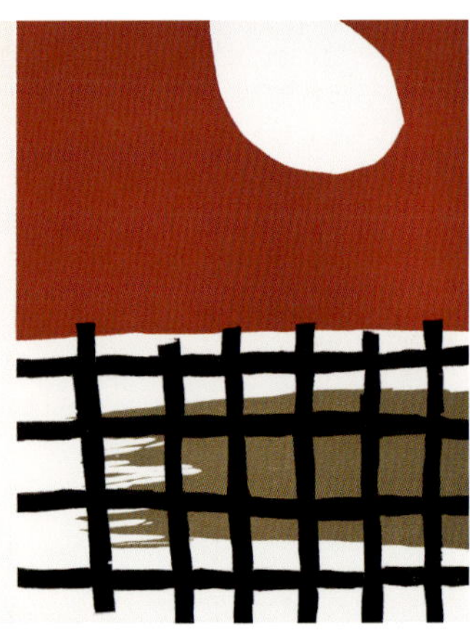

Ik moet: zoet zijn, soldaten betalen,
betaalde moed, onvergoed bloed en pijn
eisen en goedkeuren, leugens bewijzen
en leuren met jabroers en harlekijnen,
bonen van broodroof eten.

Ik moest beter weten, Marx niet lezen,
kieskeurig wezen, niet de kant kiezen
van de blauwkielen onder het kolengruis,
uit het achterhuis, de armzalige achter-
en arbeidersbuurten, neen, fijn van alure
zijn en mij spijzen met het overschone,
ten hemel wijzen en God vertonen
(dat is: op een werf van bederf werken).
En de H-bommen doen de deur dicht.
Wie biedt een simpel uitzicht,
zonder aalmoezen angst, zonder pleinen van angst?

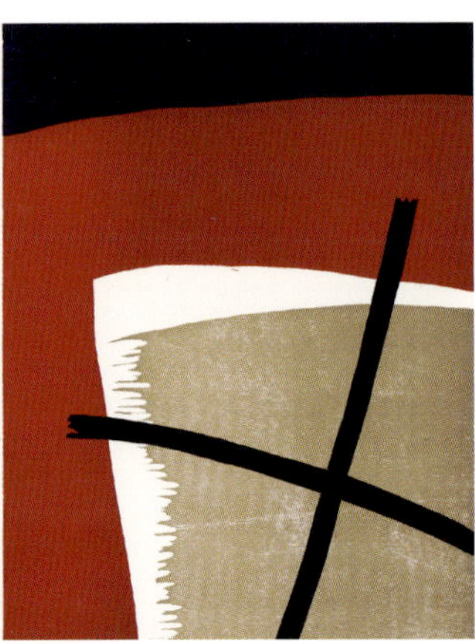

Dit is de keuze: onheuse leuzen,
delicaat gepraat van vingertoppen
op een toetsenbord met alfabet der kaballa,
of staan en weer vallen in het wisselvallig
gevecht om brood en recht en een nieuwe wereld,
met de veeltallig-veeltalige menigten:
kinderen, huismoeders, hardknuistige kerels:
een eenstemmig veemgericht van vrede.

Kameraden, wie een eerlijk besluit
in een lied uit en bij zijn klasse staan gaat,
zal door hofmeiers, honden en verstokte kohorten
gezocht en gejaagd worden, gehaat worden
als veepest. Maar het zal lang laat worden
eer hij van zijn vermaningen aflaat.

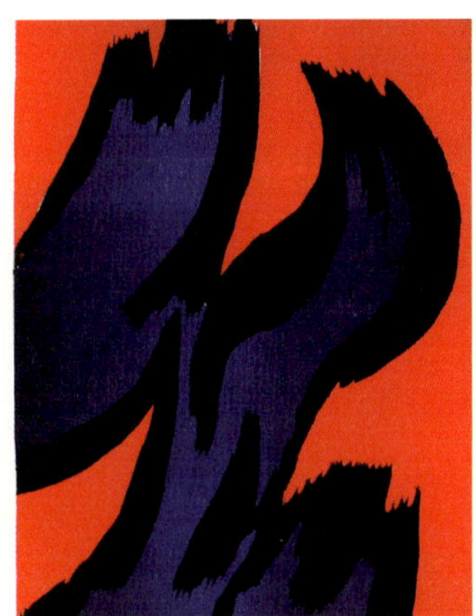

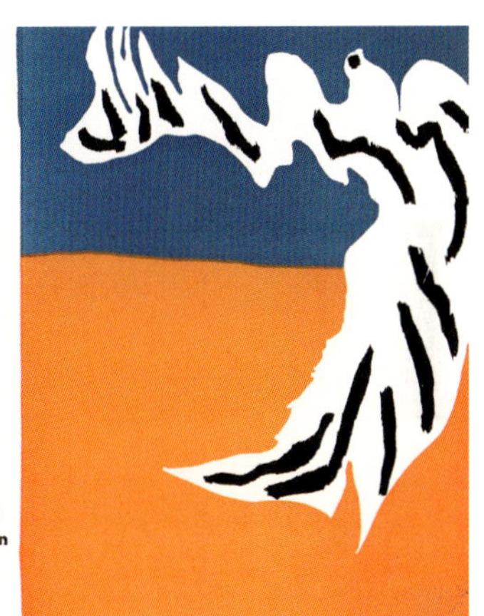

Van oudsher zien de ogen liever dons dan bloed
dat dons groeit op de duiven van Picasso:
daar steken de scherven als messen naar,
daar steken de fosforbommen de brand in,
daar steken die naar ons spugen de draak mee,
daar steekt het verleden de loftrompetten
van dode verdrukkers.

Vleselijk is onze vrede, gewone begeerte
naar een veilige wieg met een kleine stem,
een vriendelijk woord en een snee kruimig brood:
daar knaagt de dood aan, daar slaat een gele haan
de vlam van zijn vleugels aan,
daar komt men aan met een hand als brand.

Persoonlijk willen wij een vaderland,
door de koeien betreden en gegeten,
met koren en zonnige wegen, zelfs in de regen:
dat egt men met prikkeldraad,
daar legt men vulkanen aan,
daar vecht zich een waanzin van wagenraderen
door dat zware broodgraan, dat laaien zal.

Werkelijk zijn wij met velen,
een werkelijkheid met blote handen:
daar zet men de tanden in,
daar duwt men geweren in van gewin,
daar neemt men de koperen centen uit,
daar wil men de lijnen in lezen,
hoe het zal wezen.

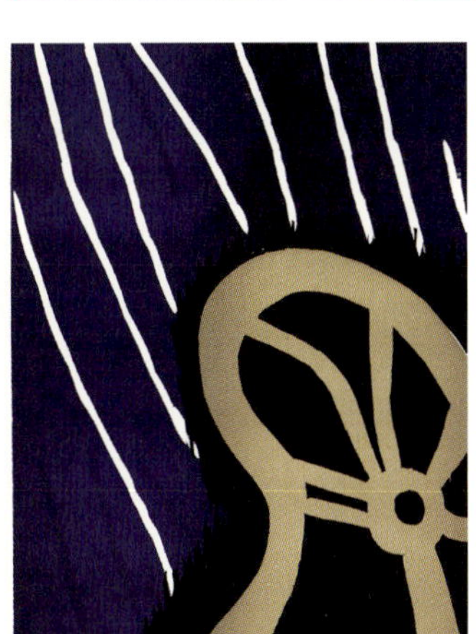

Het is bewezen dat hun rijk heeft uitgeluid:
wij zijn tot moed gedoemd, grauw van vertrouwen,
dat wij varen zullen, dit land bebouwen,
als vrijen in de fabrieken staan.
Daar helpt geen lievemoederen aan,
geen god in een heilig huis aan,
geen wichelroede, geen maan,
geen muizenval die op niets slaat,
geen huilen, geen politiestaat:
de toekomst ligt in de vuisten
van het proletariaat.

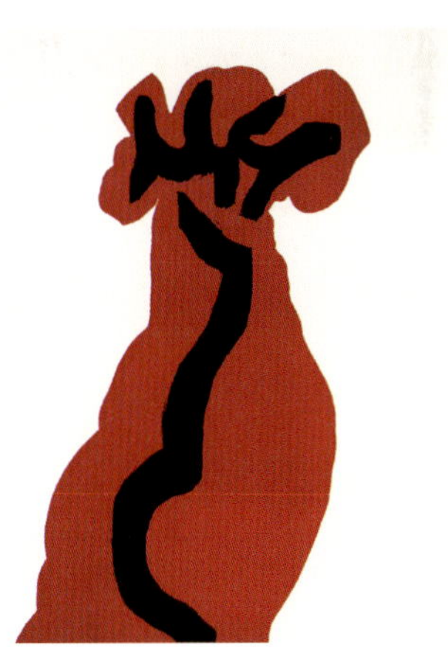

1952-1953
Colour

In this period, Constant goes further with the simplification of the motifs from the war paintings. Some titles allude to a figurative premise, while others are identified as purely abstract 'compositions'. In the works, colour is the crucial element. The colour sections slot into one another like puzzle pieces with frayed edges. Sometimes they seem to lie one on top of the other, creating a suggestion of depth. One of the paintings from this period was enlarged to monumental size for the installation *een ruimte in kleur* (A Space in Colour, p. 20-22).

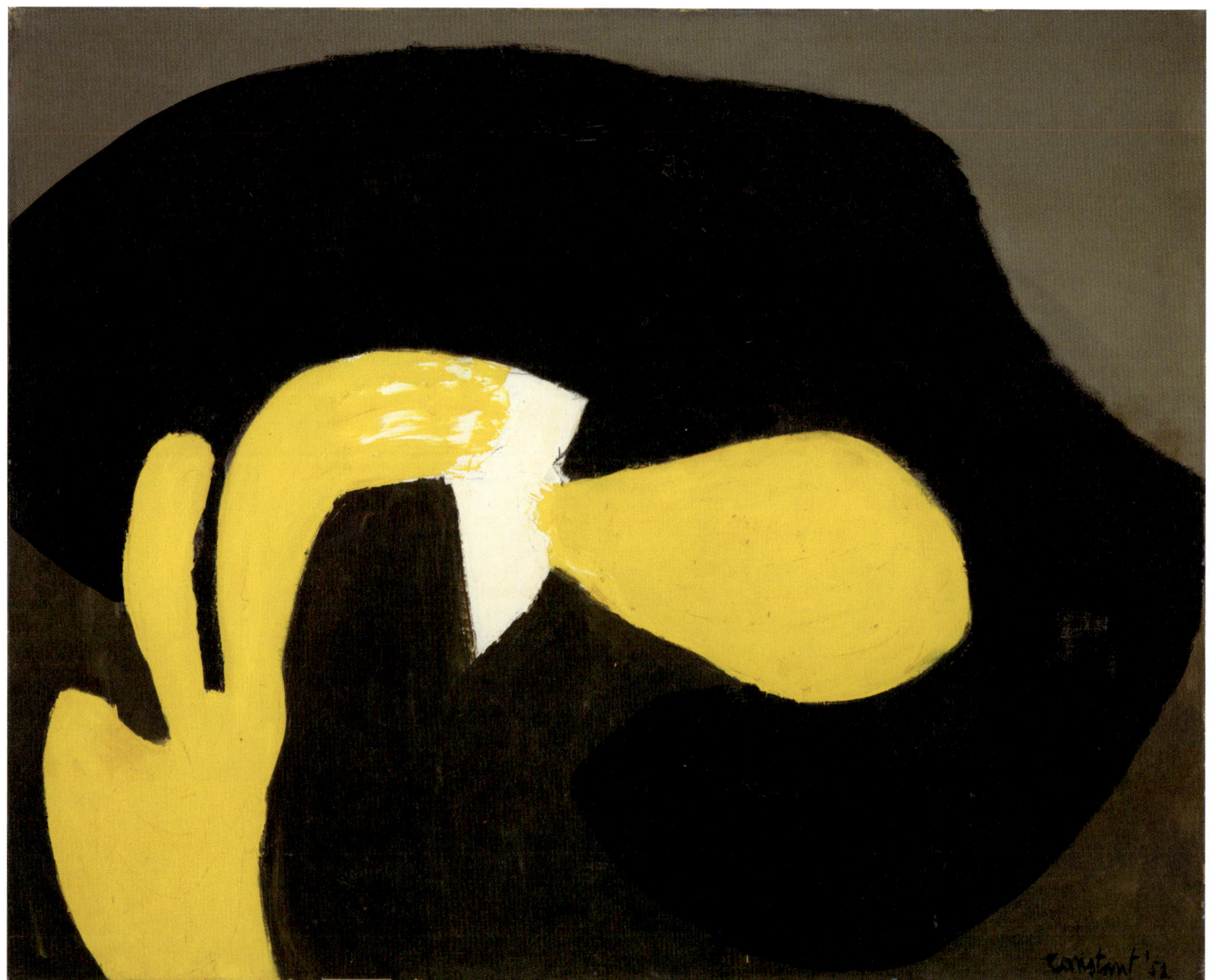

Gele cactus (Yellow Cactus), 1952
oil on linen, 110 x 143 cm
collection Fondation Constant, long-term loan to the Stedelijk Museum Schiedam

De stier (The Bull), 1952
oil on linen, 76 x 61 cm
collection Fondation Constant, long-term
loan to the Stedelijk Museum Schiedam

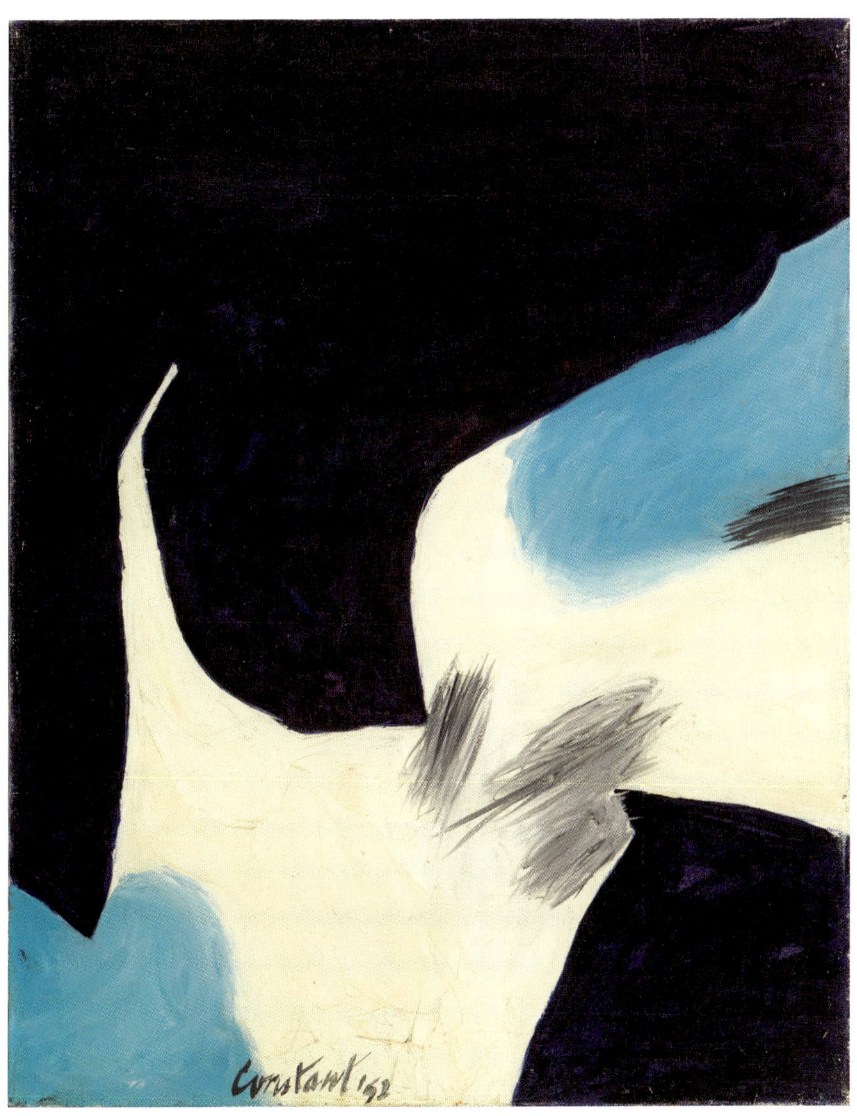

Zonder Titel – Compositie
(Untitled – Composition), 1952
oil on linen, 130 x 97.5 cm
collection Fondation Constant, long-term loan to
the Stedelijk Museum Schiedam

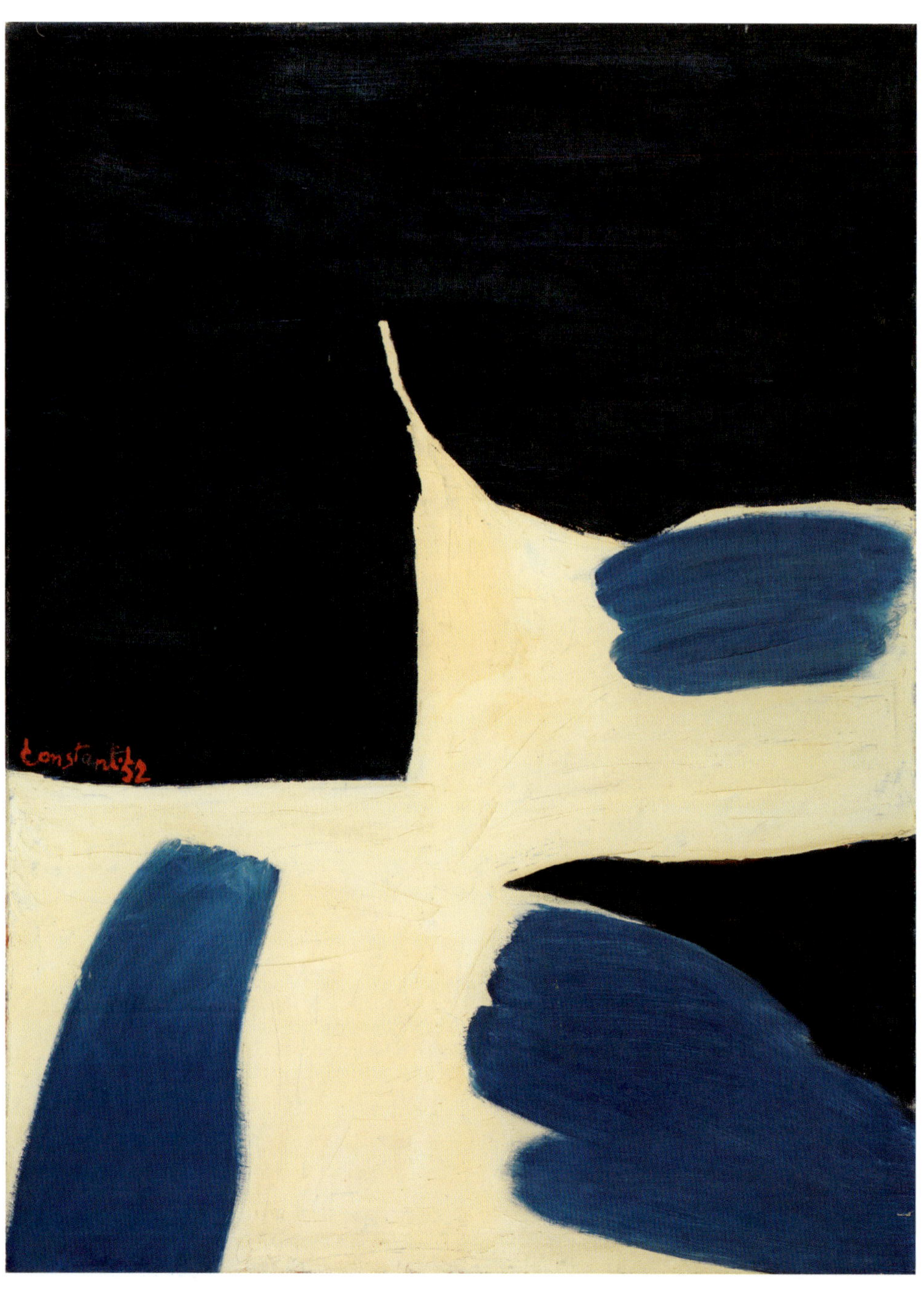

Zonder titel – Compositie blauw bruin
(Untitled – Composition Blue Brown) 1953
oil on linen, 62 x 65.5 cm
collection Fondation Constant, long-term loan to the Stedelijk Museum Schiedam

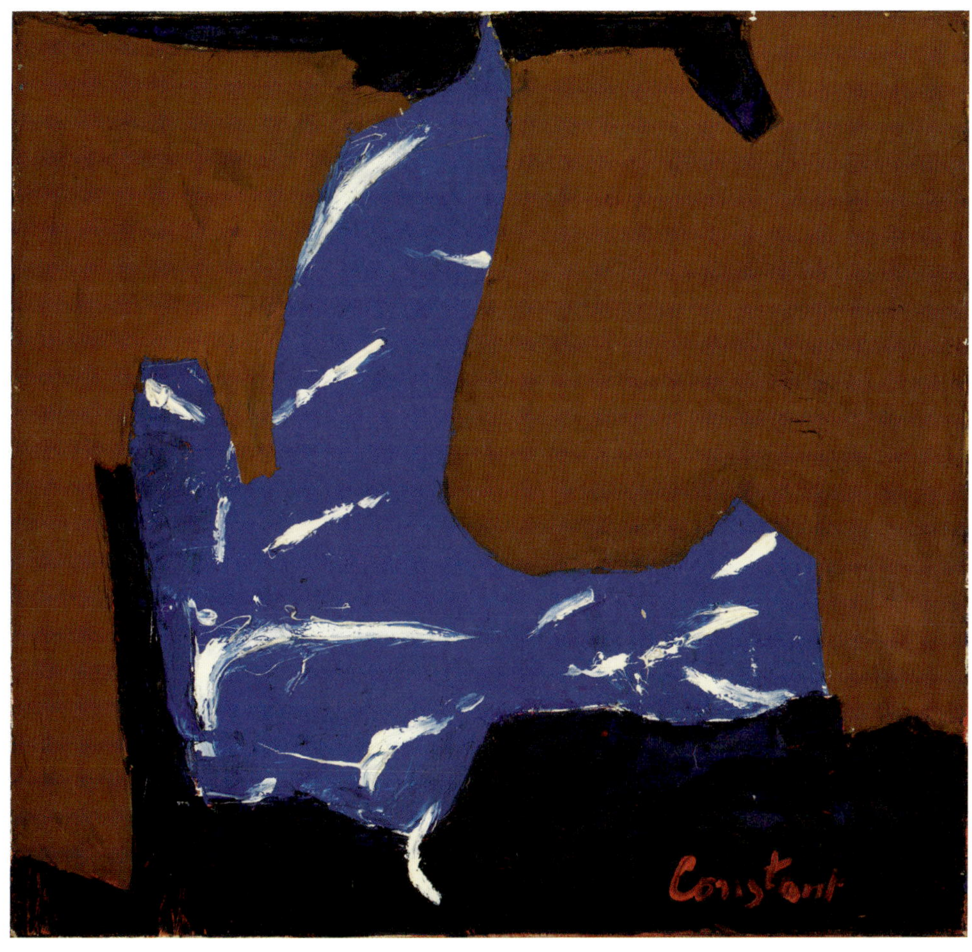

Landschap (Landscape), 1952
oil on linen, 81.5 x 63.8 cm
collection Fondation Constant, long-term loan to the Stedelijk Museum Schiedam

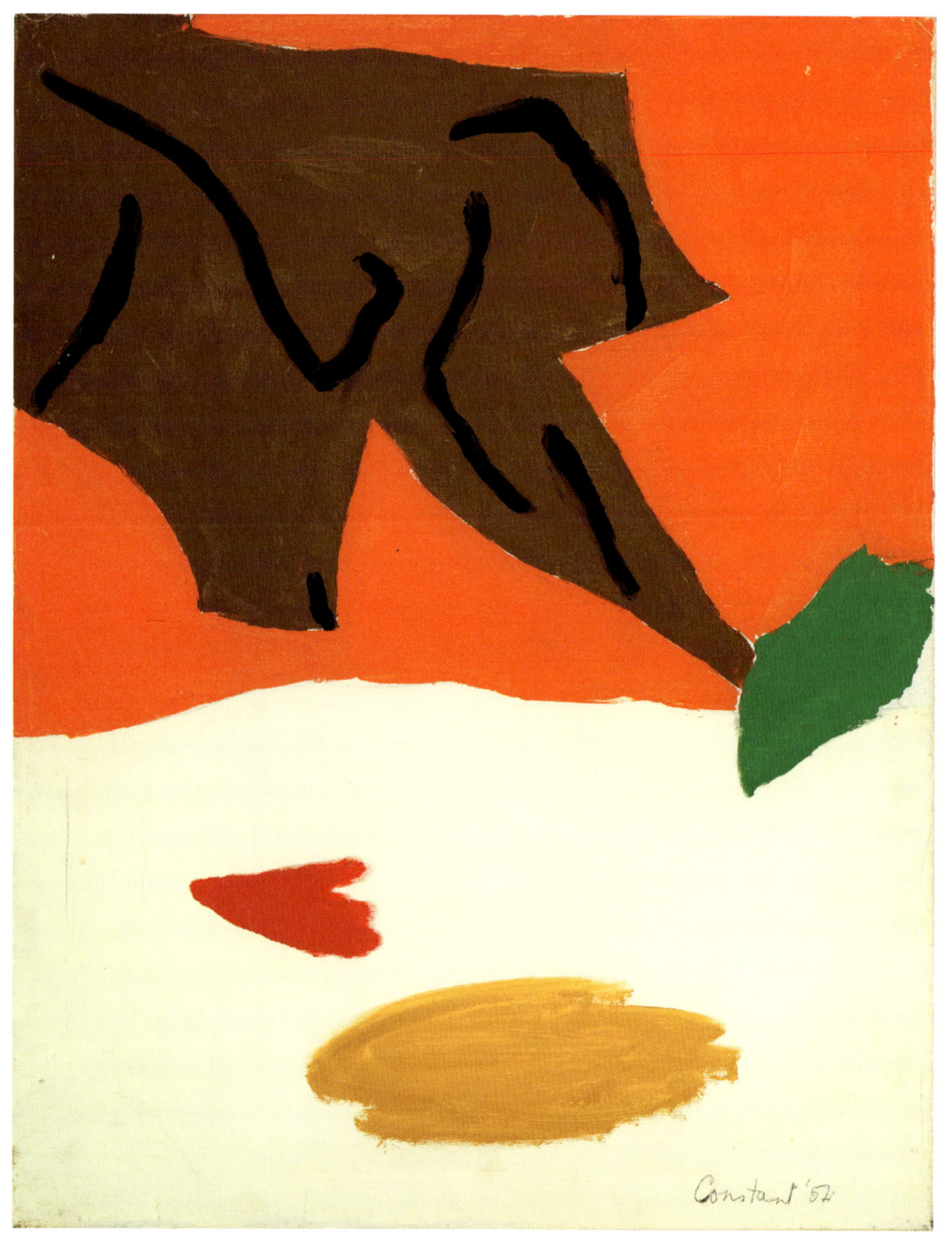

Zonder titel – Compositie met gebogen vlakken
(Untitled – Composition with Curved Planes), 1953
oil on linen, 50.5 x 60.5 cm
collection Fondation Constant, long-term loan to
the Stedelijk Museum Schiedam

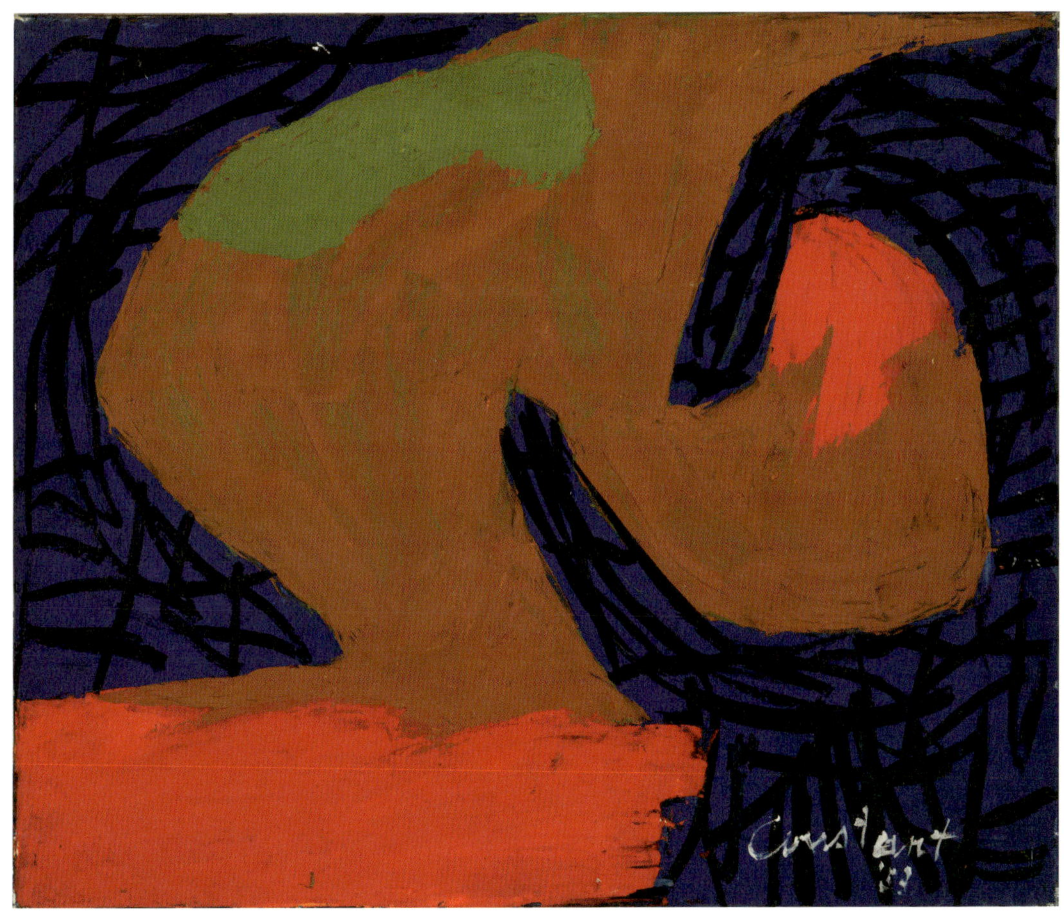

Vegetatie (Vegetation), 1952
oil on linen, 97.5 x 130 cm
collection Fondation Constant, long-term loan to
the Stedelijk Museum Schiedam

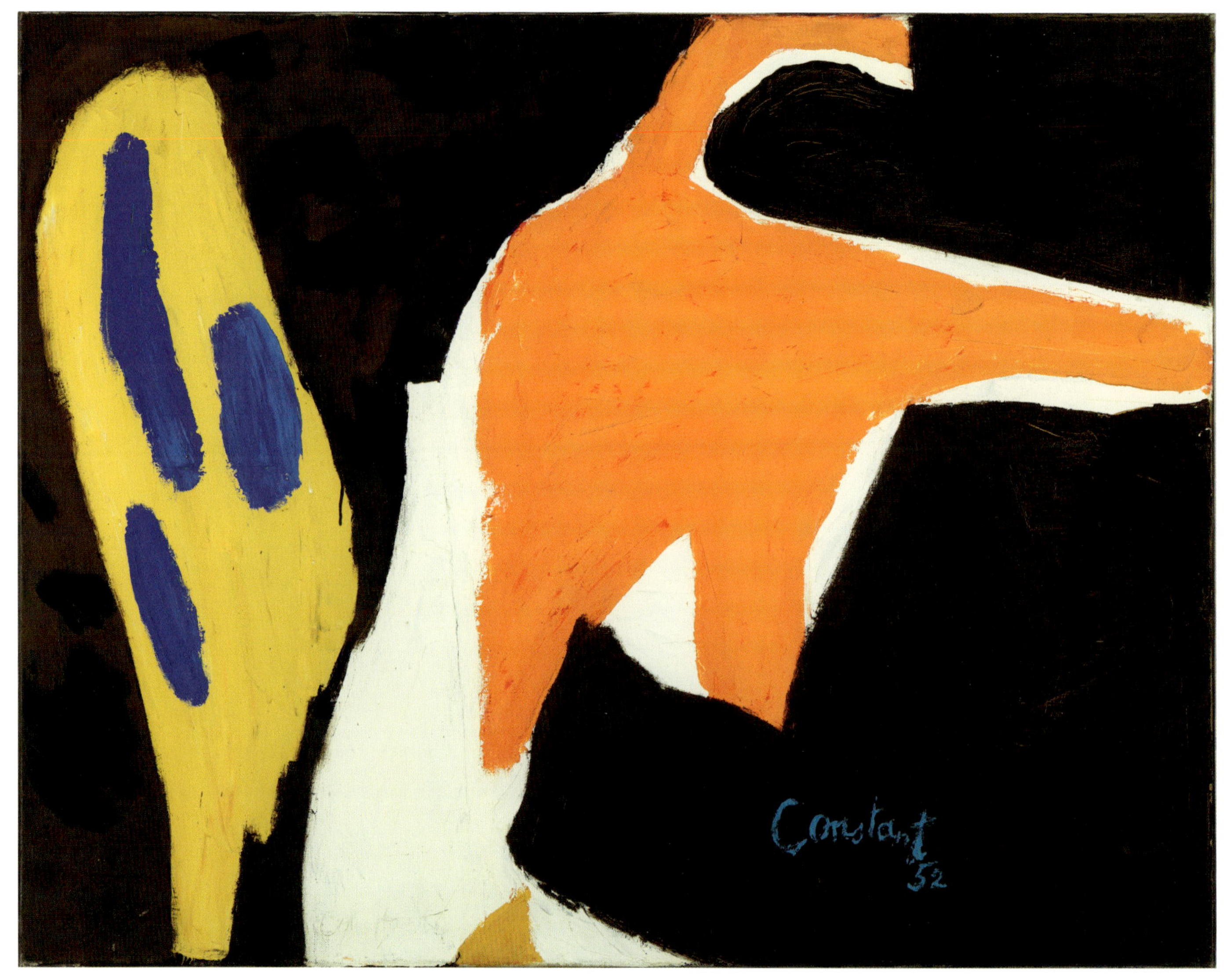

Zonder titel – Compositie met zwarte figuur
(Untitled – Composition with Black Figure), 1953
oil on linen, 61 x 75.5 cm
collection Fondation Constant, long-term loan to
the Stedelijk Museum Schiedam

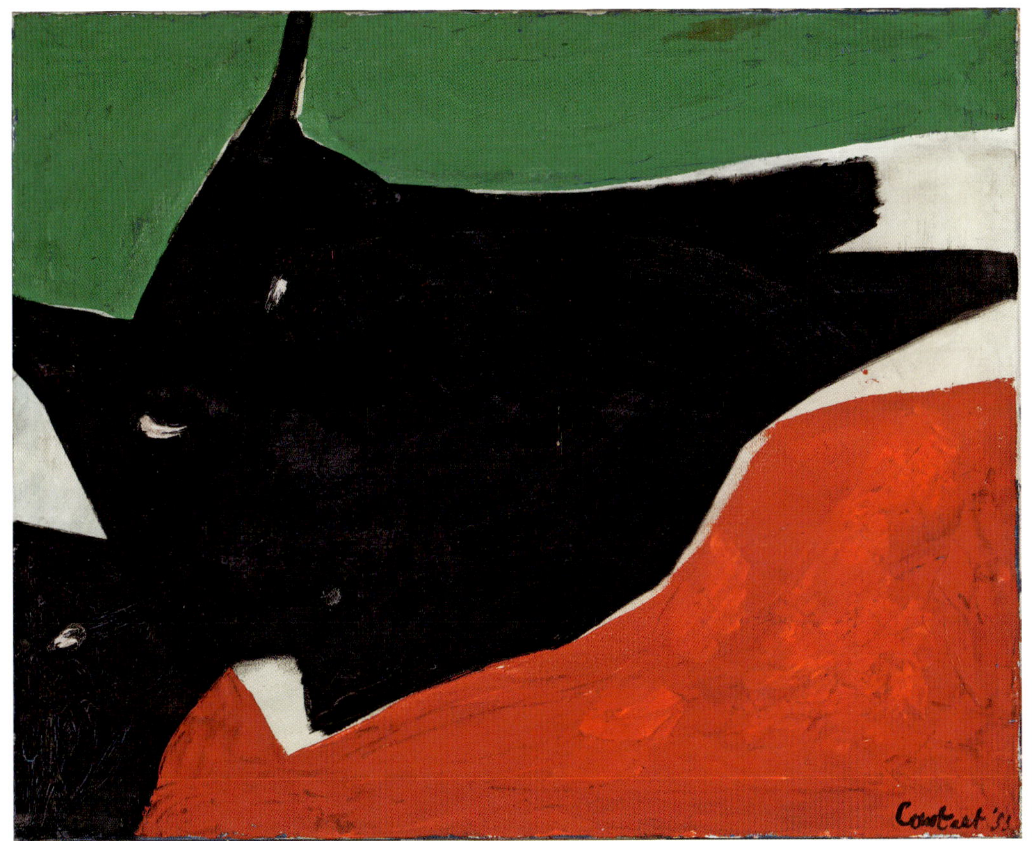

Vegetatie I (Vegetation I), 1952
oil on linen, 128 x 100 cm
collection Fondation Constant, long-term loan to the Stedelijk Museum Schiedam

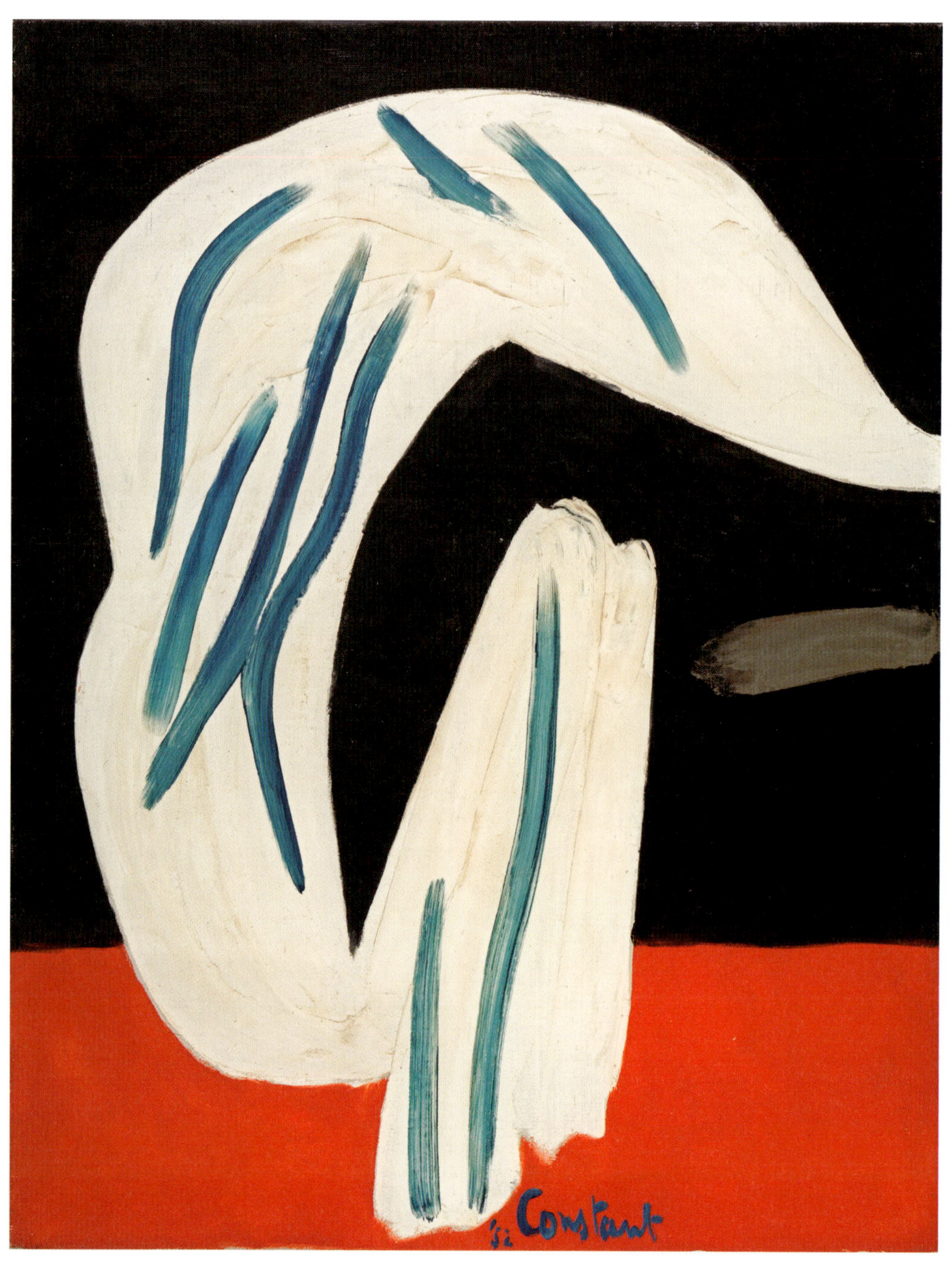

Adelaar (Eagle), 1953
oil on linen, 63.8 x 66 cm
collection Fondation Constant

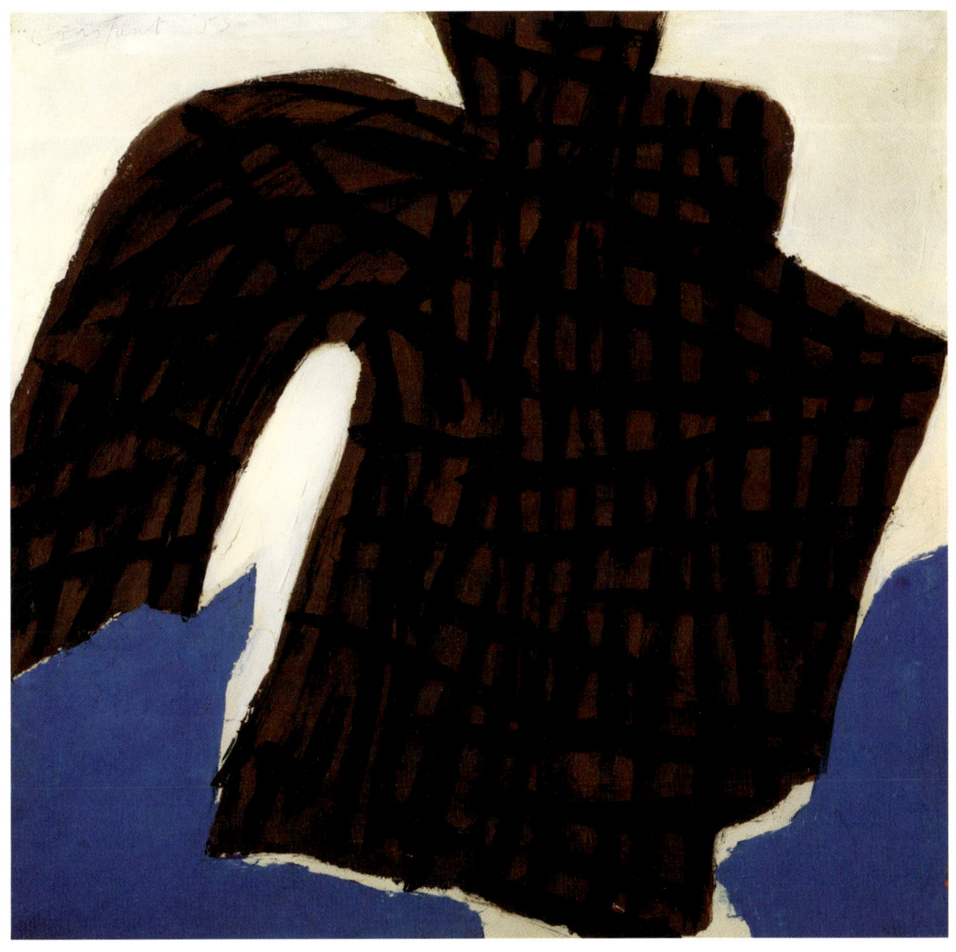

Zonder titel – Compositie blauw rood oranje
(Untitled – Composition Blue Red Orange), 1952
oil on linen, 50.5 x 60.5 cm
collection Fondation Constant, long-term loan to the Stedelijk Museum Schiedam

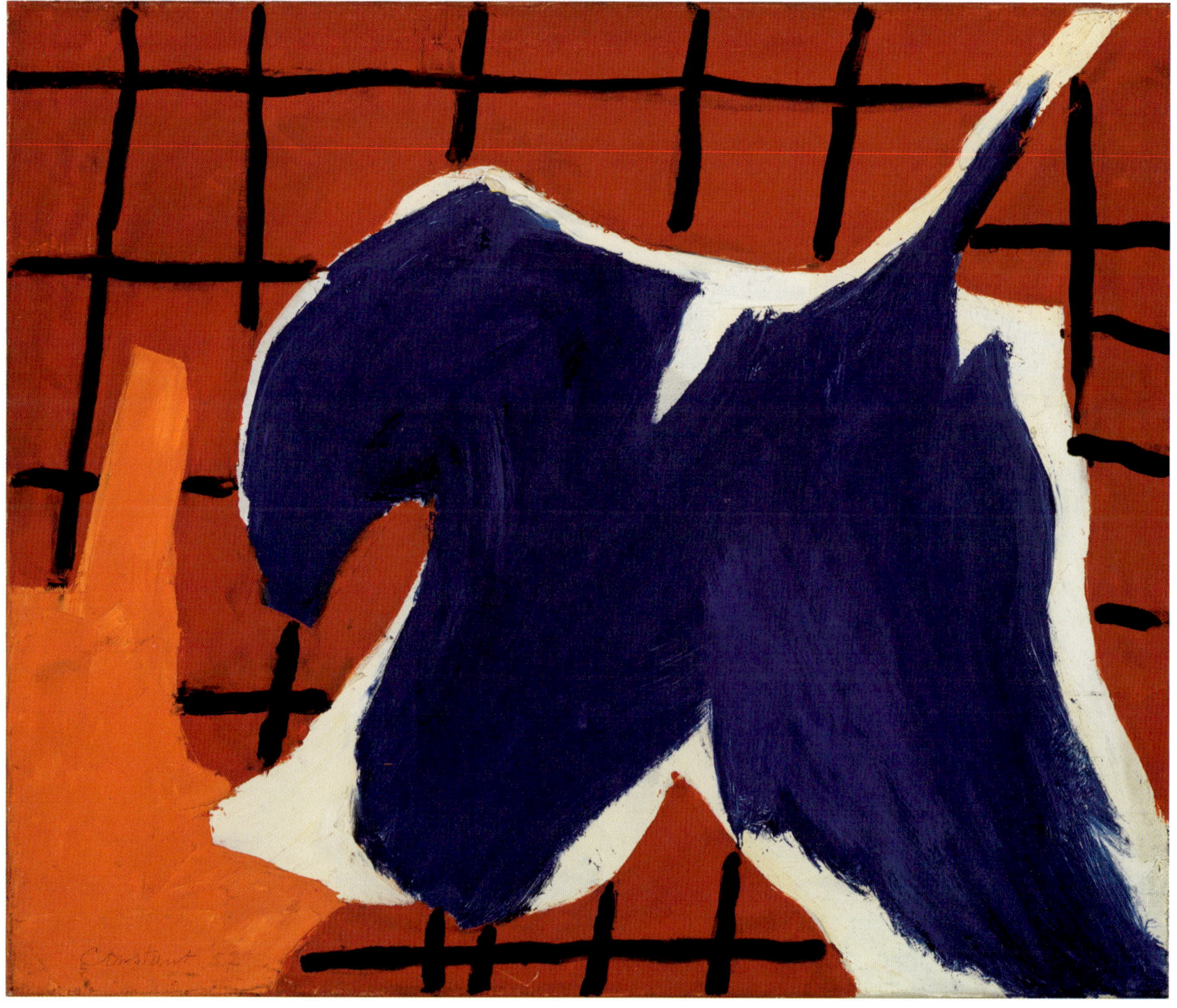

Colombe bleue (Blue Dove), 1953
oil on linen, 90 x 66 cm
collection Fondation Constant, long-term loan to
the Stedelijk Museum Schiedam

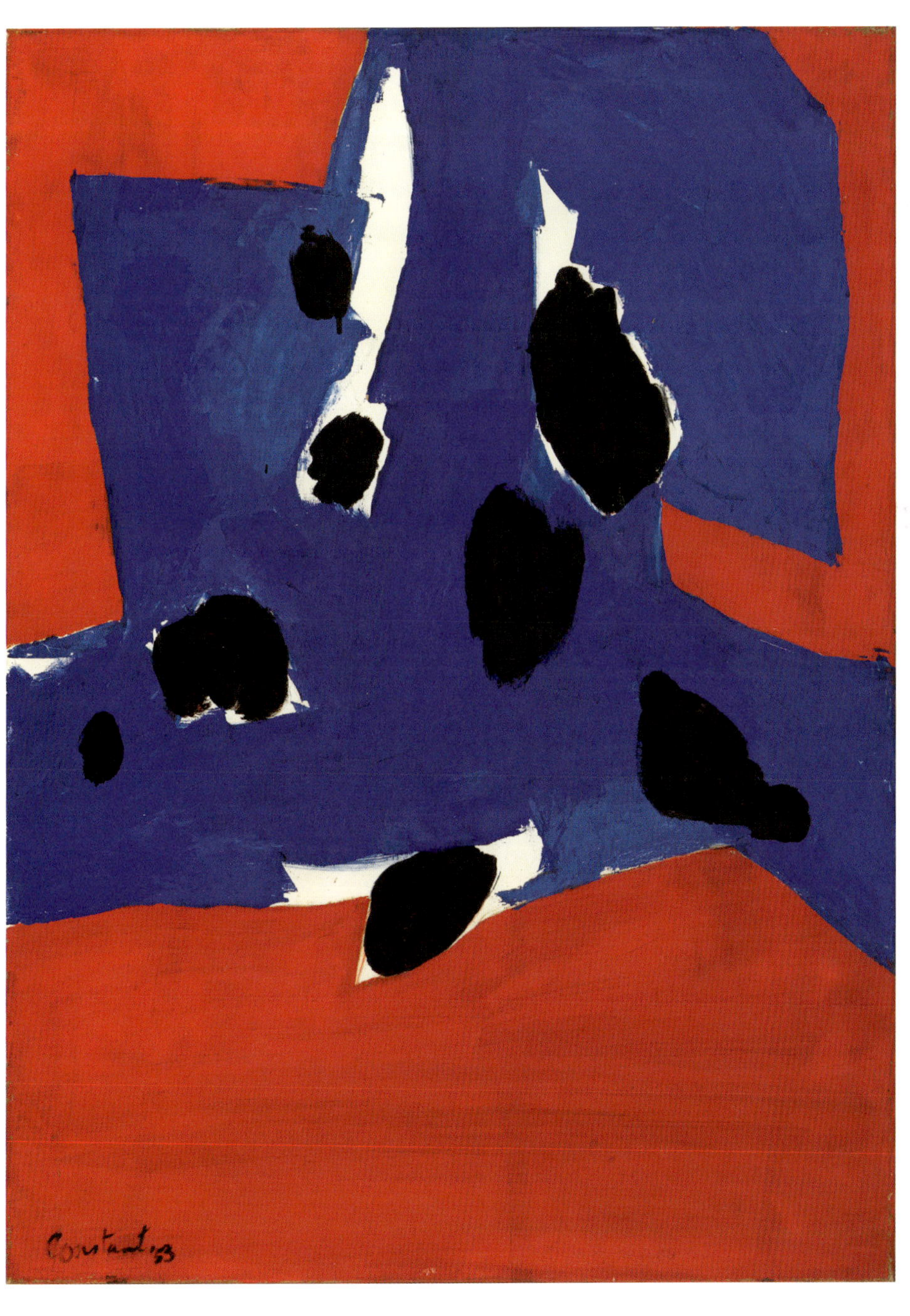

Twee figuren op blauw fond
(Two Figures on Blue Background), 1953
oil on linen, 80 x 60 cm
collection Fondation Constant, long-term loan to
the Stedelijk Museum Schiedam

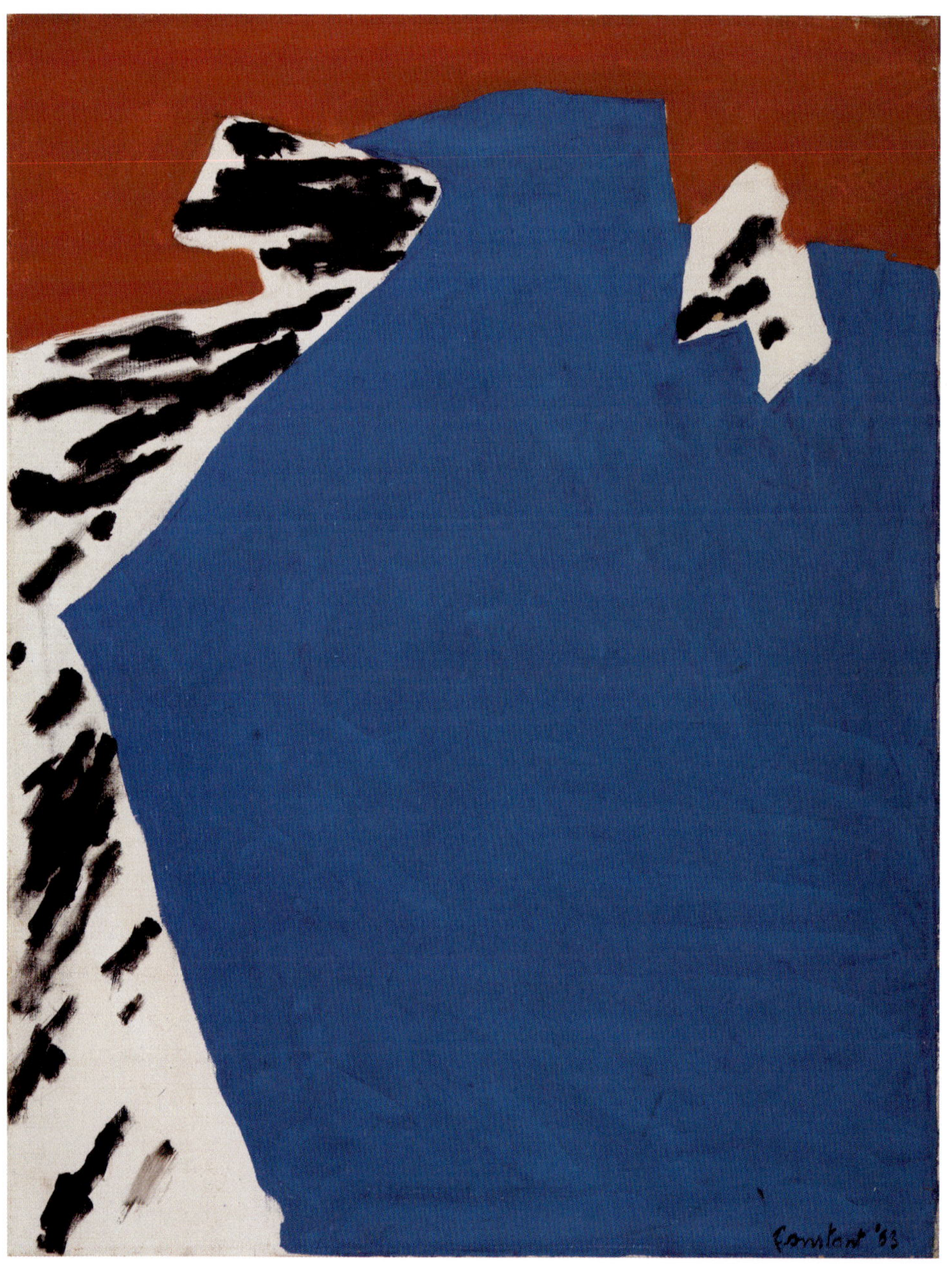

Constant with English artist
Roger Hilton, Paris, 1953
collection Fondation Constant

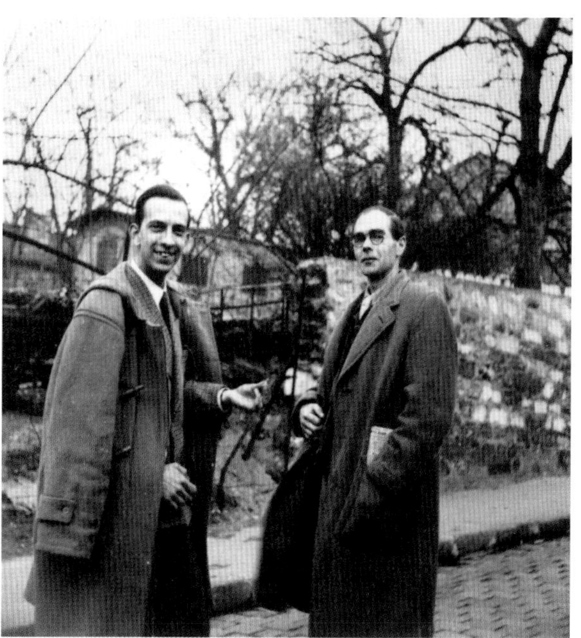

1953-1956
Art and Habitat

The spatial effect that colour can produce inspired Constant to champion an intensive collaboration between visual artists and architects. He worked with painter Stephen Gilbert and sculptor Nicolas Schöffer on founding a new artists' collective, Néovision. Their ideal was a fusion of different disciplines into a new art form that would deal with the human living environment (habitat) as a whole. The example of the pre-war avant-garde movement De Stijl (1917-1931) fuelled debate and influenced Constant's visual idiom as well. In addition, a modern material like Plexiglas offered possibilities to make this geometric visual idiom three-dimensional.

Compositie in zwart en wit
(Composition in Black and White), 1953
oil on linen, 75.2 x 62 cm
collection Fondation Constant

Compositie met oranje driehoek
(Composition with Orange Triangle), 1953
oil on linen, 99.7 x 90.2 cm
collection Gemeentemuseum Den Haag,
The Hague

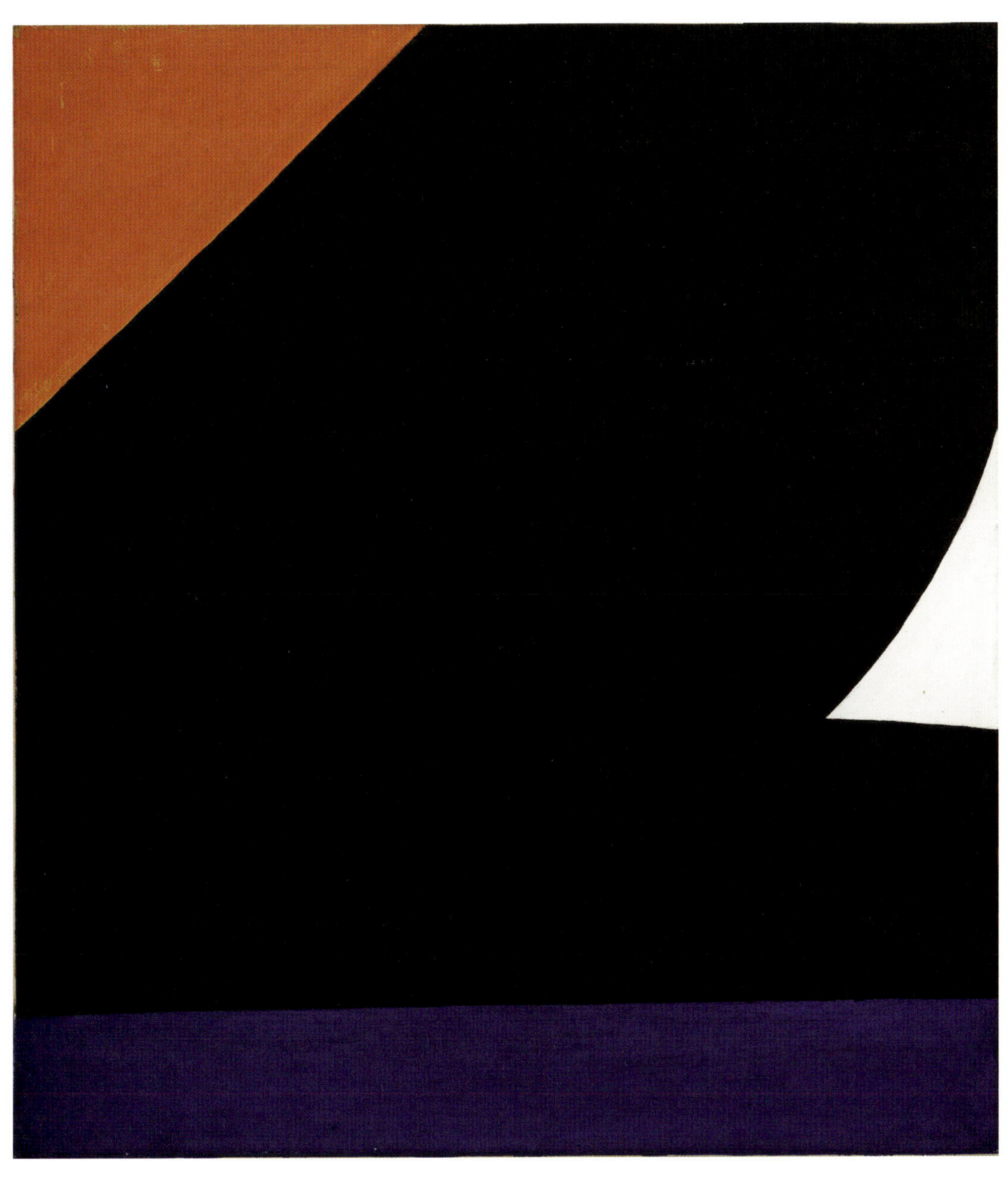

Witte piek (White Peak), 1952
oil on linen, 135 x 145.5 cm
collection Fondation Constant, long-term loan to
the Stedelijk Museum Schiedam

Collage met kleurvlakken
(Collage with Coloured Planes), 1953
collage with gouache on paper, 44.2 x 61.8 cm
collection Fondation Constant

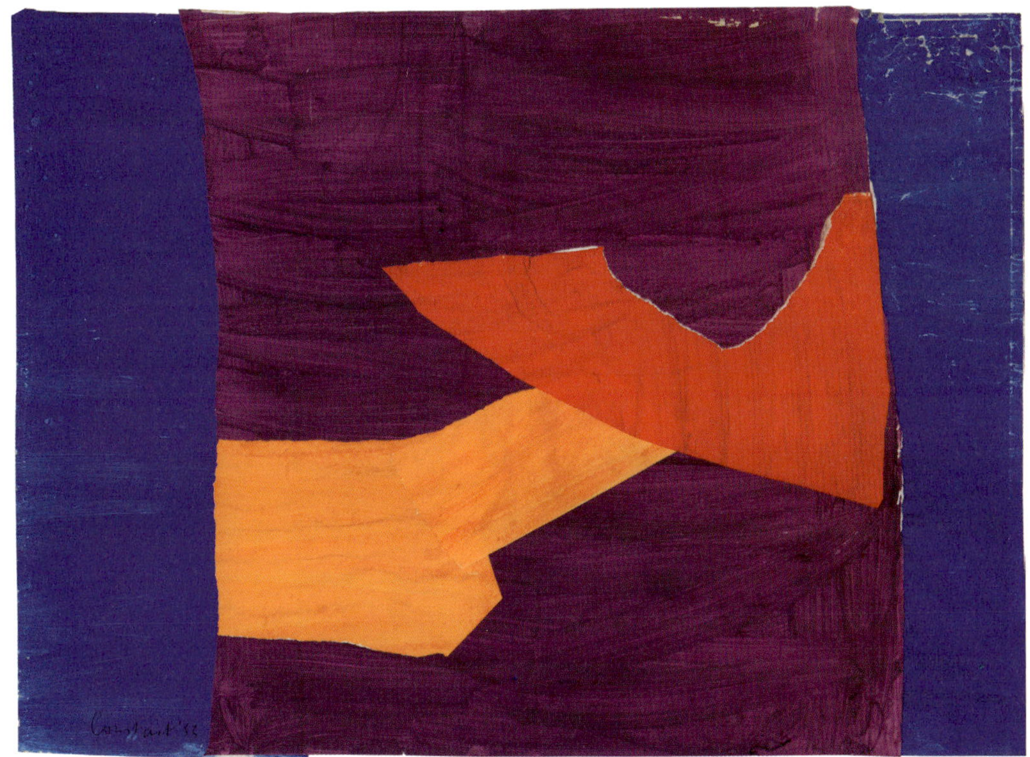

Compositie met vierkanten
(Composition with Squares), 1953
collage with gouache on fiberboard, 57 x 57 cm
collection Heirs of Carel Visser

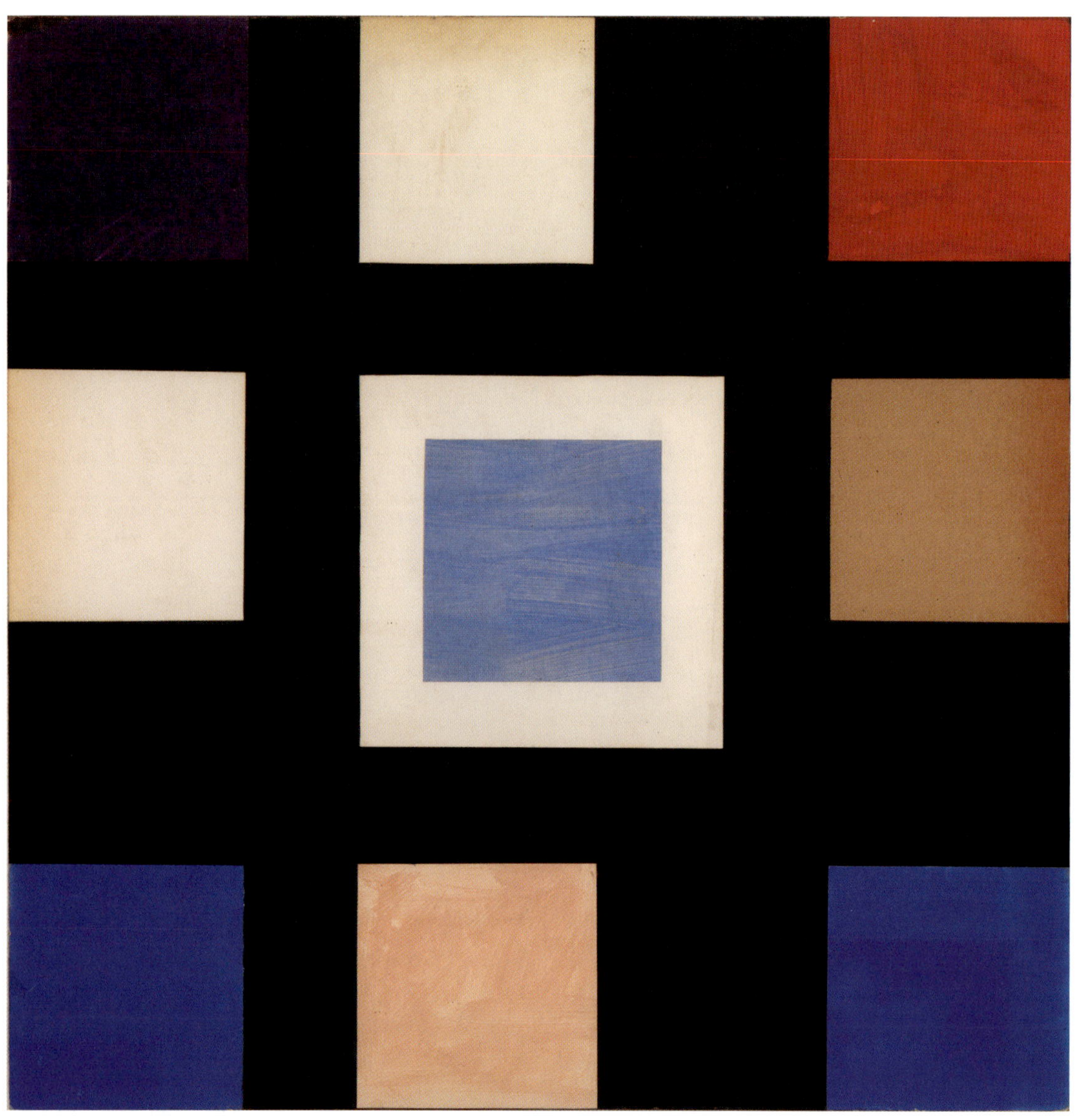

Constructie met gekleurde vlakken
(Construction with Coloured Planes), 1954
Plexiglas and black steel, 119.5 x 62 x 57.2 cm
collection Fondation Constant, long-term loan to
the Stedelijk Museum Schiedam

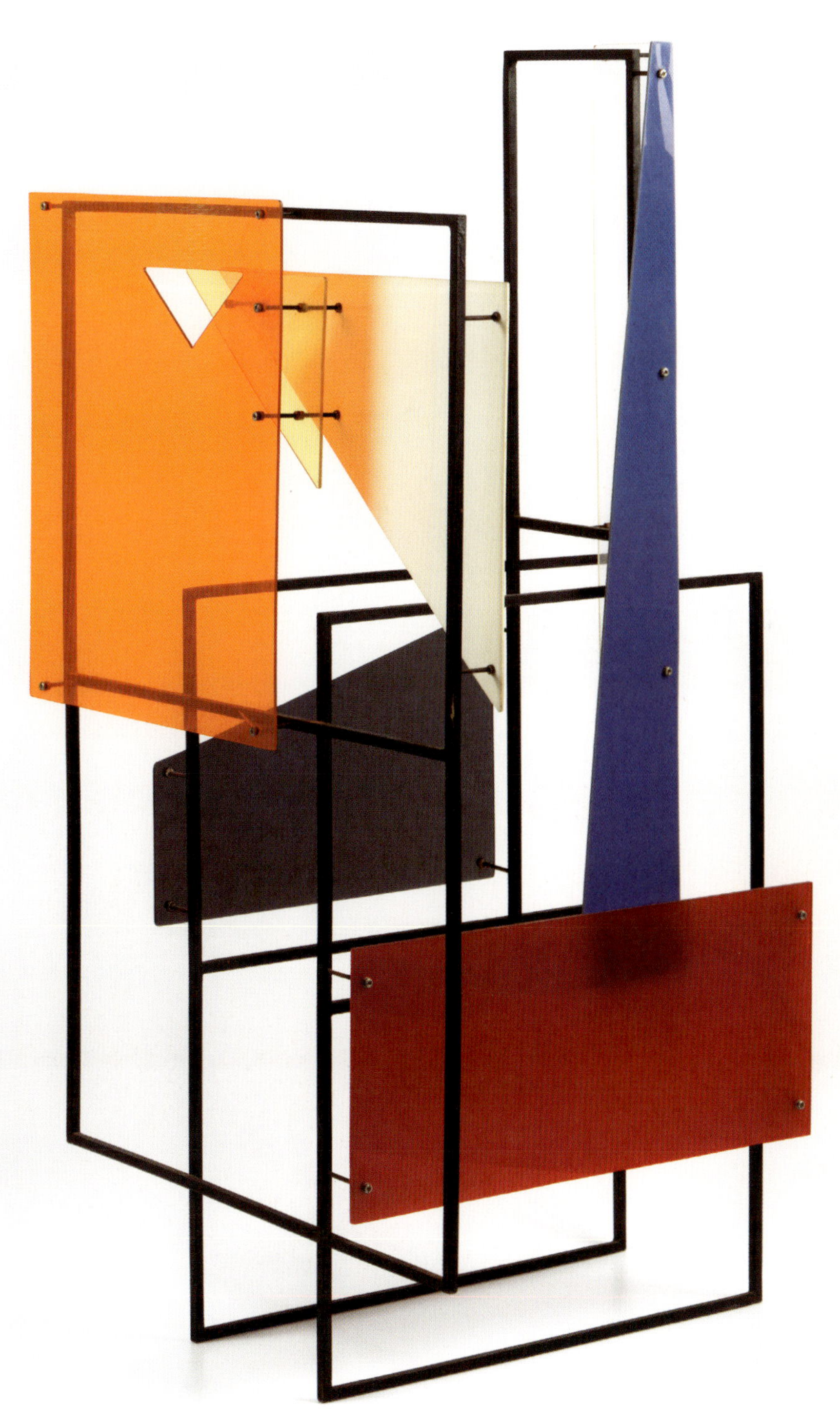

Construction aux plans transparents
(Construction with Transparent Planes), 1954
Plexiglas and aluminium, 75.5 x 75.5 x 54 cm
collection Museu d'Art Contemporani de Barcelona,
MACBA Foundation, Barcelona

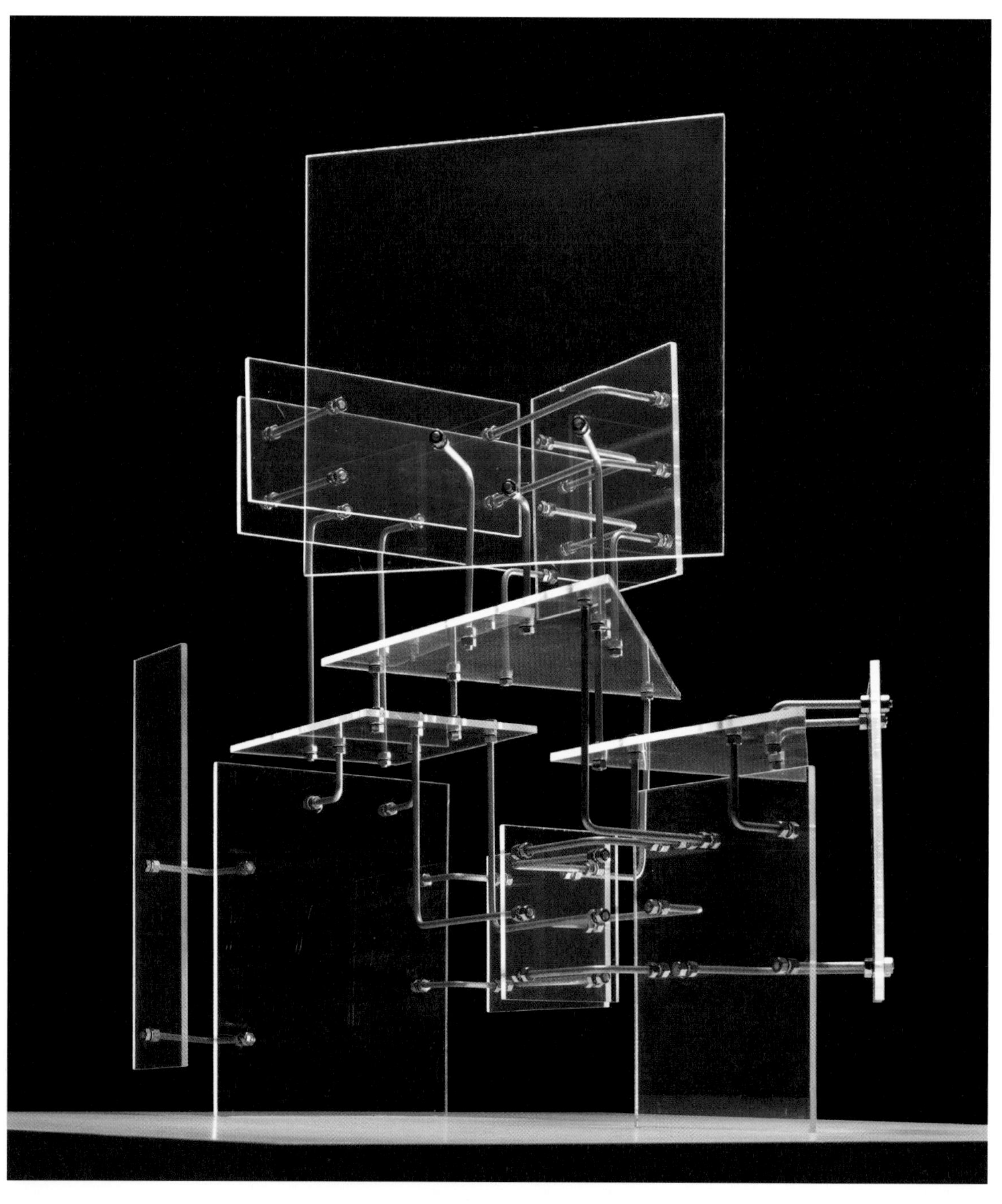

Variations rythmiques (Rhythmic Variations), 1953
oil on panel, 121.7 x 121.7 cm
collection Cultural Heritage Agency of the Netherlands, long-term loan to the Cobra Museum of Modern Art, Amstelveen (see comment on p. 159)

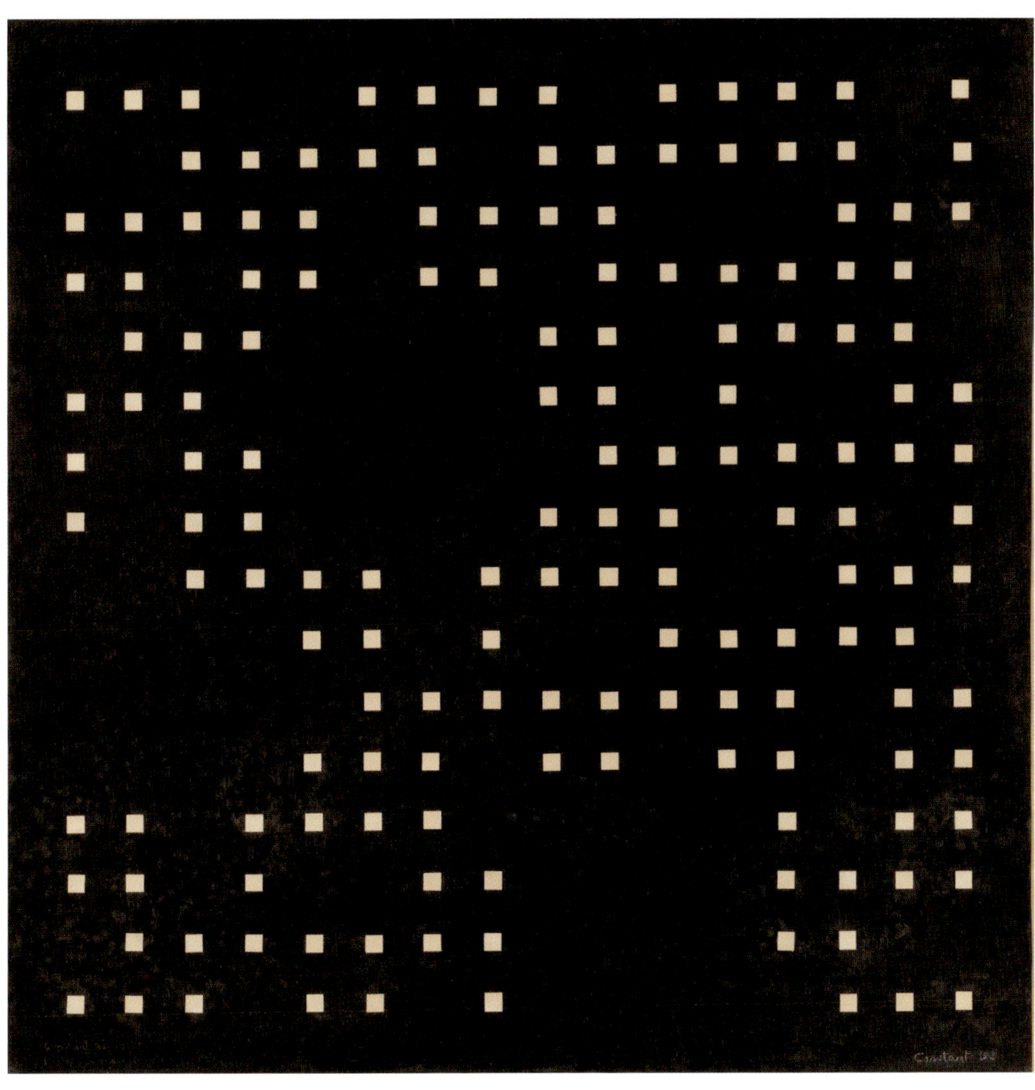

Compositie met blauwe lijnen
(Composition with Blue Lines), 1953
oil on plywood panel, 122.2 x 121.7 cm
collection Kröller-Müller Museum, Otterlo

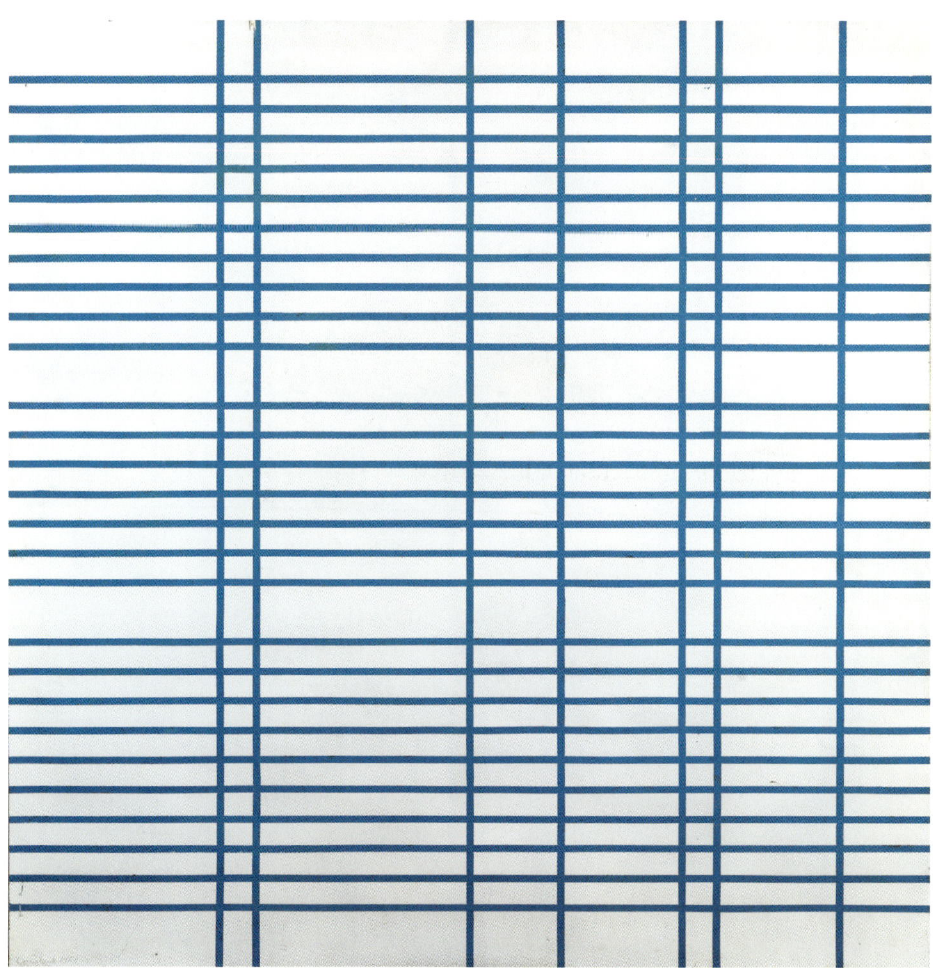

Curtain Fabric, 1953-1955
produced by Handelsonderneming
Van Rije junior for the Bijenkorf
silkscreen on cotton, 132.5 x 390 cm
collection Stedelijk Museum Amsterdam

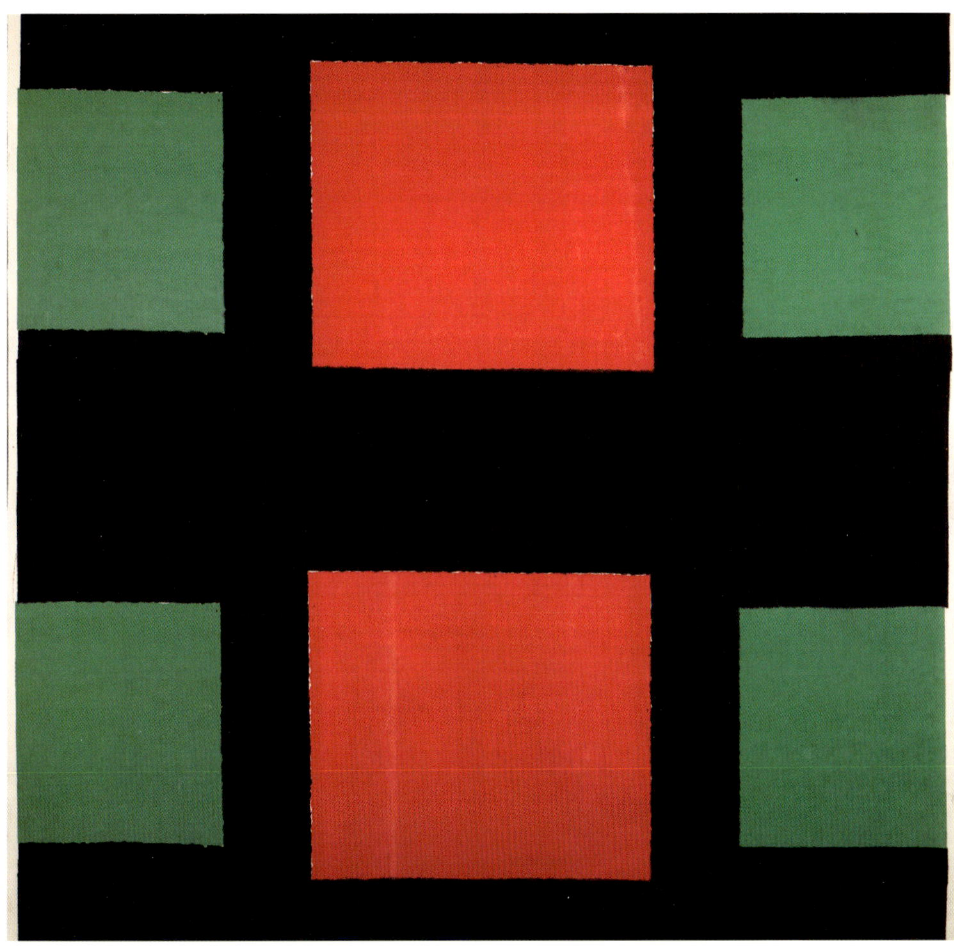

Design for Curtain Fabric, 1956
gouache on paper, 49.7 x 58 cm
collection Cultural Heritage Agency of the Netherlands, long-term loan to the Stedelijk Museum Schiedam

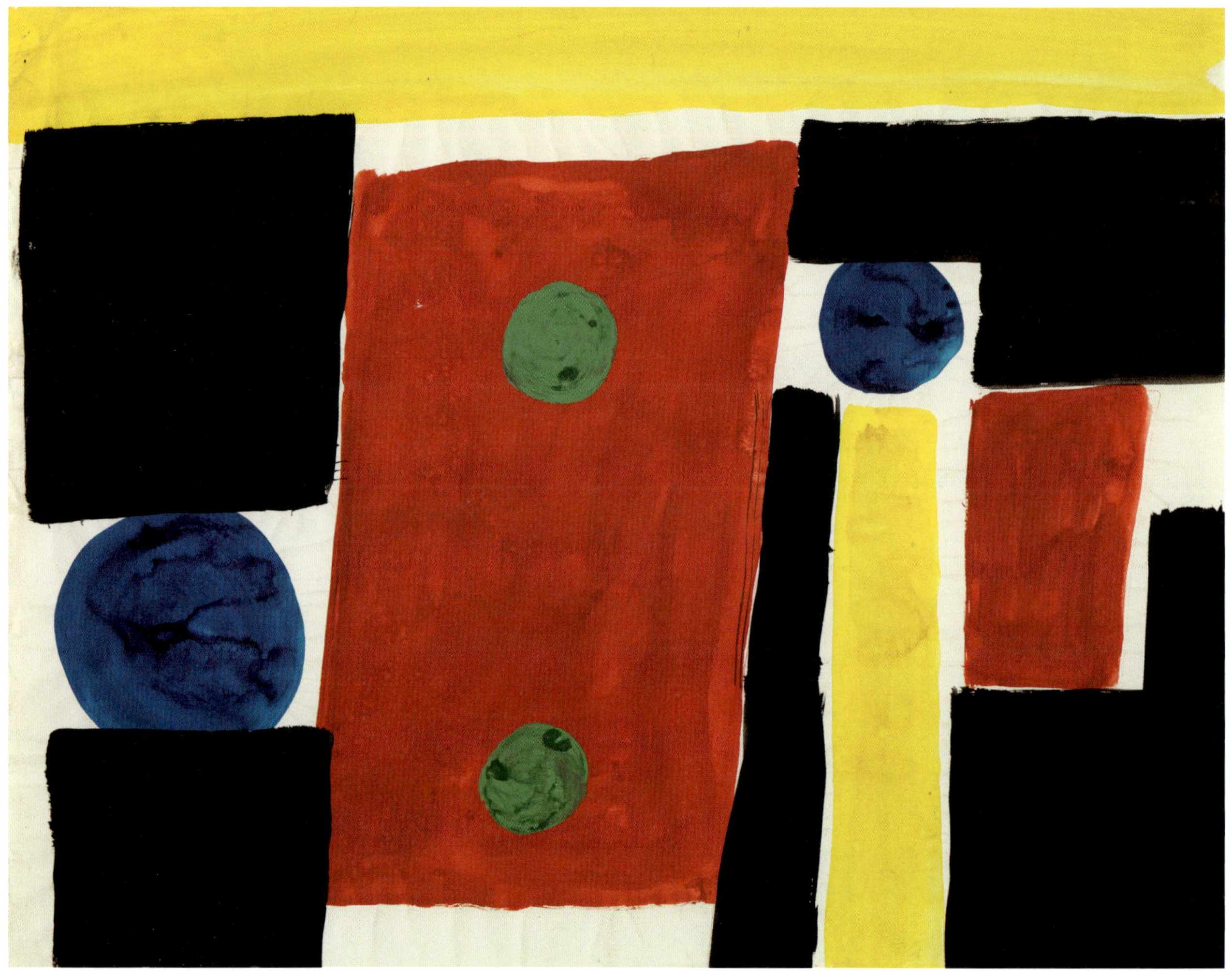

Stofontwerp h (Fabric Design h), 1956
gouache on paper, 41.9 x 47.8 cm
collection Fondation Constant

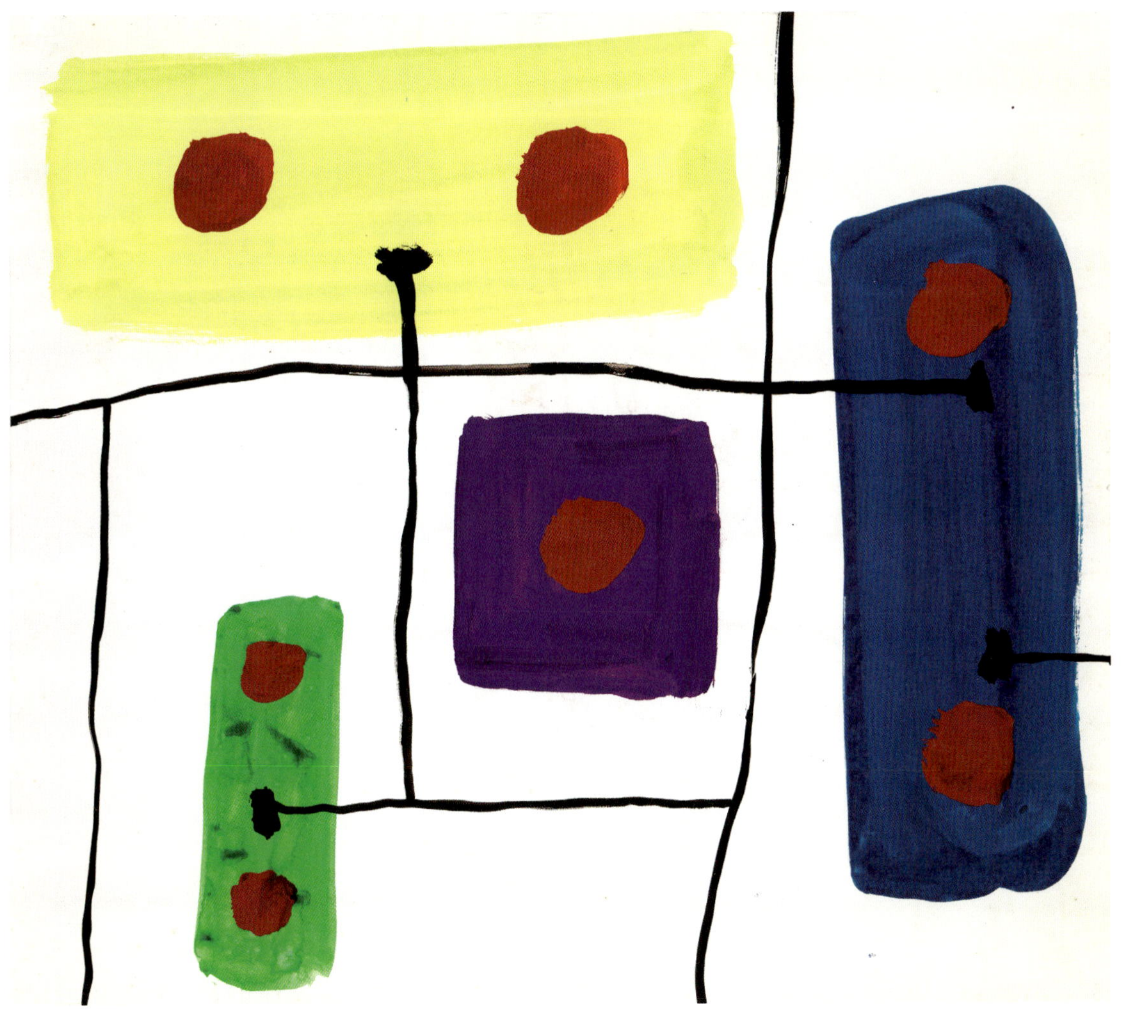

1956-1957
Life Will Reside in Poetry

The geometric element vanished from Constant's work as quickly as it had come. 'What I seek', he would later write, 'is the undetermined form, the form with a thousand faces, the form without beginning and without end' (p. 155). As a form without beginning or end, the wheels from the Cobra and the war paintings returned; as a material, paint was literally given free rein. With his lecture 'Tomorrow Life Will Reside in Poetry' in 1956 (p. 153) he called for the construction of a poetic living environment. He led by example with a series of elegant occasional furniture, manufactured by 't Spectrum, and vibrant textile designs for the Stoomweverij Nijverheid weaving mill.

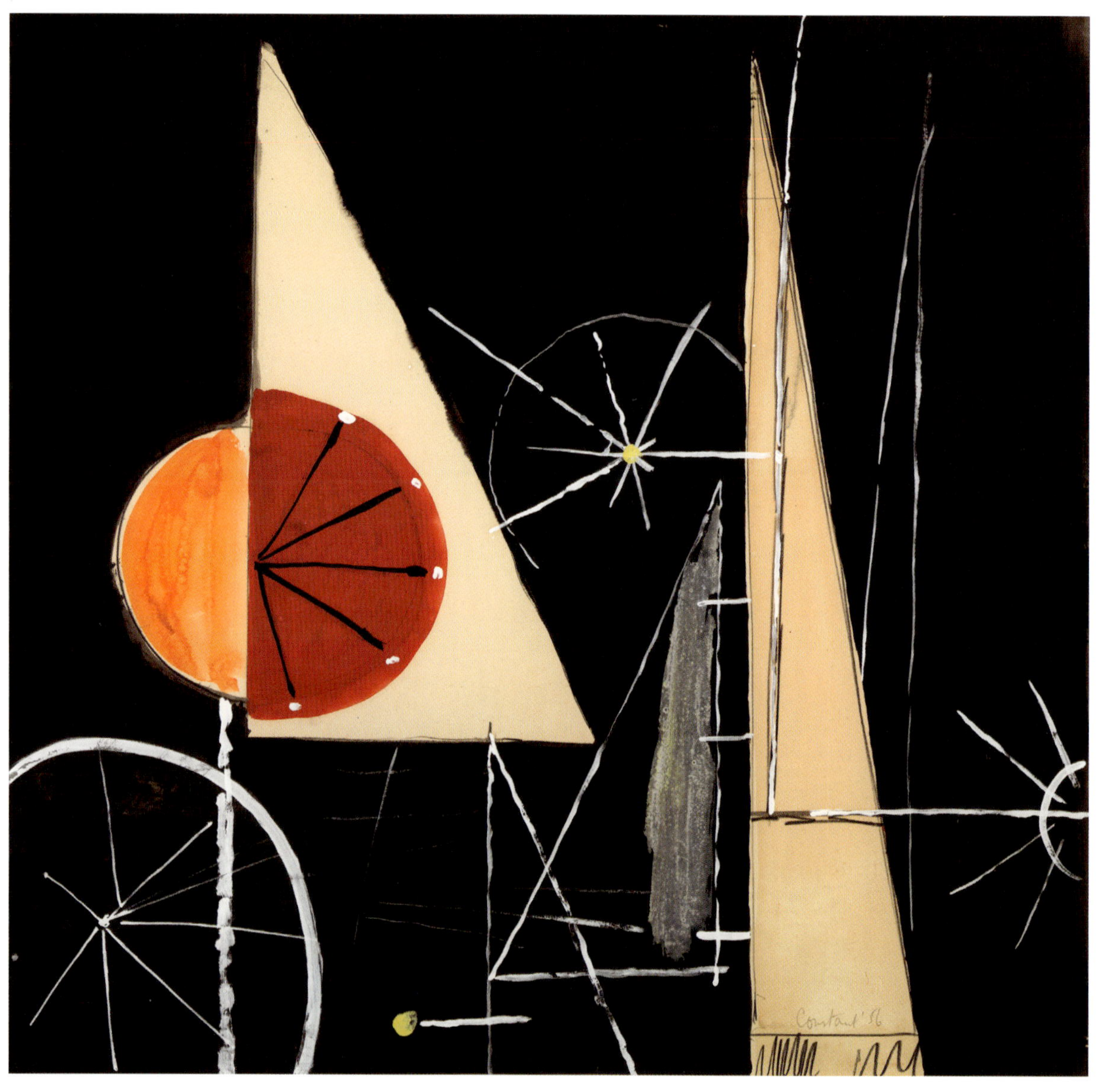

Zonder titel – Compositie met driehoek
(Untitled – Composition with Triangle), 1956
gouache on paper, 68 x 71.5 cm
collection ProWinko, Switzerland

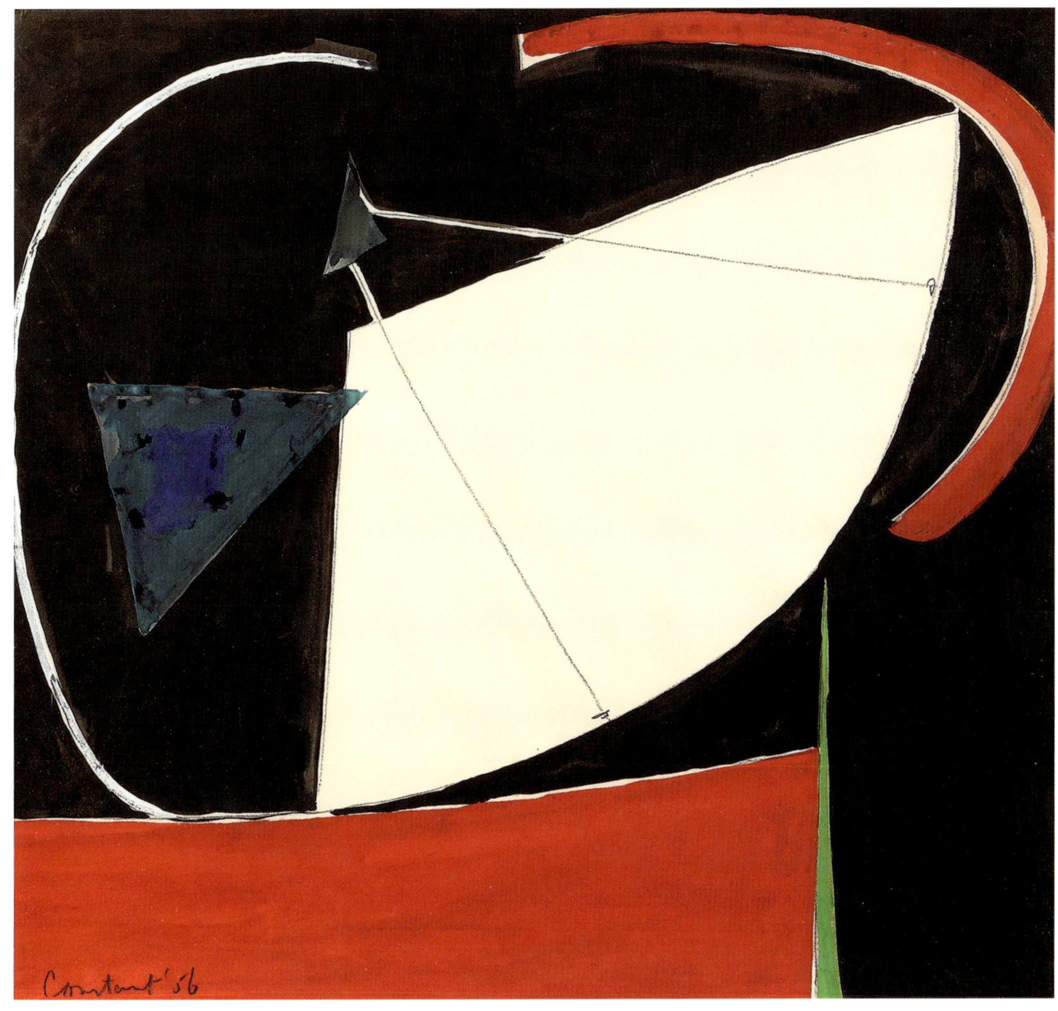

The Blue Triangle, 1956
gouache and crayon on paper, 68.1 x 73.9 cm
collection G. Dreesmann, Amsterdam

Ronde vorm (Round Shape), 1956
watercolour and pencil on paper, 67.4 x 71 cm
collection Gemeentemuseum Den Haag,
The Hague

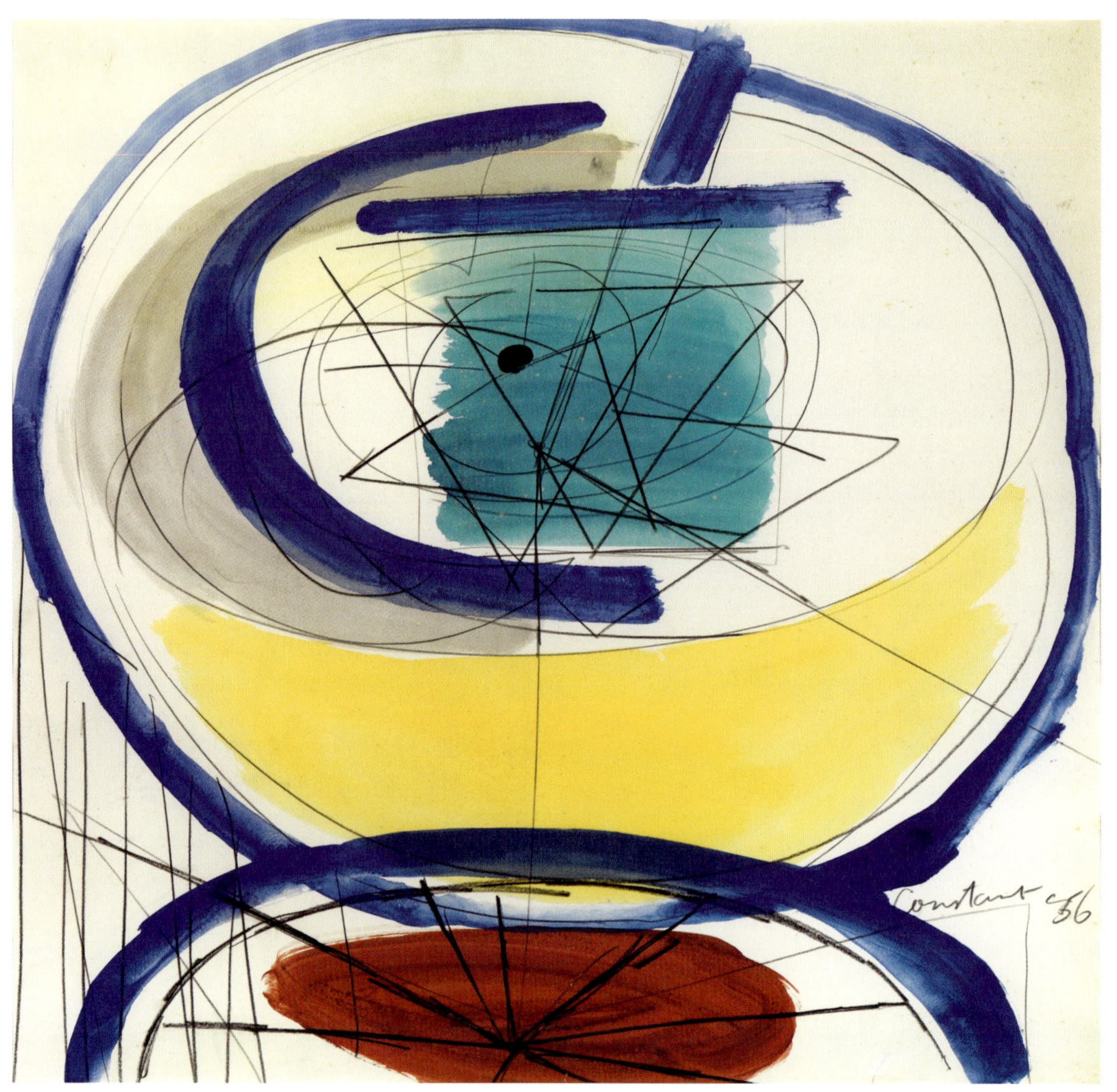

Observatorium (Observatory), 1956
Plexiglas and brass, 52 x ∅ 48.5 cm
collection Fondation Constant

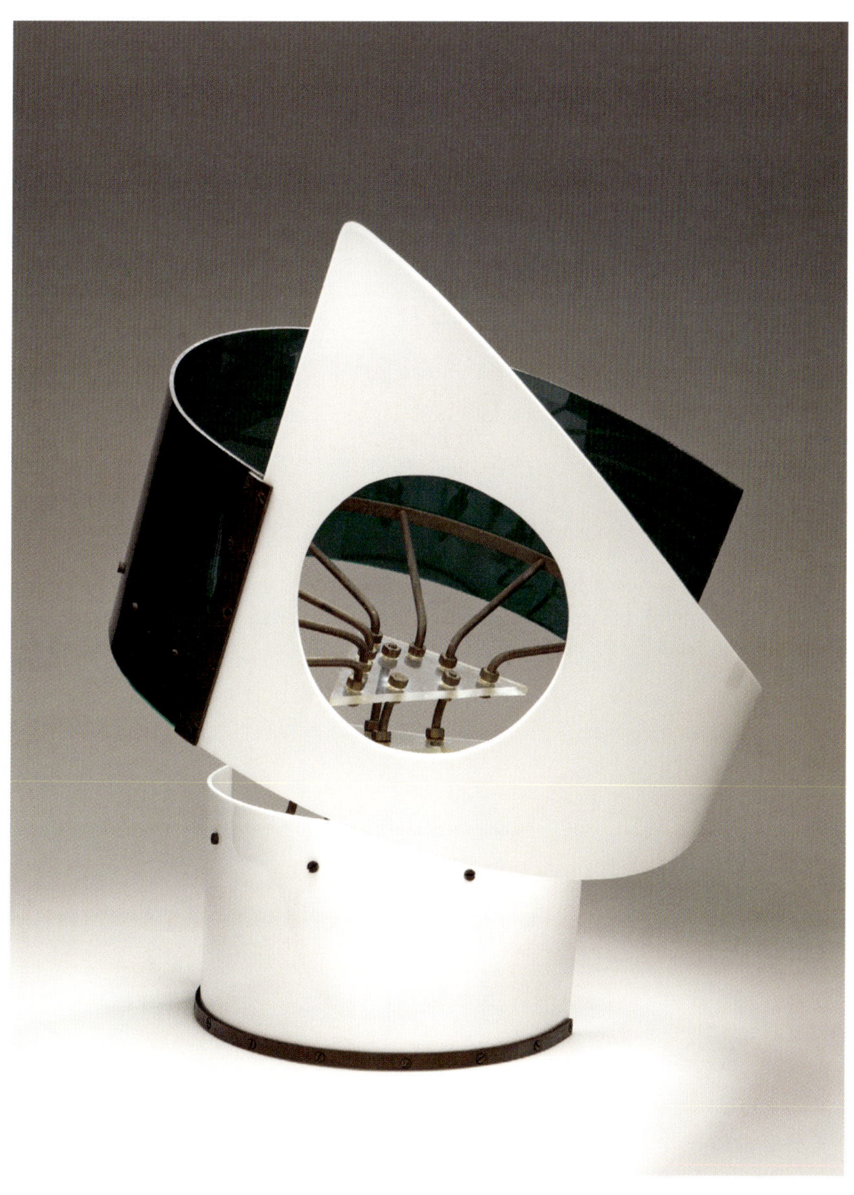

La fleur mécanique (The Mechanical Flower), 1956-1959
copper, lead, plastic, Plexiglas and stone,
140 x 61 x 48 cm
collection Rijksmuseum Twenthe, Enschede

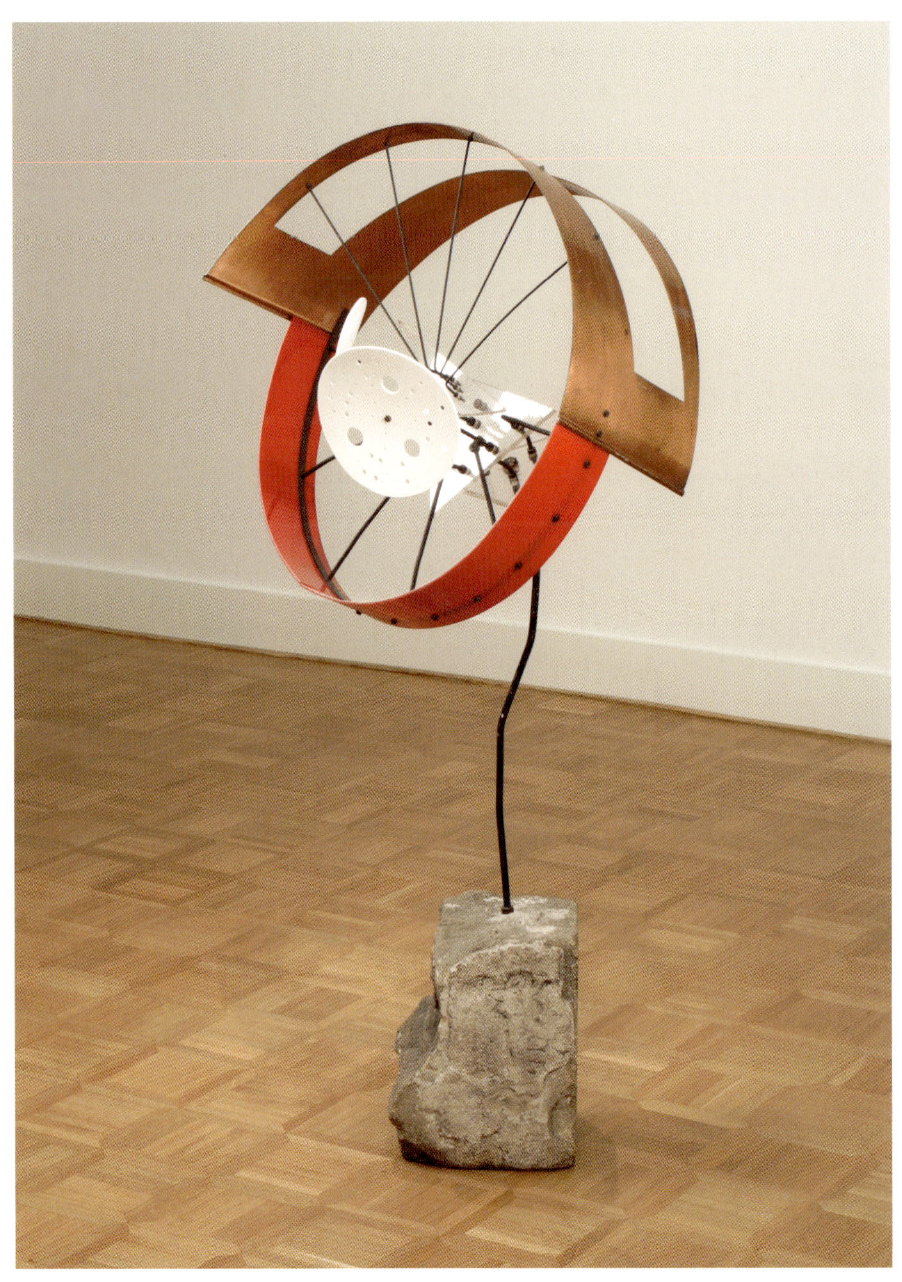

De lansen (Souvenir d'Uccello)
(The Lances [Souvenir d'Uccello]), 1956
oil on linen, 95 x 110 cm
collection Fondation Constant, long-term loan to
the Stedelijk Museum Schiedam

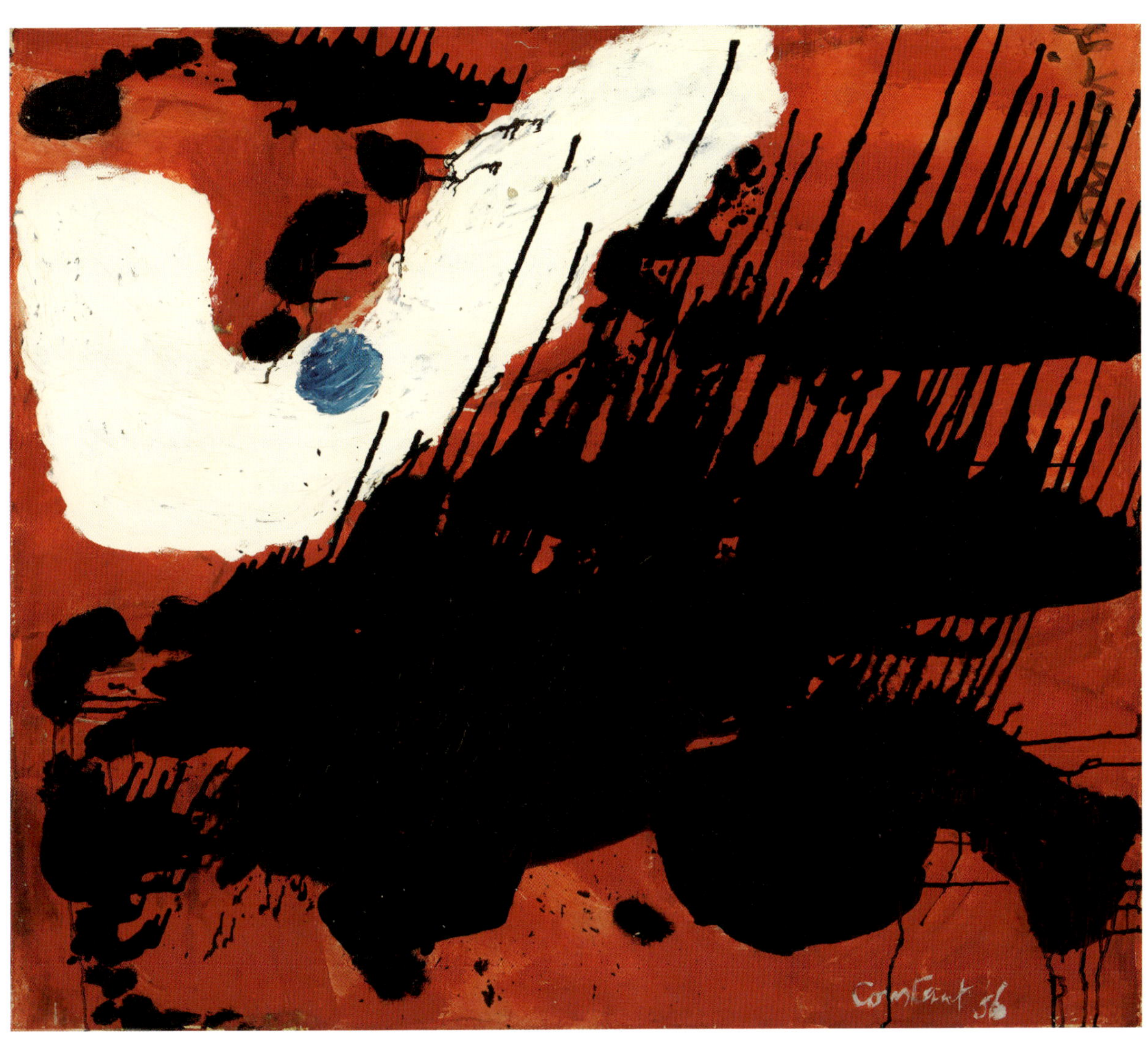

Construction dans un volume
(Wire Construction in Prism), 1957
black steel, iron, brass and paint,
142 x 49.5 x 21.5 cm
collection Fondation Constant, long-term loan to
the Stedelijk Museum Schiedam

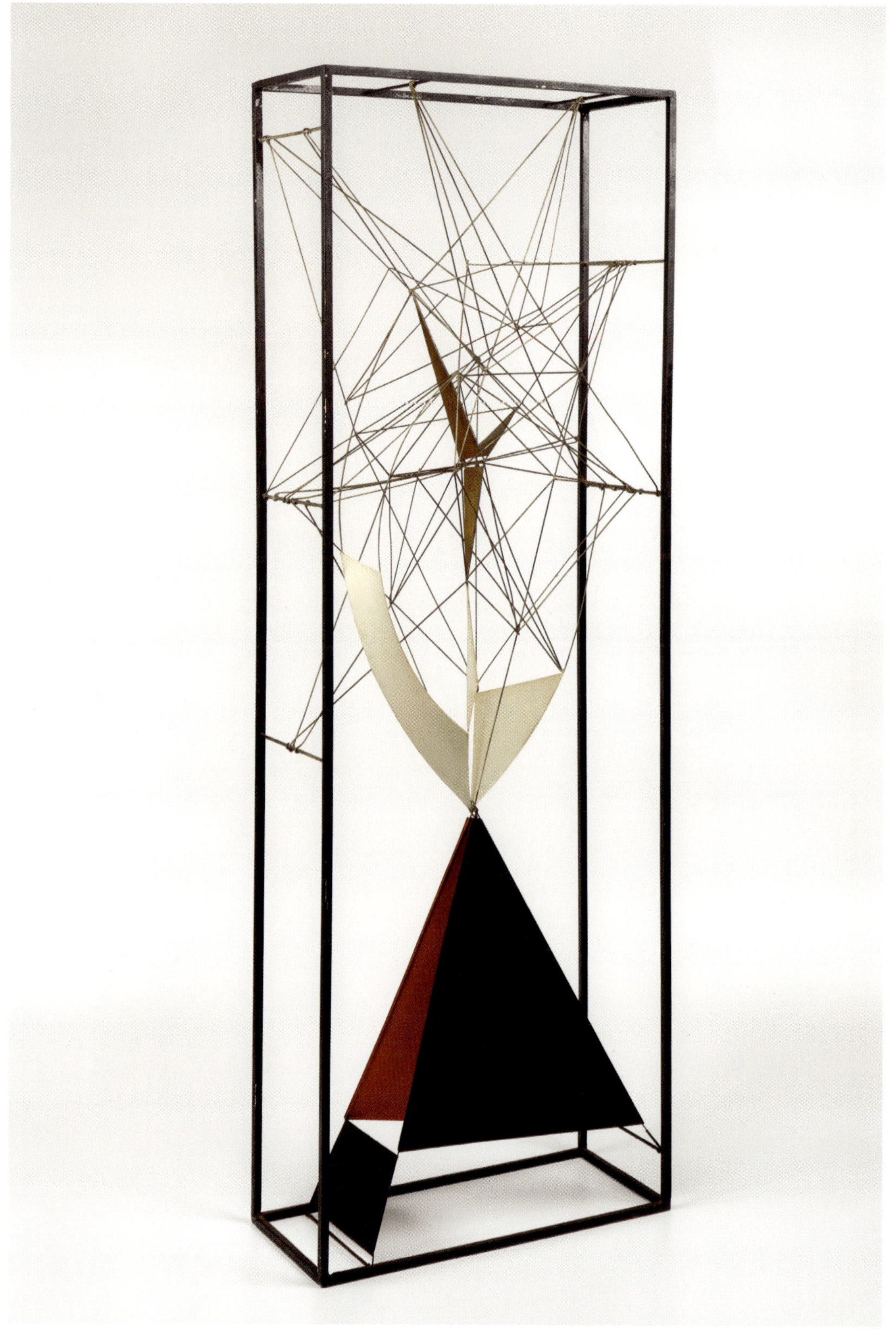

Zonder titel (Untitled), 1956
oil on linen, 59.9 x 70.1 cm
collection G. Dreesmann, Amsterdam

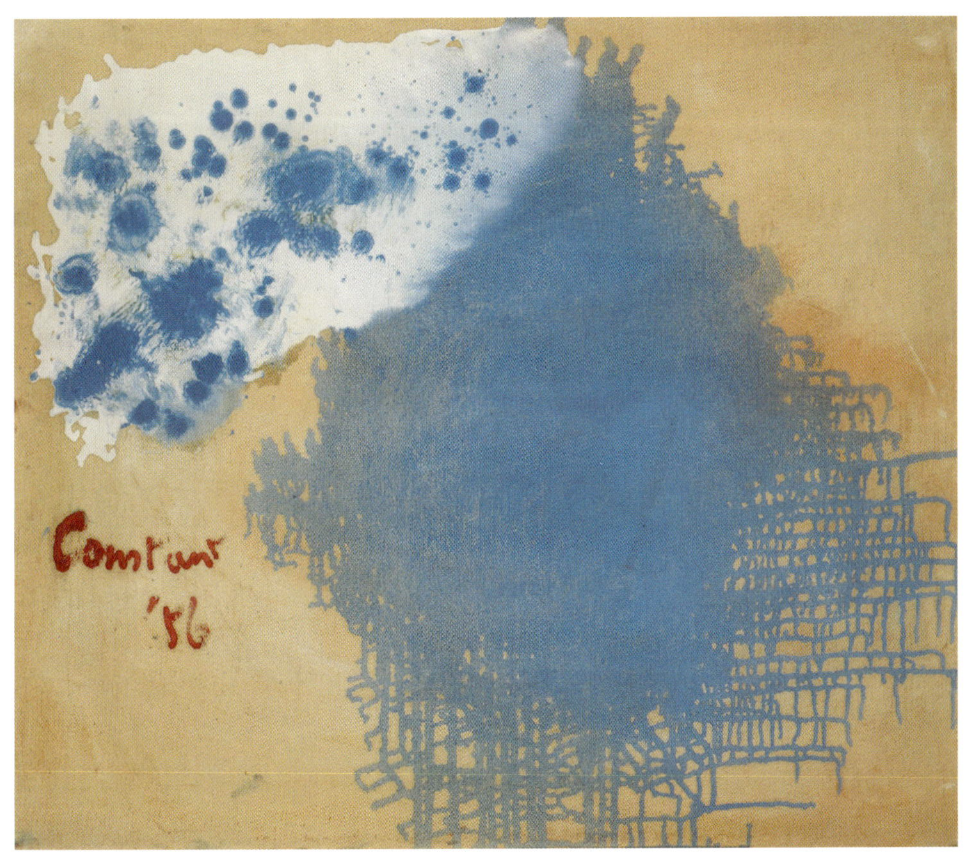

Constant and Anton Rooskens, model for the décor of the ballet *The Process (Kafka)* commissioned by the Dutch National Ballet, 1955 wood, paint, iron, nylon, collage and paper, 18.5 x 31 x 18.7 cm
collection Fondation Constant, donation heirs of Anton Rooskens

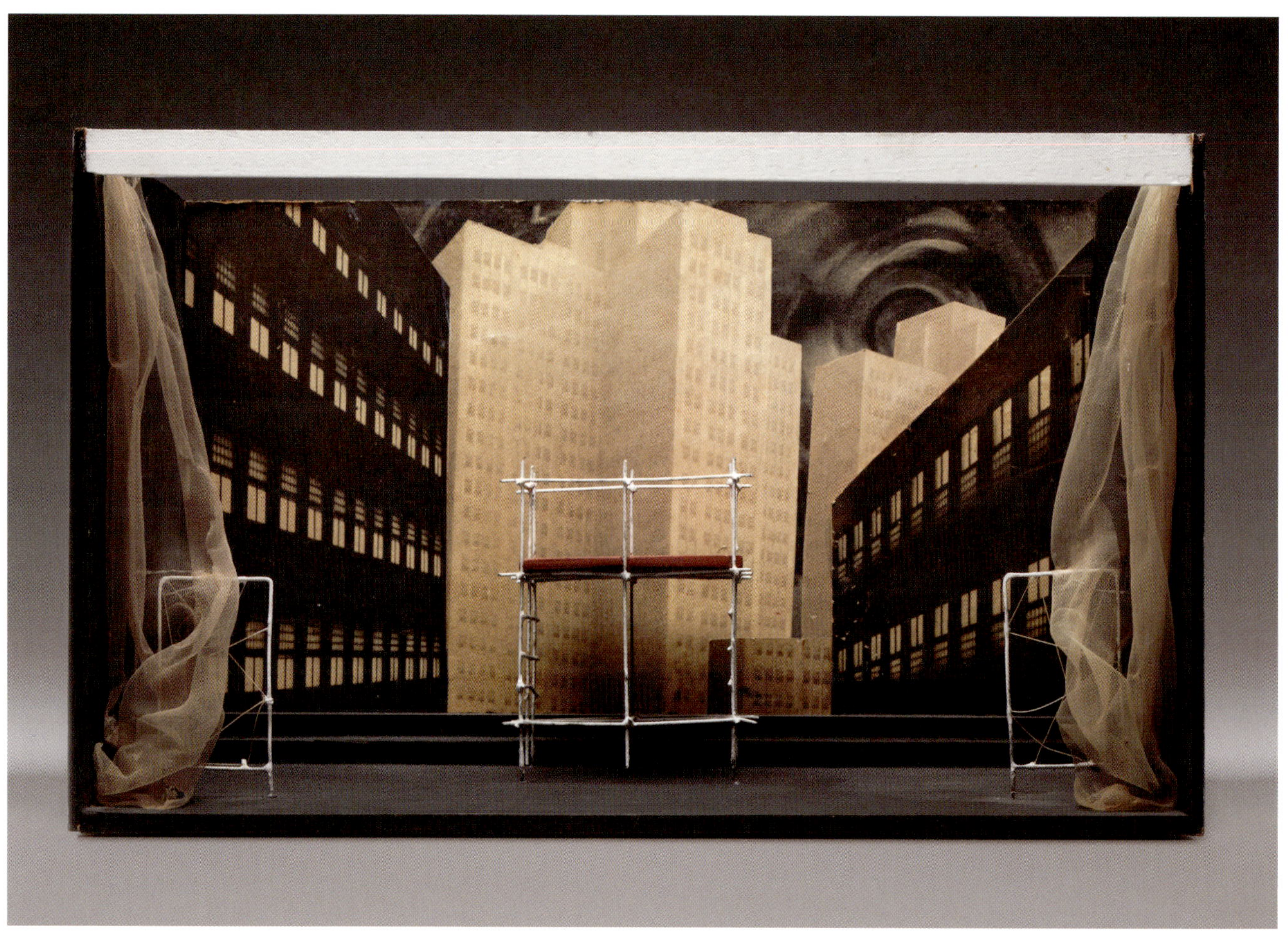

Model IJhorst, design 1953
painted steel wire support and Securit glass table top, 45.5 x ∅ 64.5 cm
collection Fondation Constant

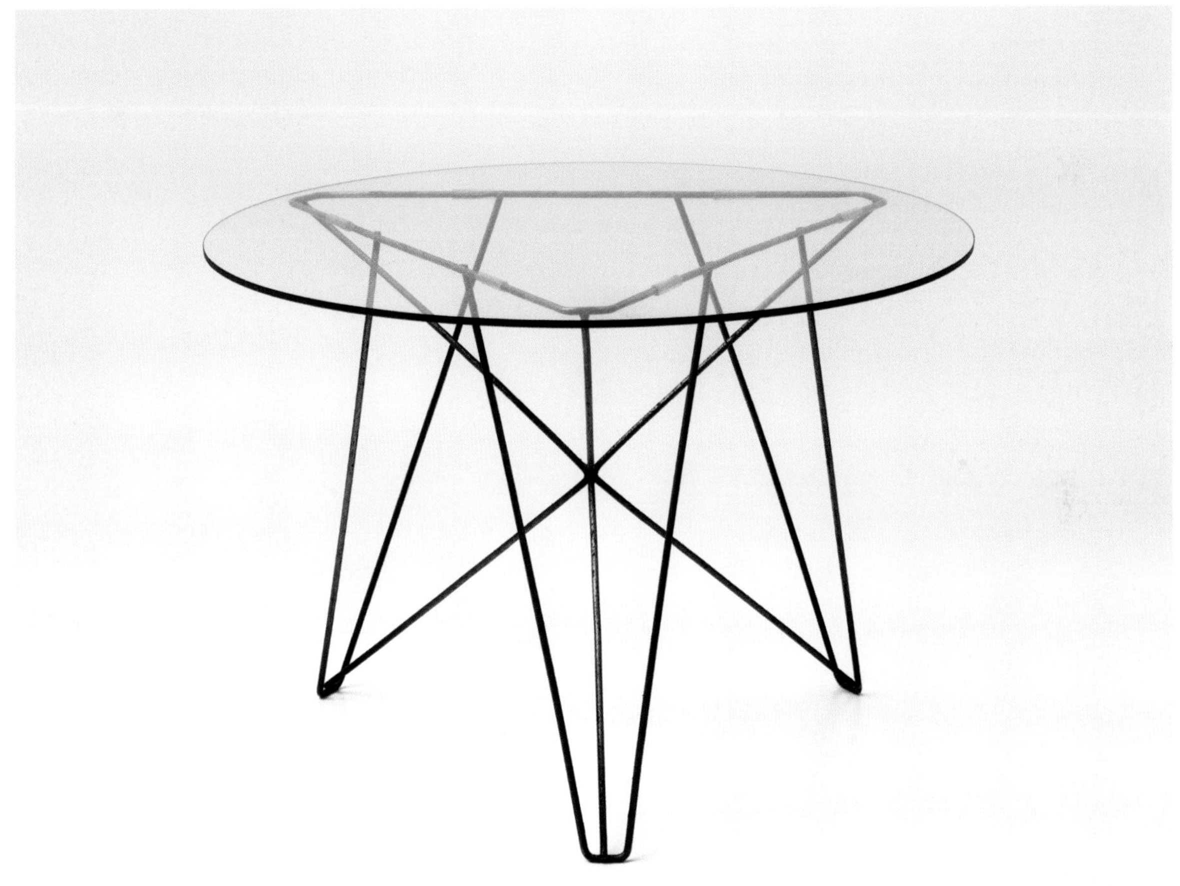

Delft wall rack, 1956
produced by 't Spectrum
painted steel wire, red, 17.5 x 78.5 x 20 cm
painted steel wire, yellow, 17.5 x 79 x 20.5 cm
painted steel wire, black (large version), 17.5 x 77.5 x 20 cm
painted steel wire, black (small version), 17 x 53 x 19.5 cm
collection www.ArtBrokerDesign.com

Table 'IJhorst', 1956
produced by 't Spectrum
painted steel wire, painted wood,
43.5 x 35.5 cm
collection Titus Darley and Monique Laenen

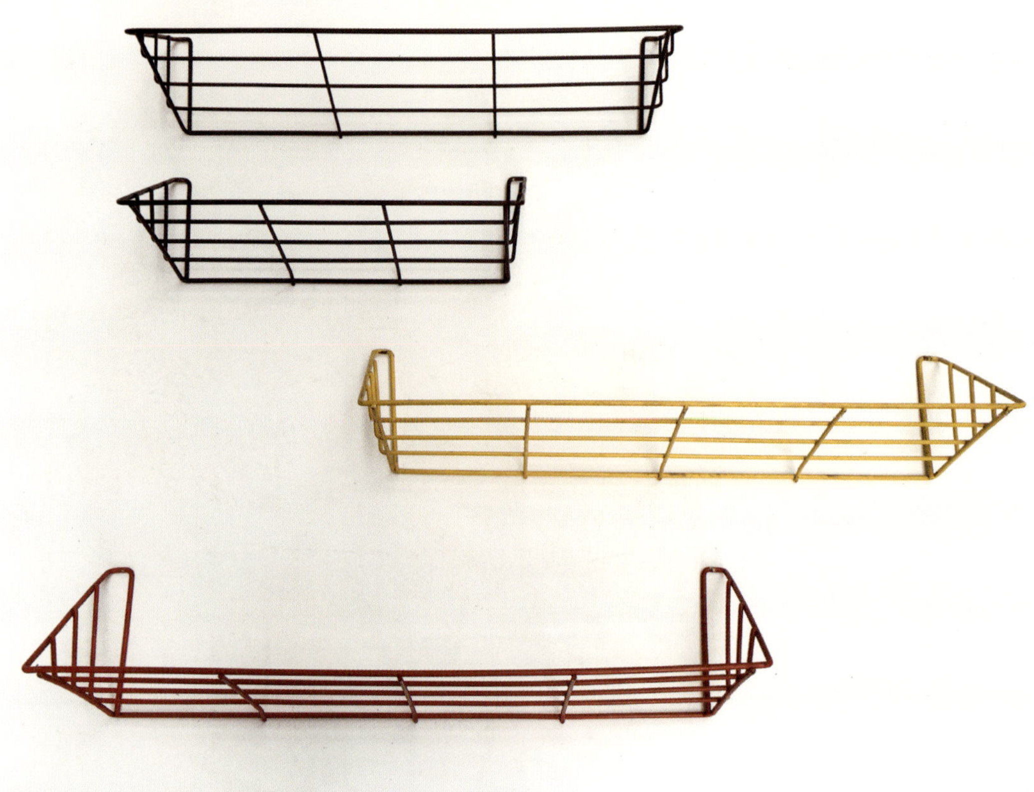

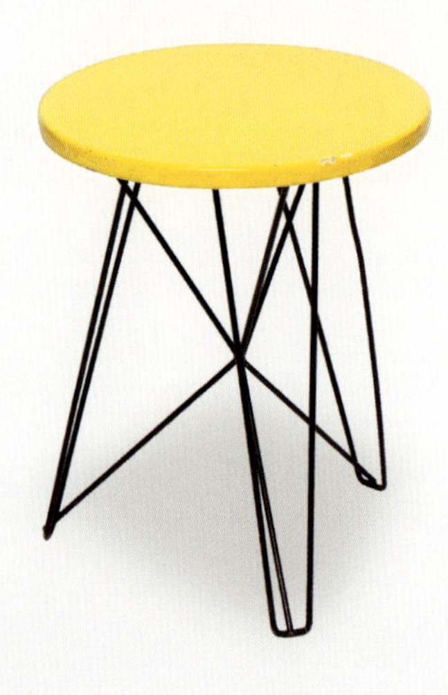

Fabric Design 1, 1956
gouache on paper, 32.5 x 38.4 cm
collection Fondation Constant

Fabric Design 28, 1956
gouache on paper, 32.6 x 39.8 cm
collection Fondation Constant

Fabric Design 25, 1956
gouache on paper, 32.6 x 35.6 cm
collection Fondation Constant

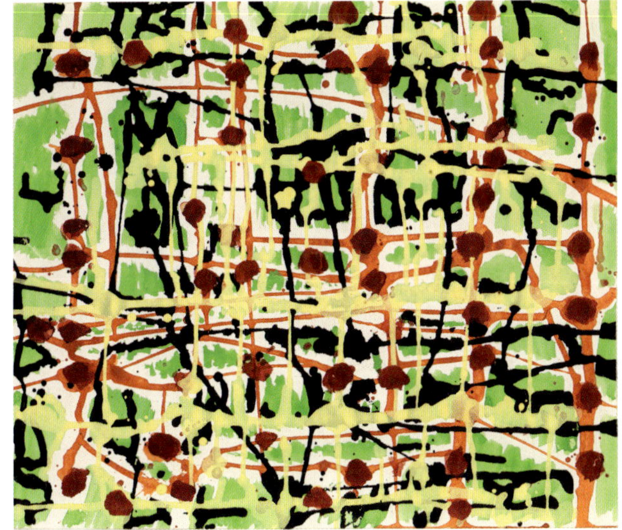

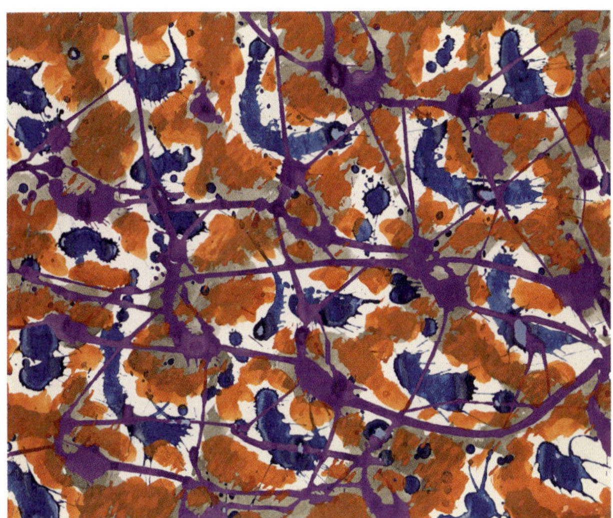

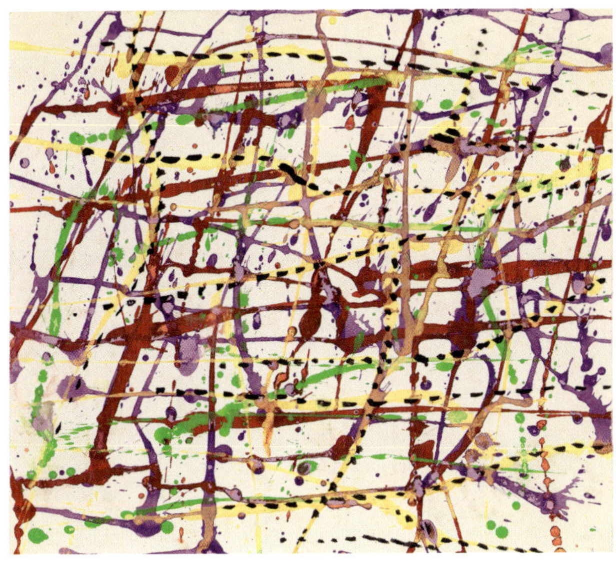

Fabric Design g, 1956
gouache on paper, 28.6 x 36 cm
collection Fondation Constant

Fabric Design d, 1956
gouache on paper, 32.6 x 38 cm
collection Fondation Constant

Fabric Design b, 1956
gouache on paper, 32.5 x 34.9 cm
collection Fondation Constant

Fabric Design c, 1956
gouache on paper, 29.1 x 37.6 cm
collection Fondation Constant

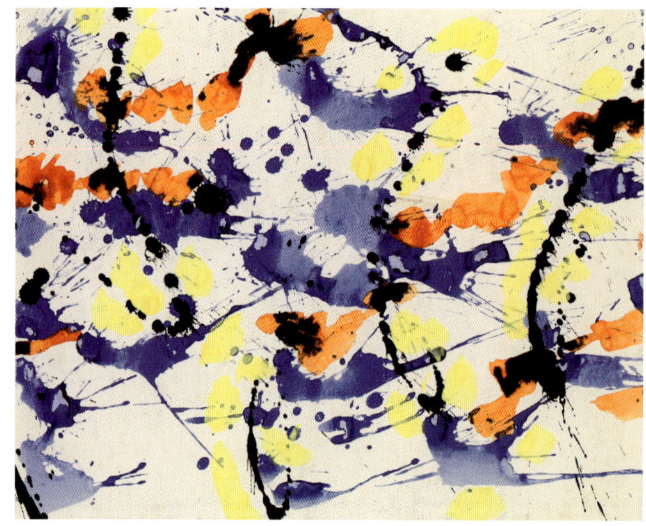

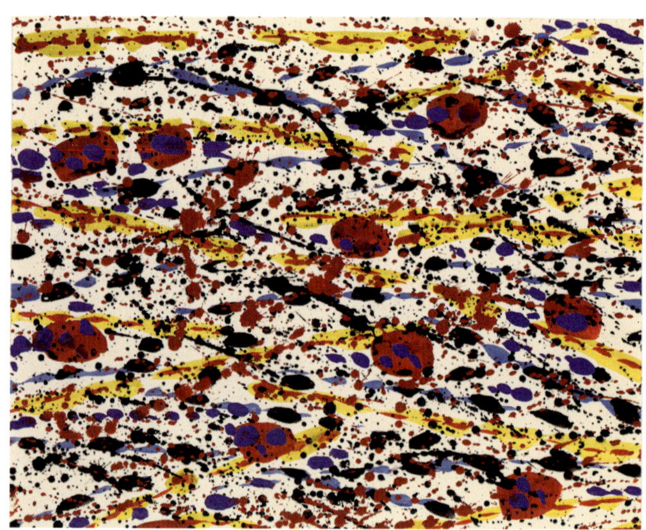

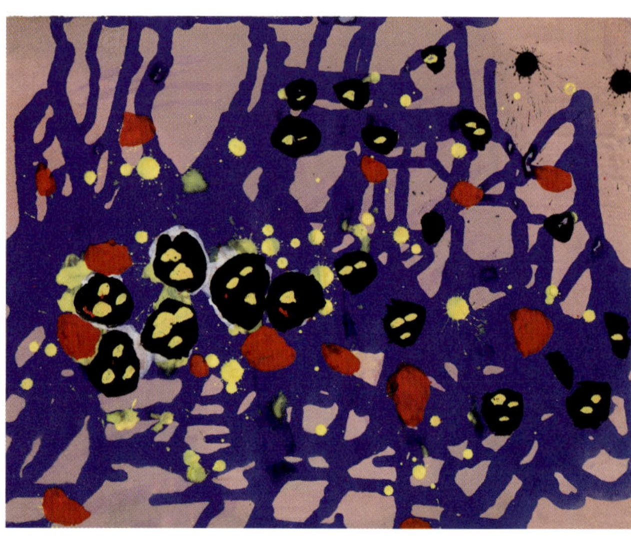

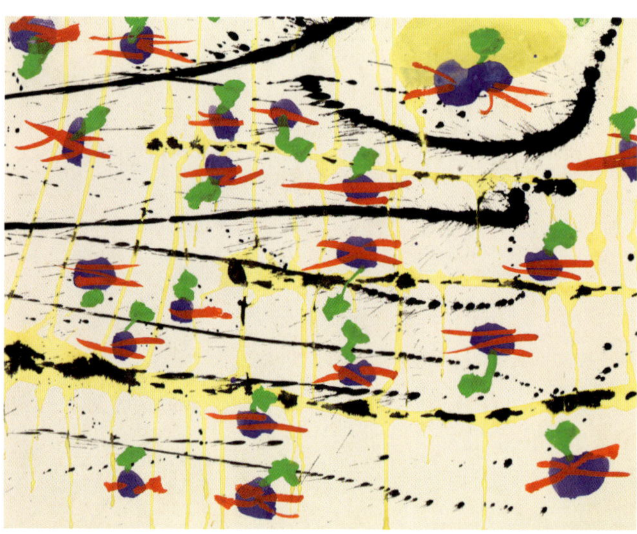

Chilla I (Clothing Fabric), 1957
manufactured by N.V. Stoomweverij Nijverheid, Enschede
silk screen on cotton, 92.5 x 414 cm
collection Stedelijk Museum Amsterdam

Chilla III (Clothing Fabric), 1957
manufactured by N.V. Stoomweverij Nijverheid, Enschede
silk screen on cotton, 92.3 x 102 cm
collection Stedelijk Museum Amsterdam

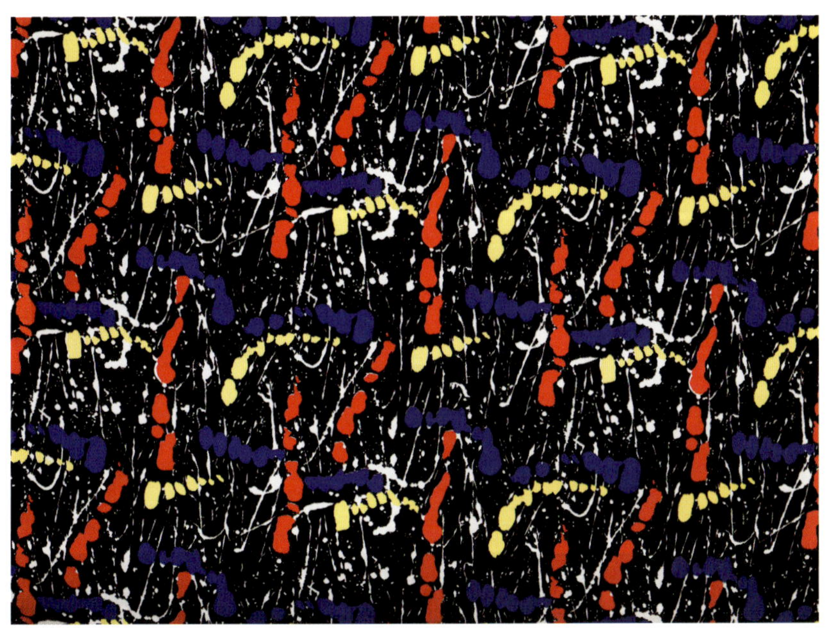

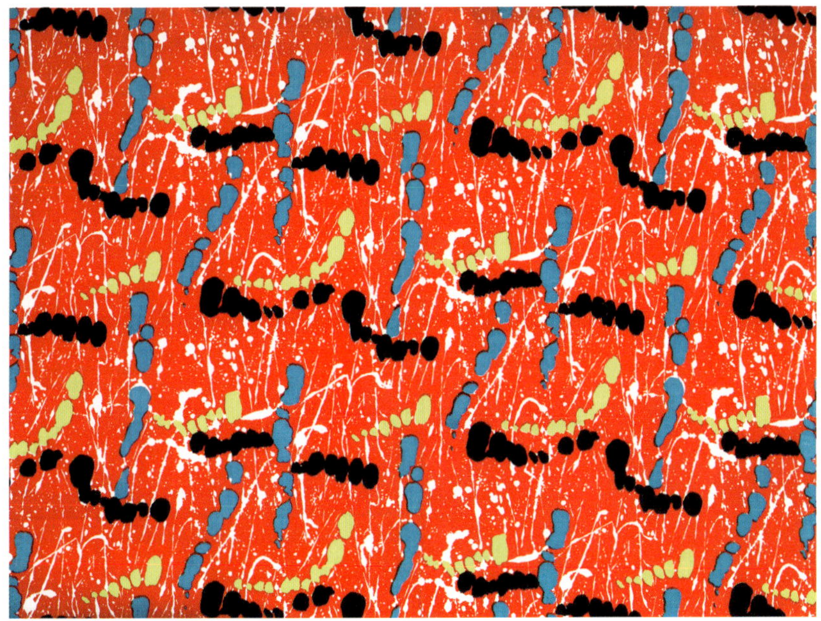

Chilla II (Clothing Fabric), 1957
manufactured by N.V. Stoomweverij Nijverheid, Enschede
silk screen on cotton, 92.5 x 435 cm
collection Stedelijk Museum Amsterdam

Chilla IV (Clothing Fabric), 1957
manufactured by N.V. Stoomweverij Nijverheid, Enschede
silk screen on cotton, 90 x 100 cm
collection Stedelijk Museum Amsterdam

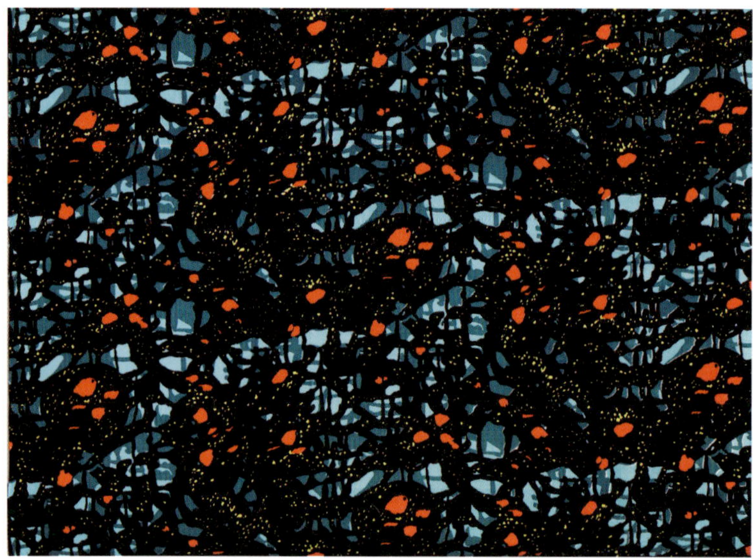

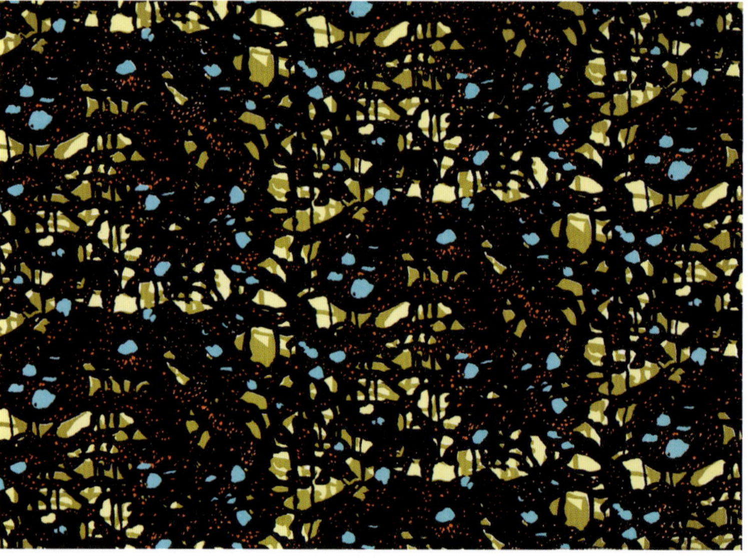

La ville noyée (Drowned City), 1956
oil on linen, 146.5 x 112.7 cm
collection De Heus-Zomer

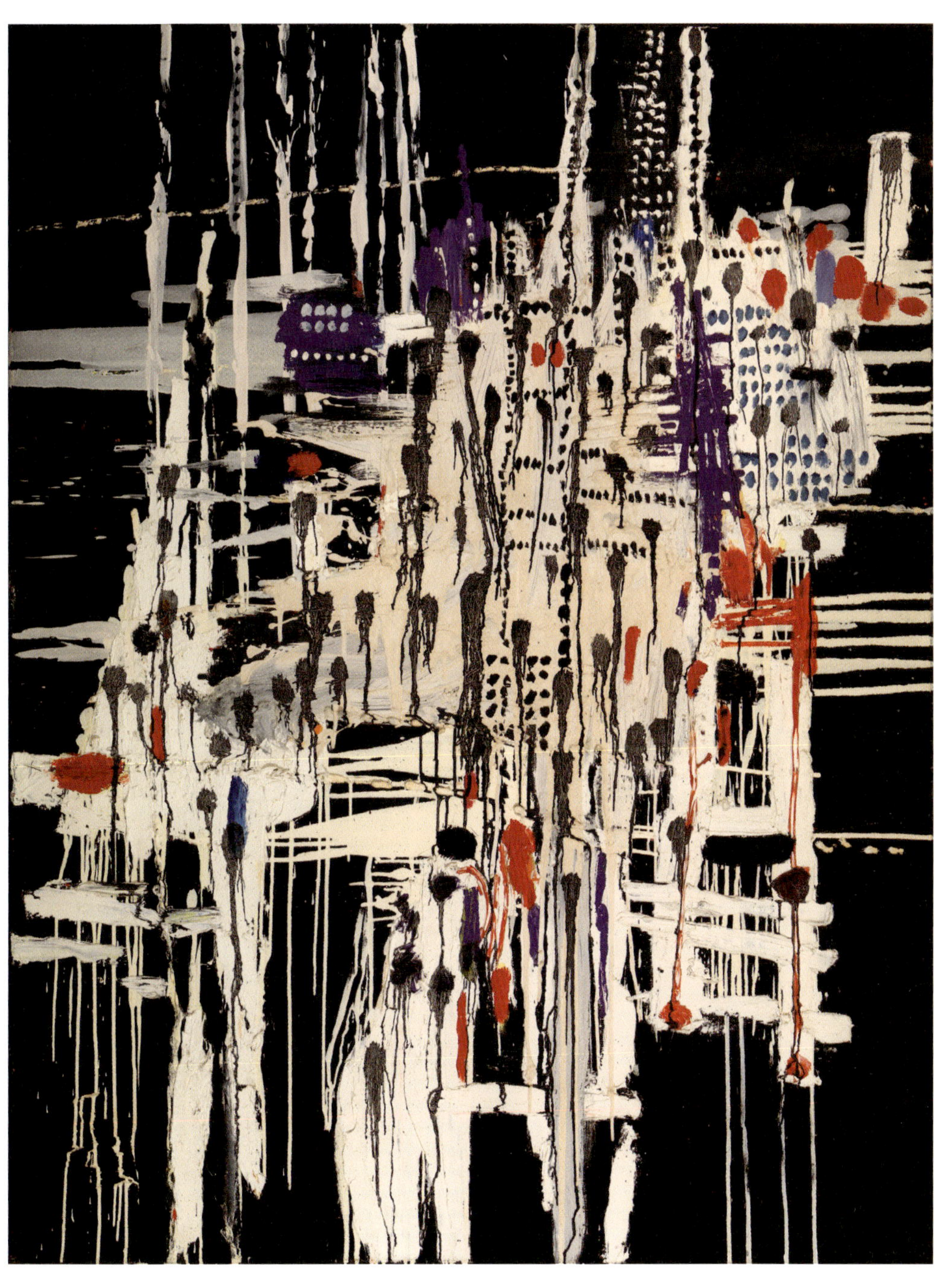

Constructie met halve cirkels
(Construction with Semicircles), 1958
aluminium, Plexiglas, 60 x ∅ 76 cm
collection Kröller-Müller Museum, Otterlo,
Government Acquisition 1965

1957-1961
Space Travel

The second half of the 1950s was dominated by the space race between the Soviet Union and the United States. It was one of the fronts on which the Cold War was fought. The technological developments made possible by space travel opened unprecedented possibilities for the future. Engineering and future became almost synonymous. The commission Constant was given to create a sculpture for the 'Lunar Valley' at the 'E55' reconstruction exhibition brought his work into direct contact with space travel. The result was an intriguing group of space paintings and sculptures that simultaneously reflect his admiration for 1920s Russian Constructivism.

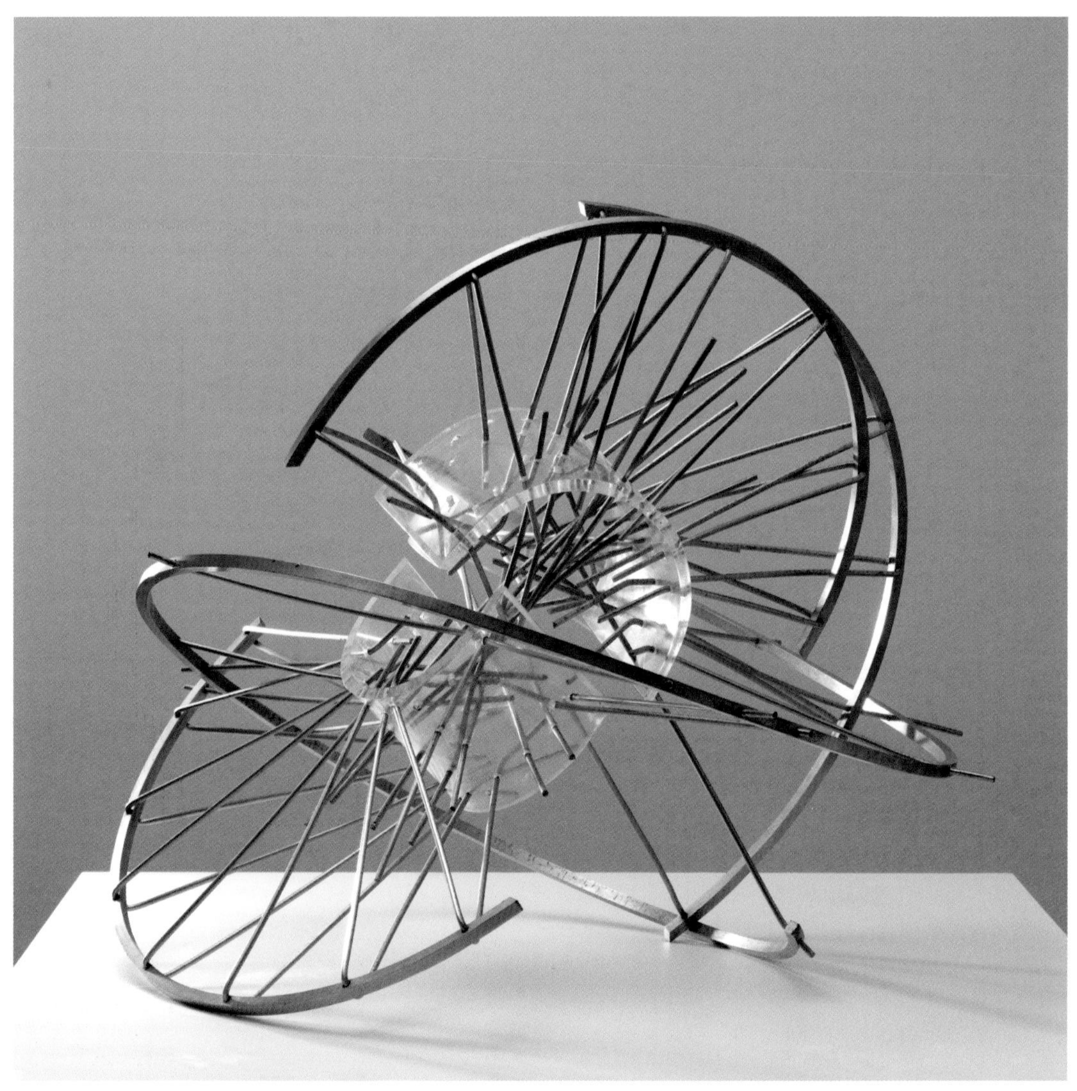

Ruimte en beweging (Space and Movement), 1955 -1956
copper, steel, Plexiglas, ink, plywood base and wood stain,
97 x 76 x 77 cm
collection Stedelijk Museum Amsterdam

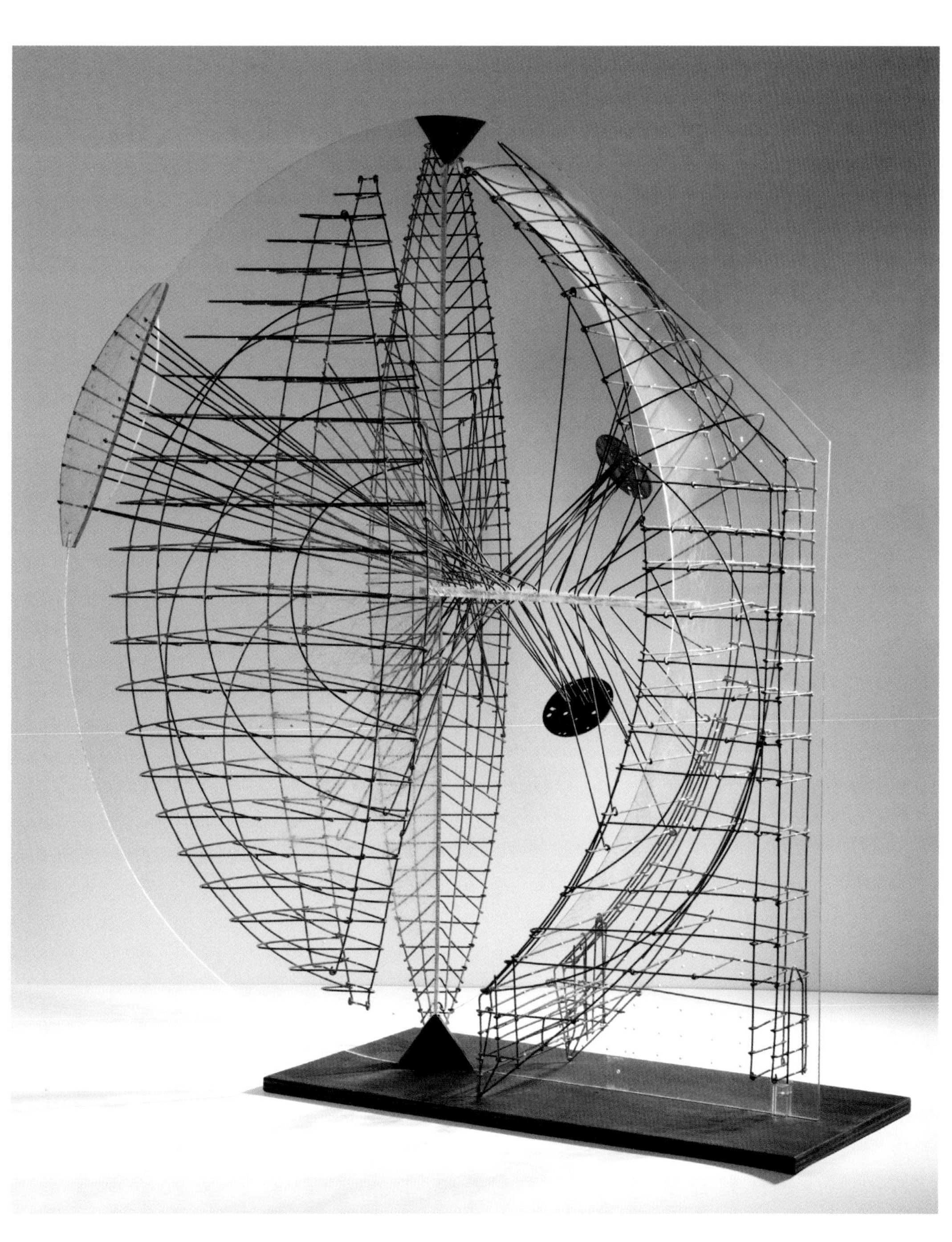

Ruimtecircus (Space Circus), 1956/1961
iron wire, 69 x 59 x 59 cm
collection Rijksmuseum, Amsterdam

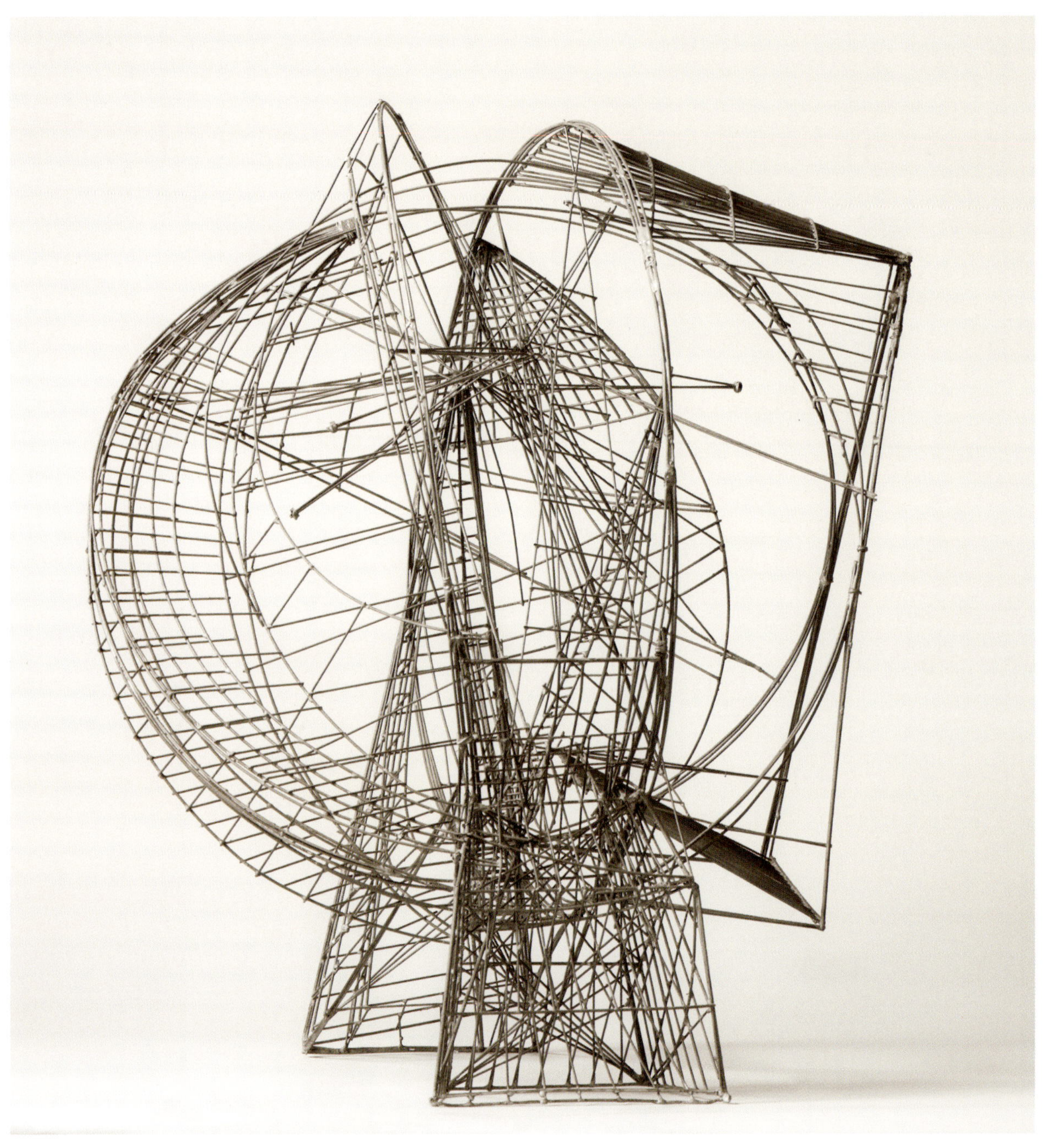

Draadconstructie – Construction turbulente
(Wire Construction), 1958
iron wire, 93 x 96 x 84 cm
collection Kunstmuseum Bochum

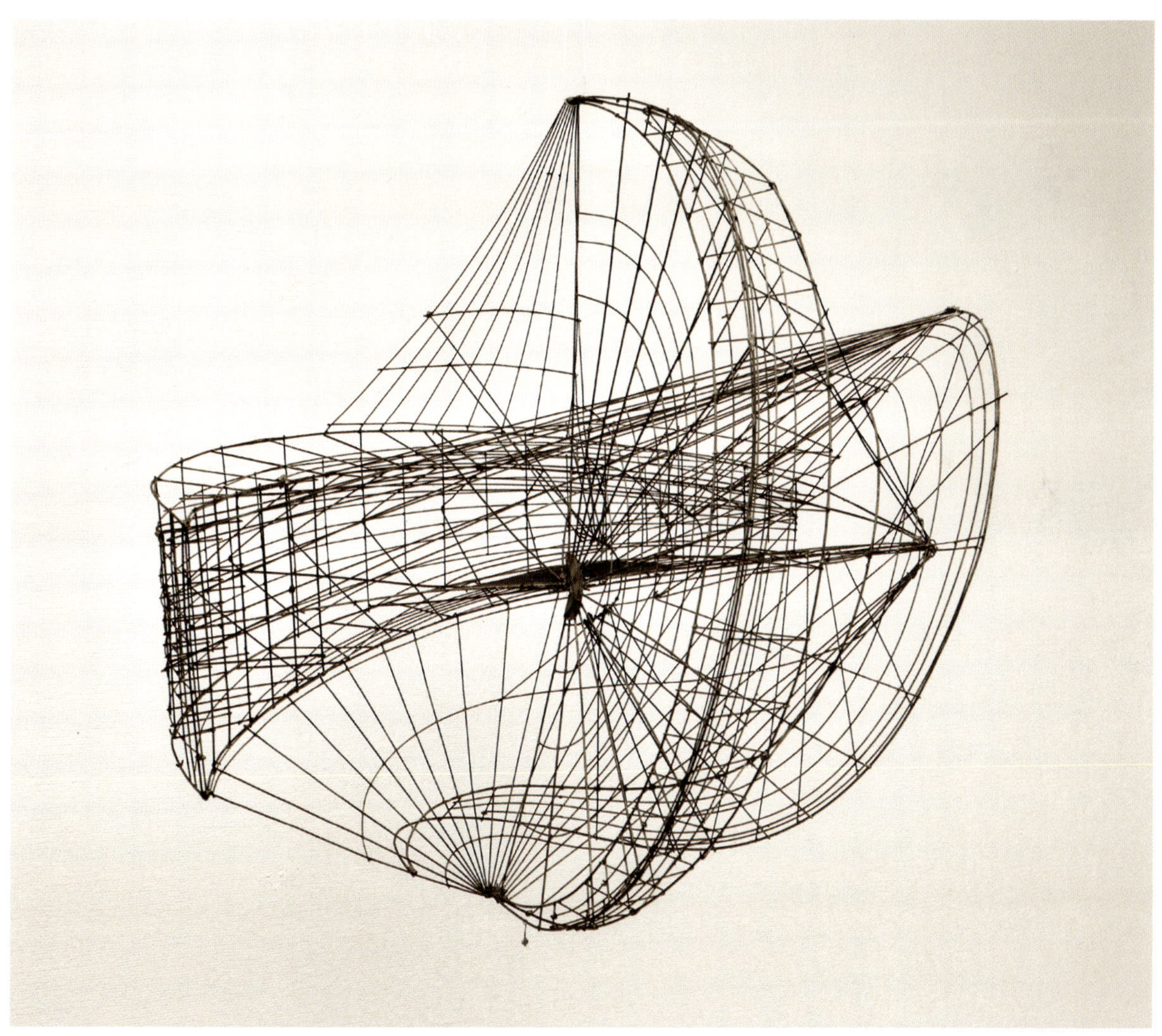

Eivormige constructie – Divergerende Strahlen II
(Ovoid Construction – Divergent Rays II), 1957
Plexiglas, stainless steel and stone, 94 x 67 x 64 cm
collection Fondation Constant, long-term loan to
the Cobra Museum of Modern Art, Amstelveen

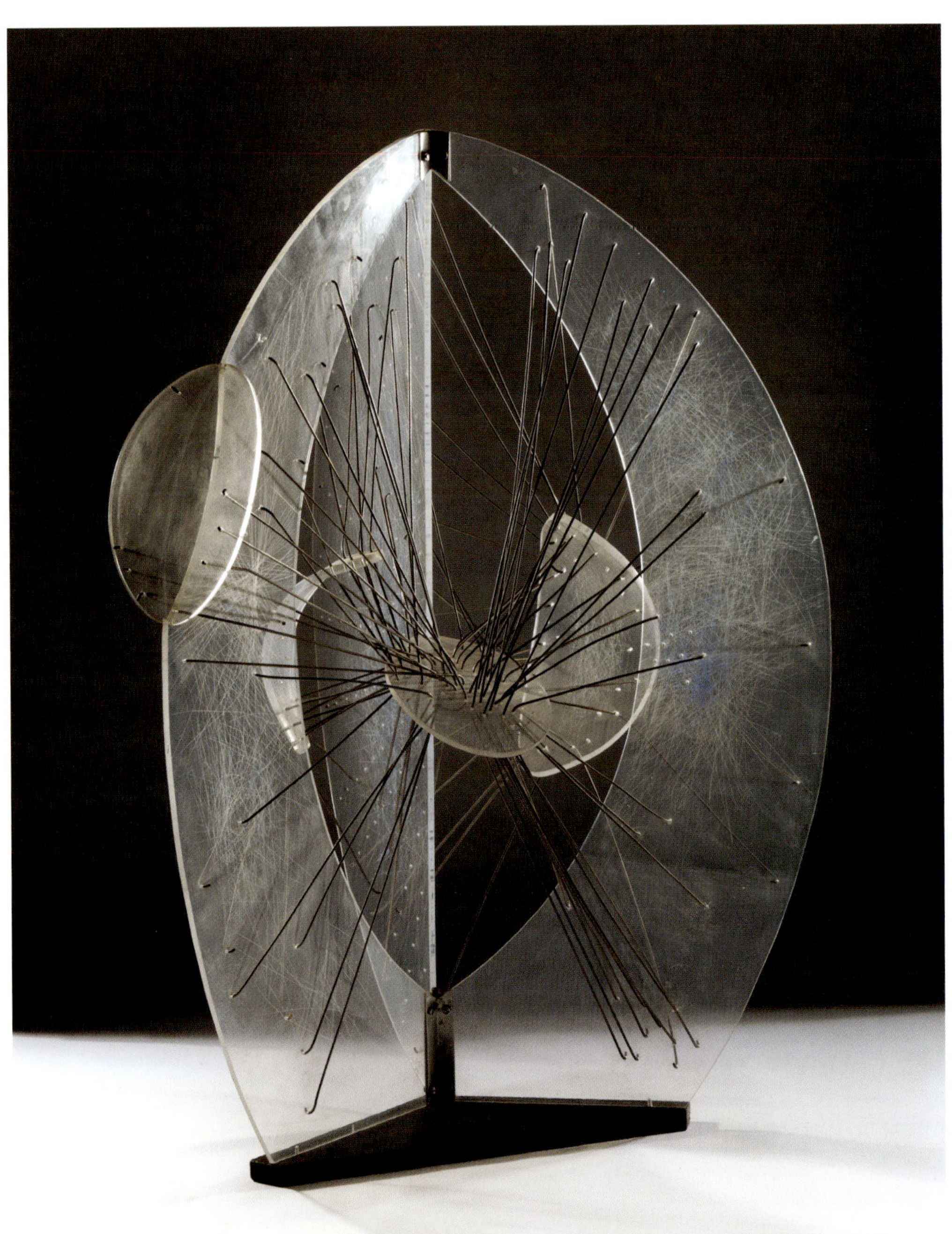

Eivormige constructie – Divergerende Strahlen I
(Ovoid construction – Divergent Rays I), 1957
Plexiglas and steel wire, 60 x 50 x 50 cm
collection Rijksmuseum Twenthe, Enschede

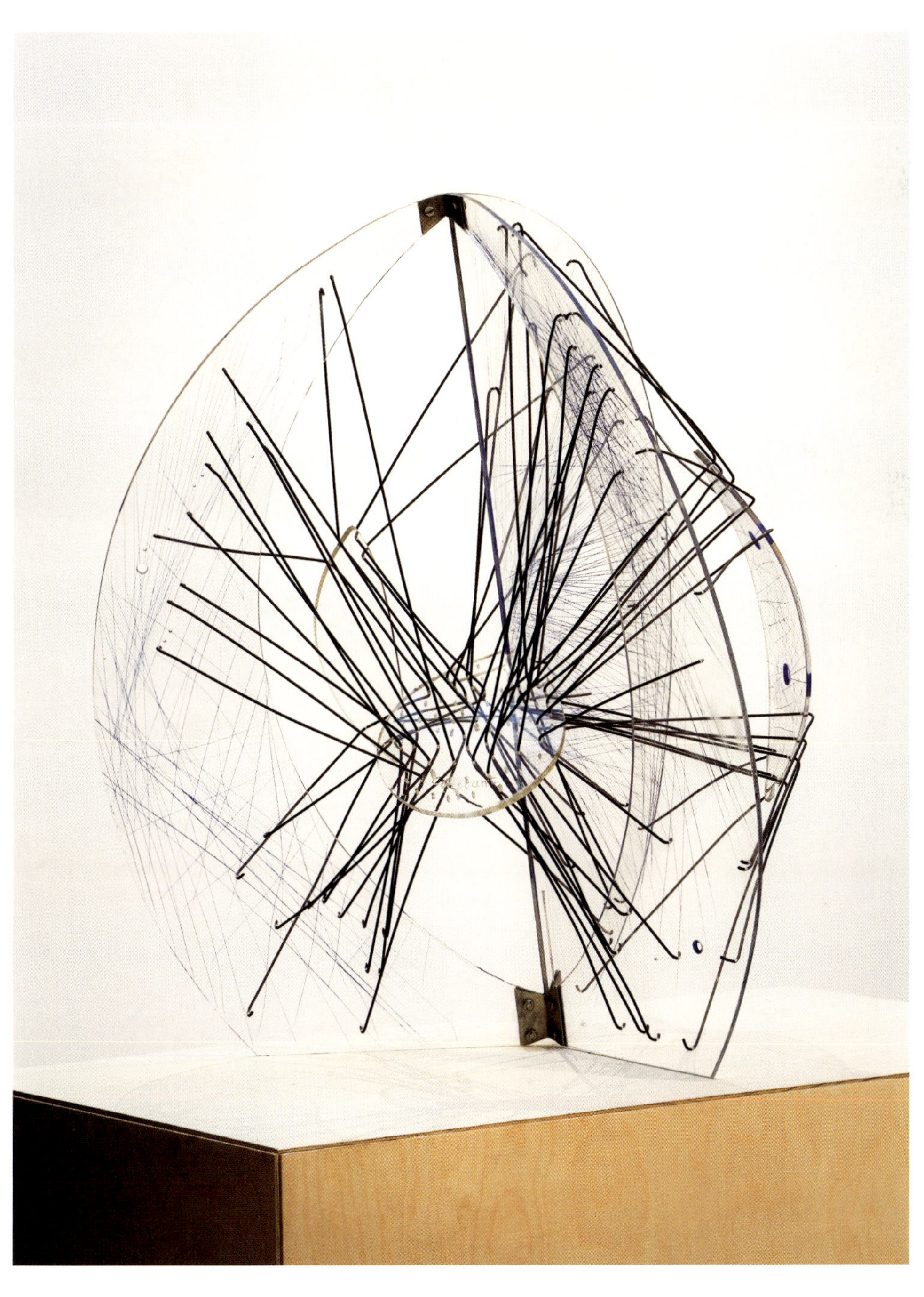

Nébulose mécanique – liggend / hangend
(Nébulose mécanique – lying / hanging), 1958
Plexiglas and brass, 35 x 96 x 73 cm
collection Fondation Constant, long-term loan to
the Stedelijk Museum Schiedam

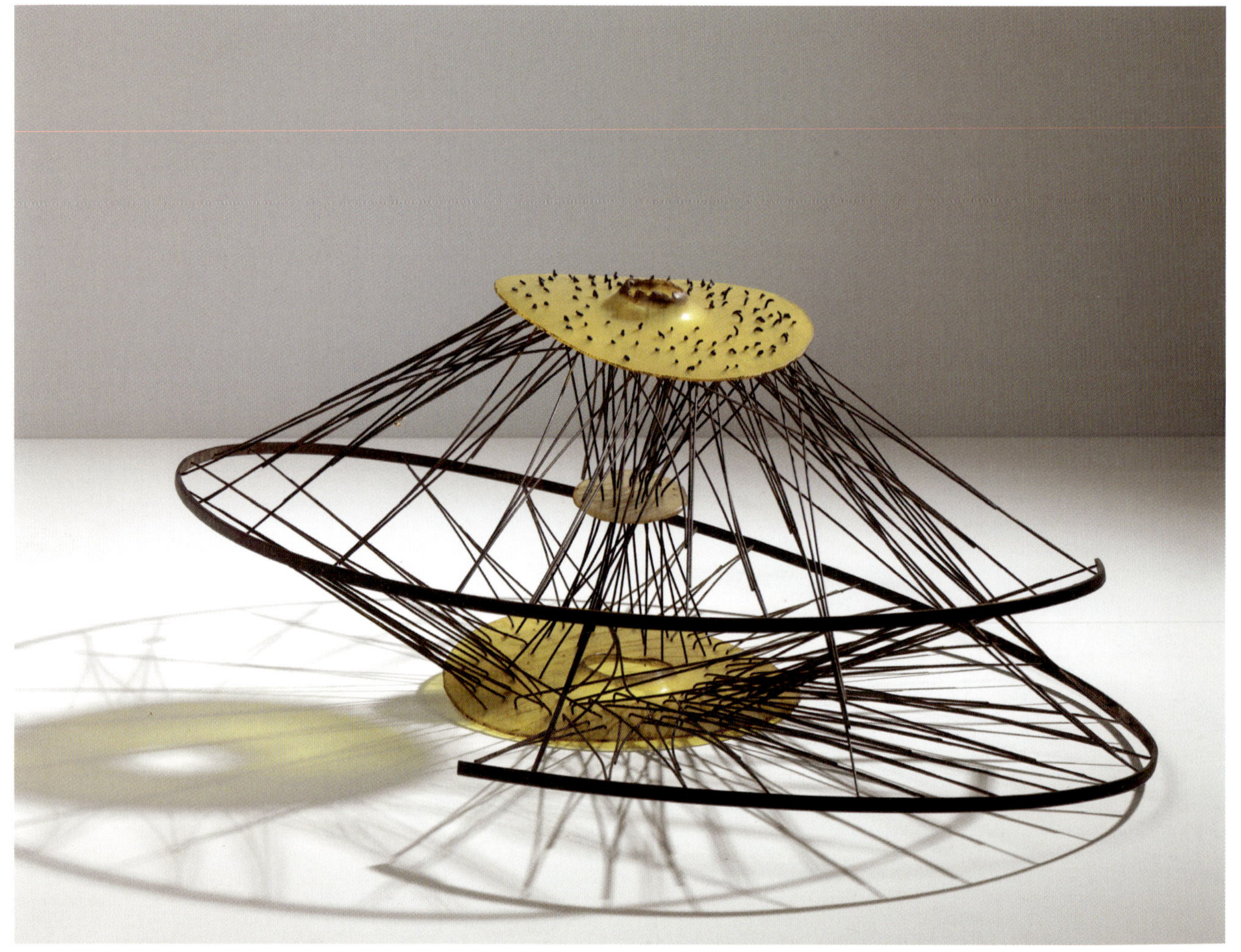

Lijn zonder einde (Infinite Line), 1958
Plexiglas, paint, aluminium and brass wire,
145 x 70 x 70 cm
collection Fondation Constant, long-term loan
to the Cobra Museum of Modern Art, Amstelveen

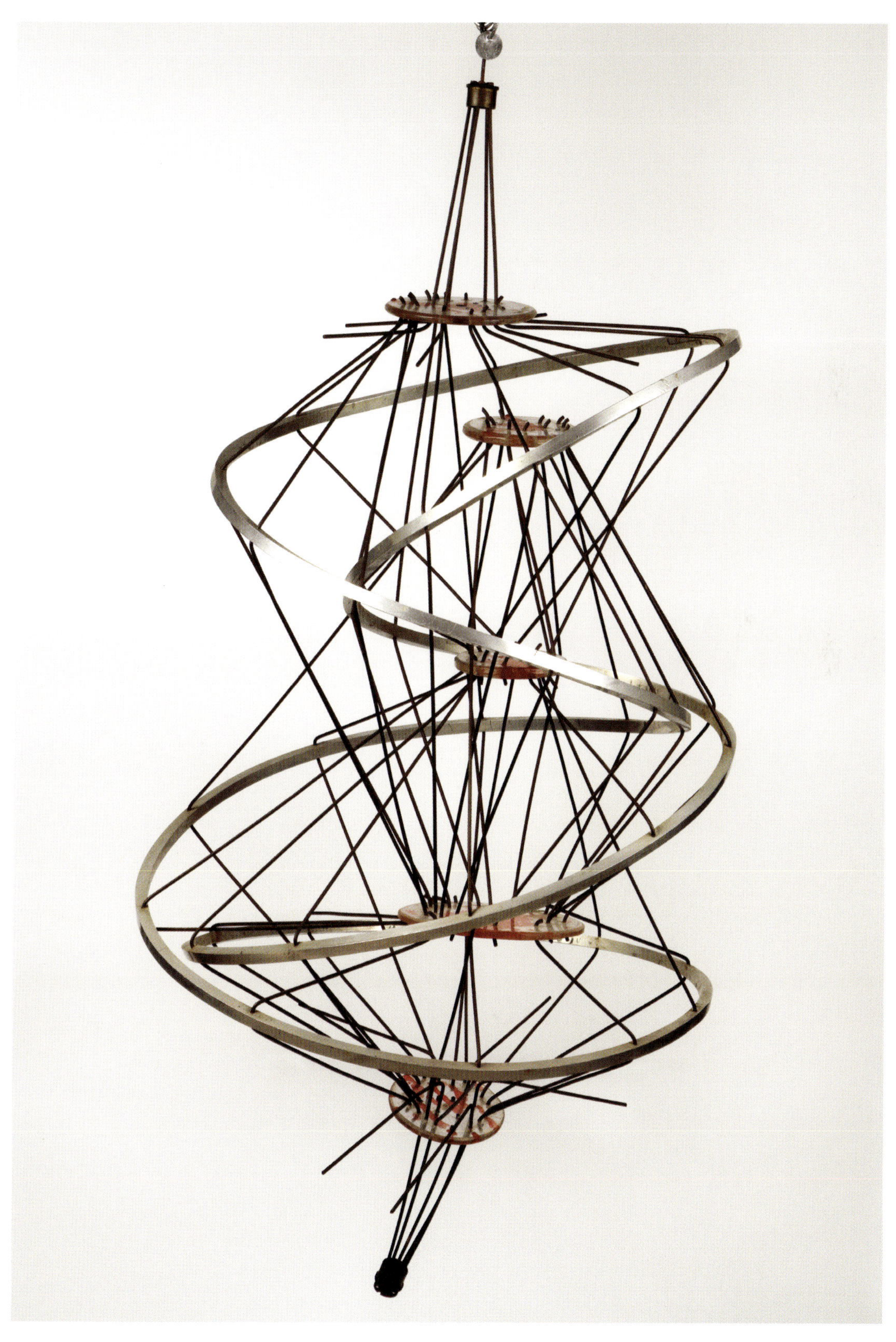

Nébulose mécanique III, 1958
Plexiglas, steel, wooden base, 65 x 53 x 43 cm
collection Kröller-Müller Museum, Otterlo,
donation Ida and Piet Sanders, Schiedam

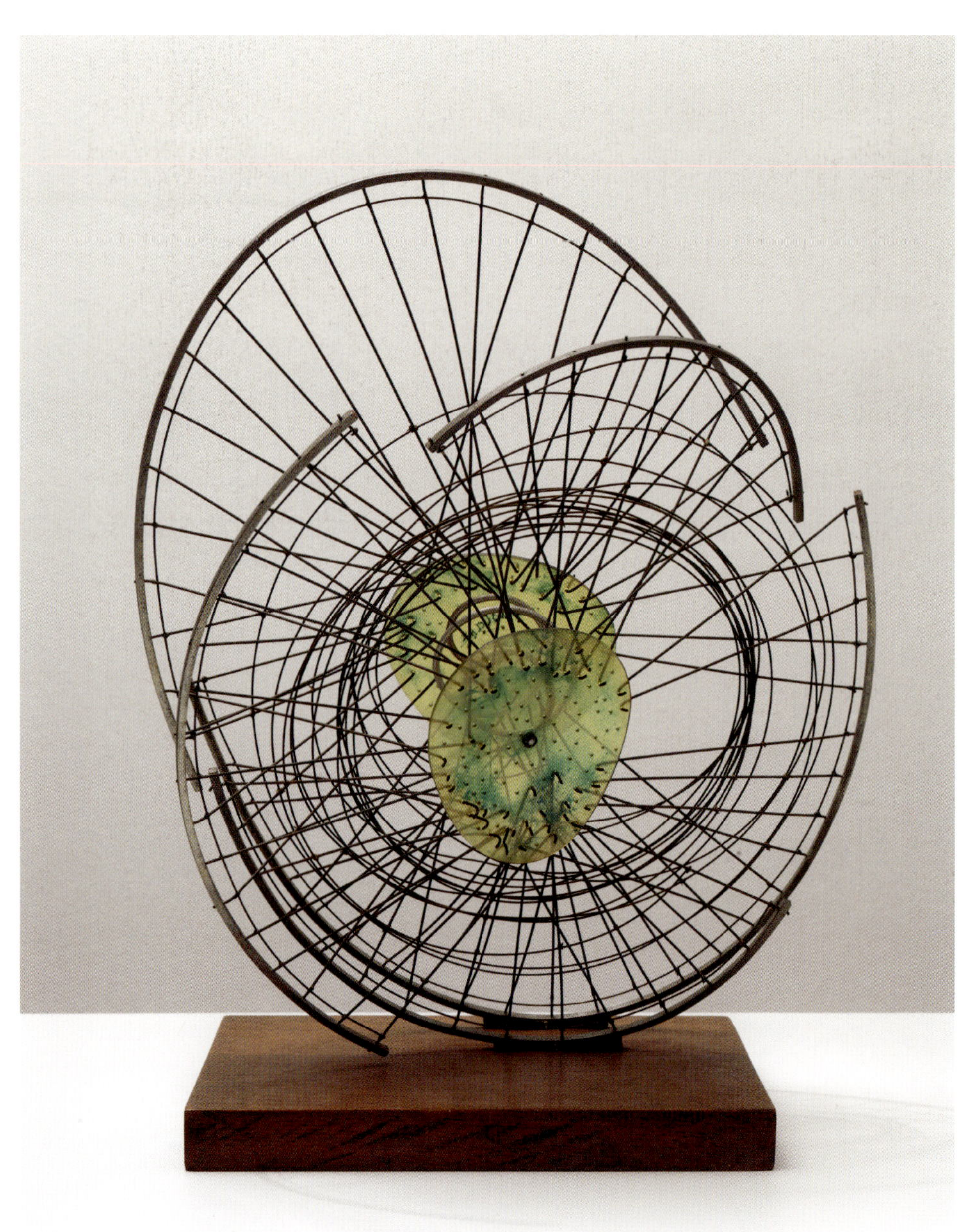

Sterrenbeeld (Constellation), 1956
oil on linen, 35.6 x 50 cm
collection Fondation Constant, long-term loan to
the Stedelijk Museum Schiedam

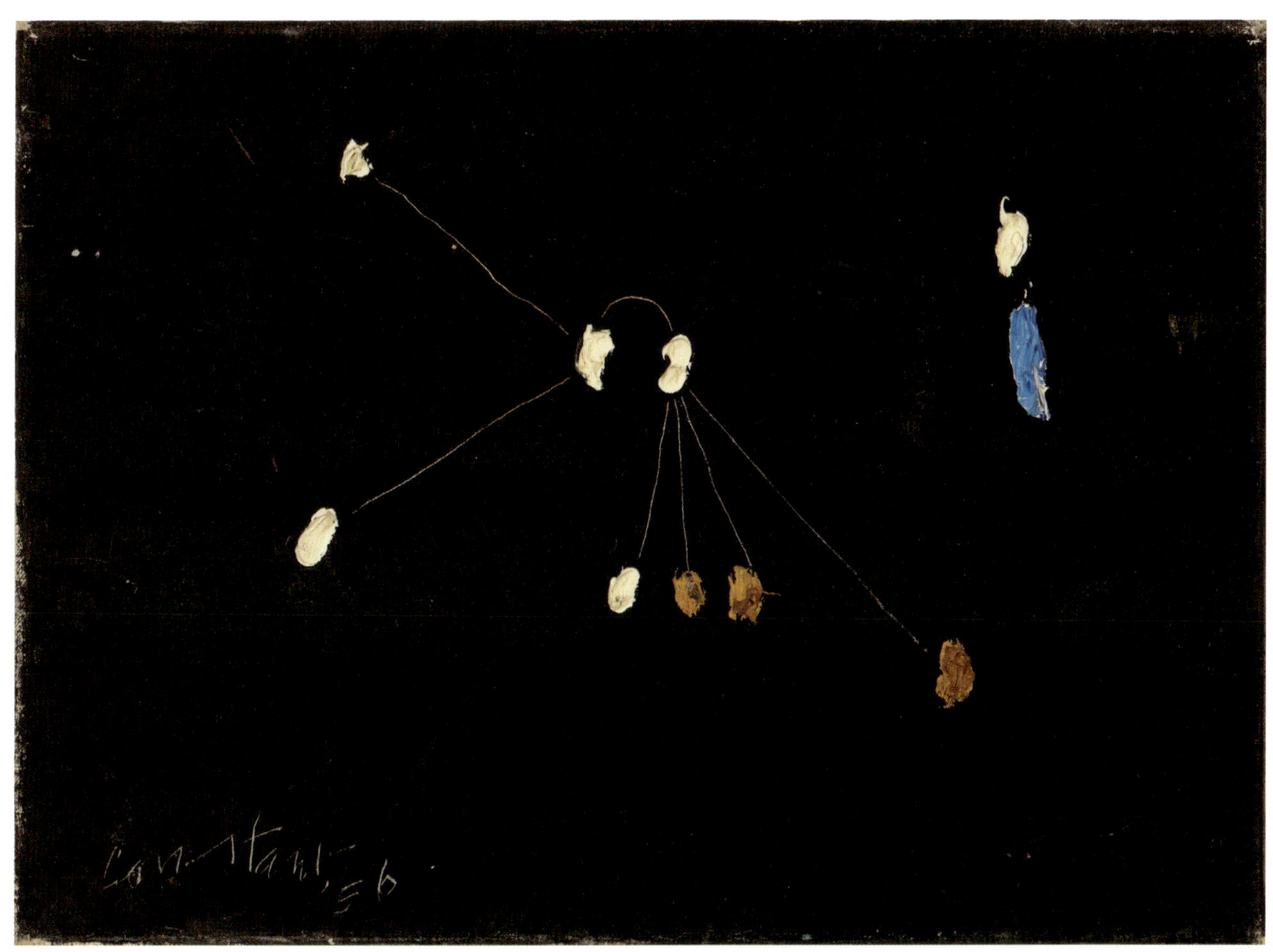

Kosmisch landschap (Cosmic Landscape), 1956
oil on panel, 19.5 x 43.5 cm
collection Fondation Constant

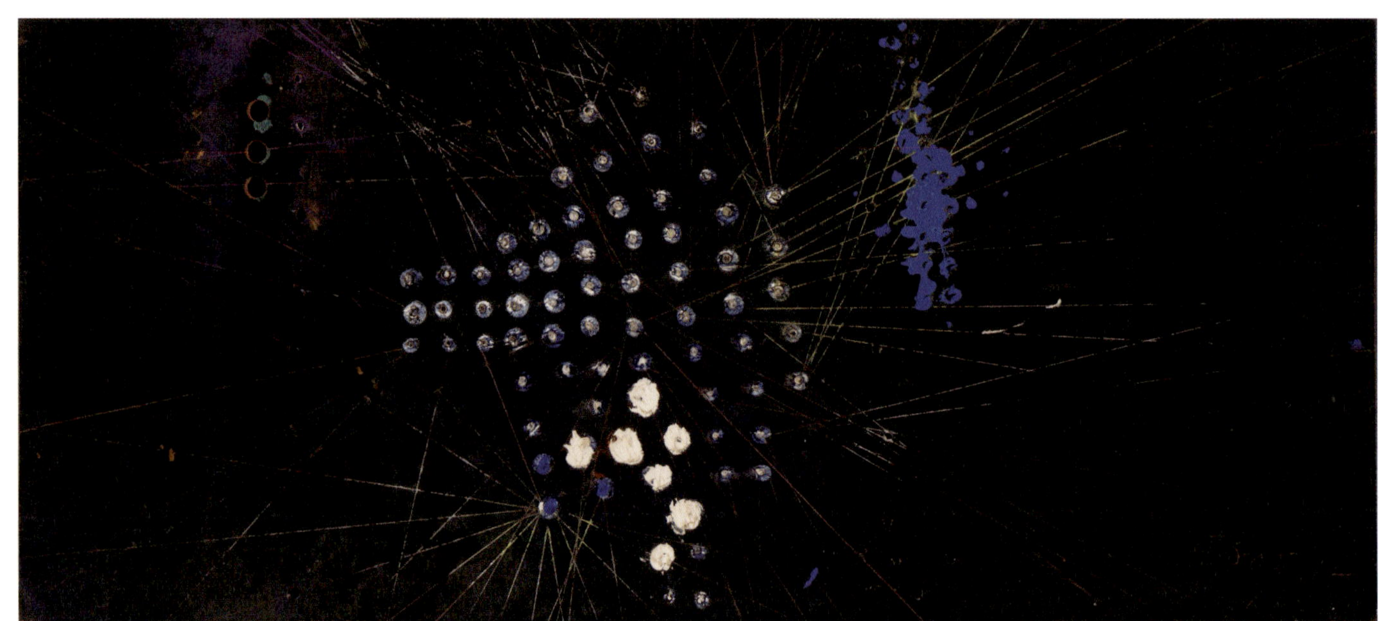

Structures dans l'espace (Structures in Space), 1958
oil on panel, 19.5 x 41 cm
collection Fondation Constant

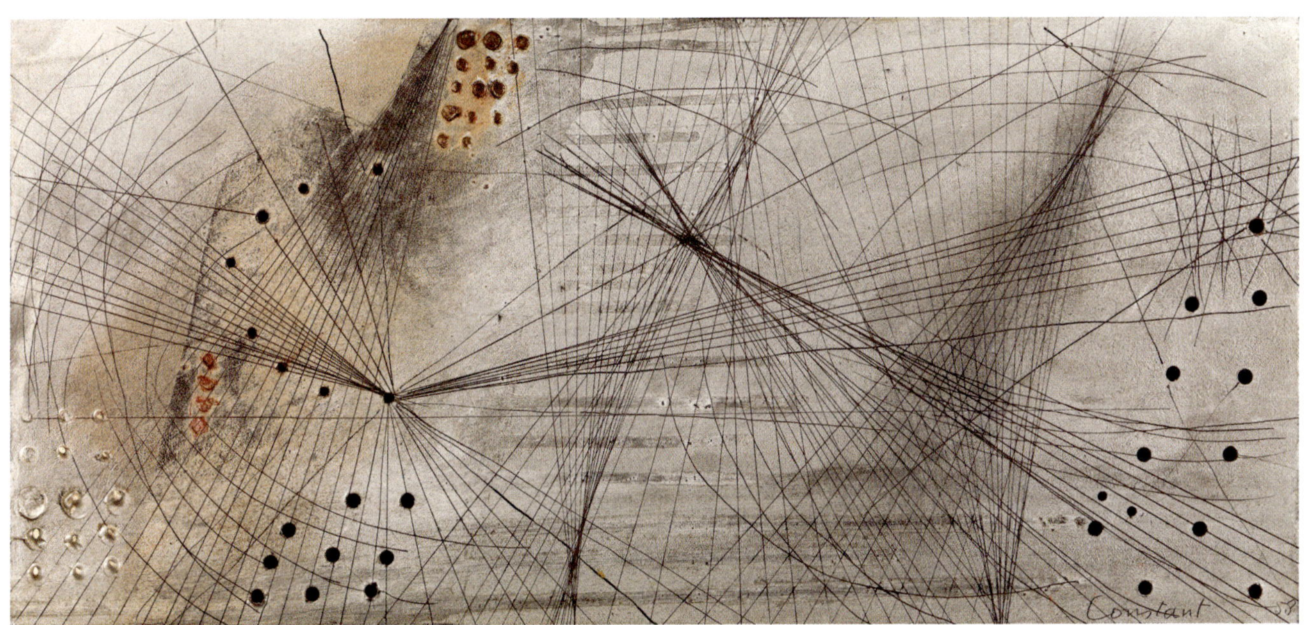

Ruimtelandschap (Space Landscape), 1957
oil on panel, 26.8 x 30.1 cm
collection Fondation Constant

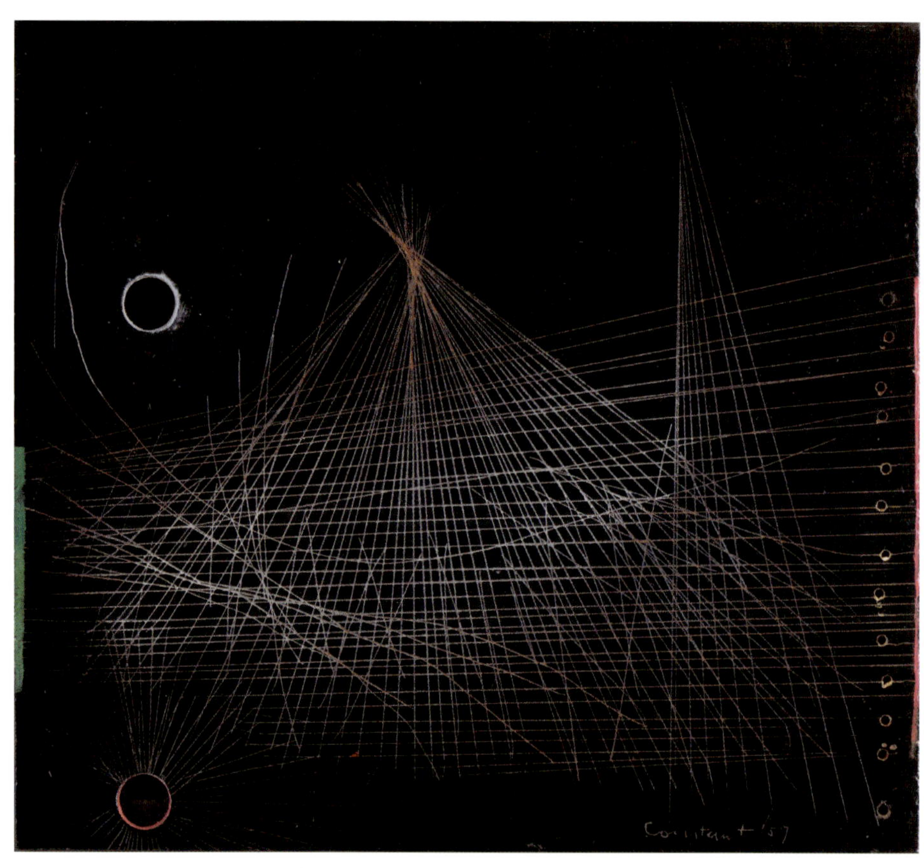

Voyage dans l'espace (Space Travel), 1957
oil on panel, 31 x 42 cm
collection Fondation Constant

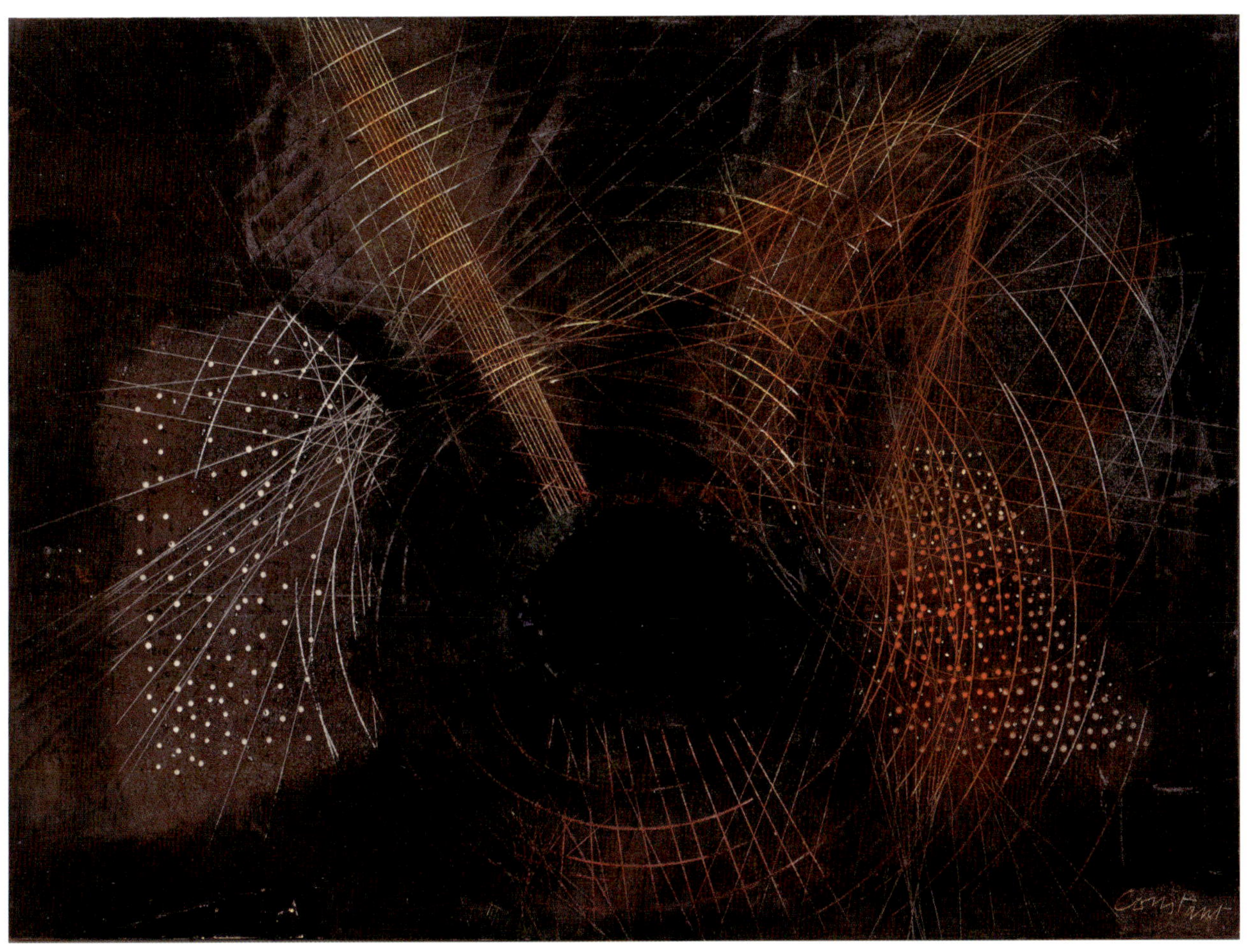

Spatiovore IV, 1959
Plexiglas, steel, paint and wood, 28 x 68.2 x 52.2 cm
collection Kröller-Müller Museum, Otterlo,
Government Acquisition 1965

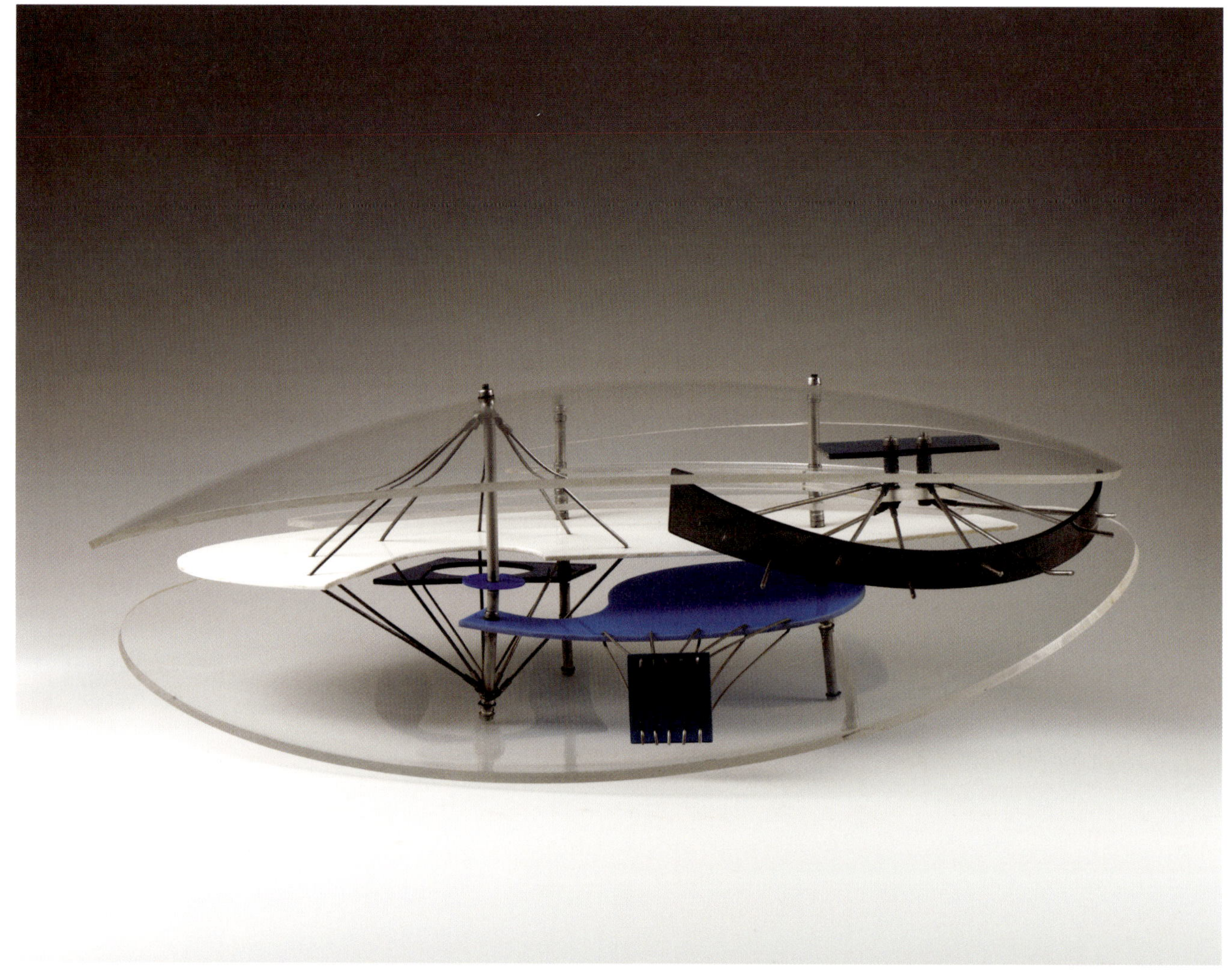

Spatiovore V, 1959
Plexiglas, brass, metal and screw thread,
29 x 62 x 49 cm
Rabo Art Collection, Utrecht

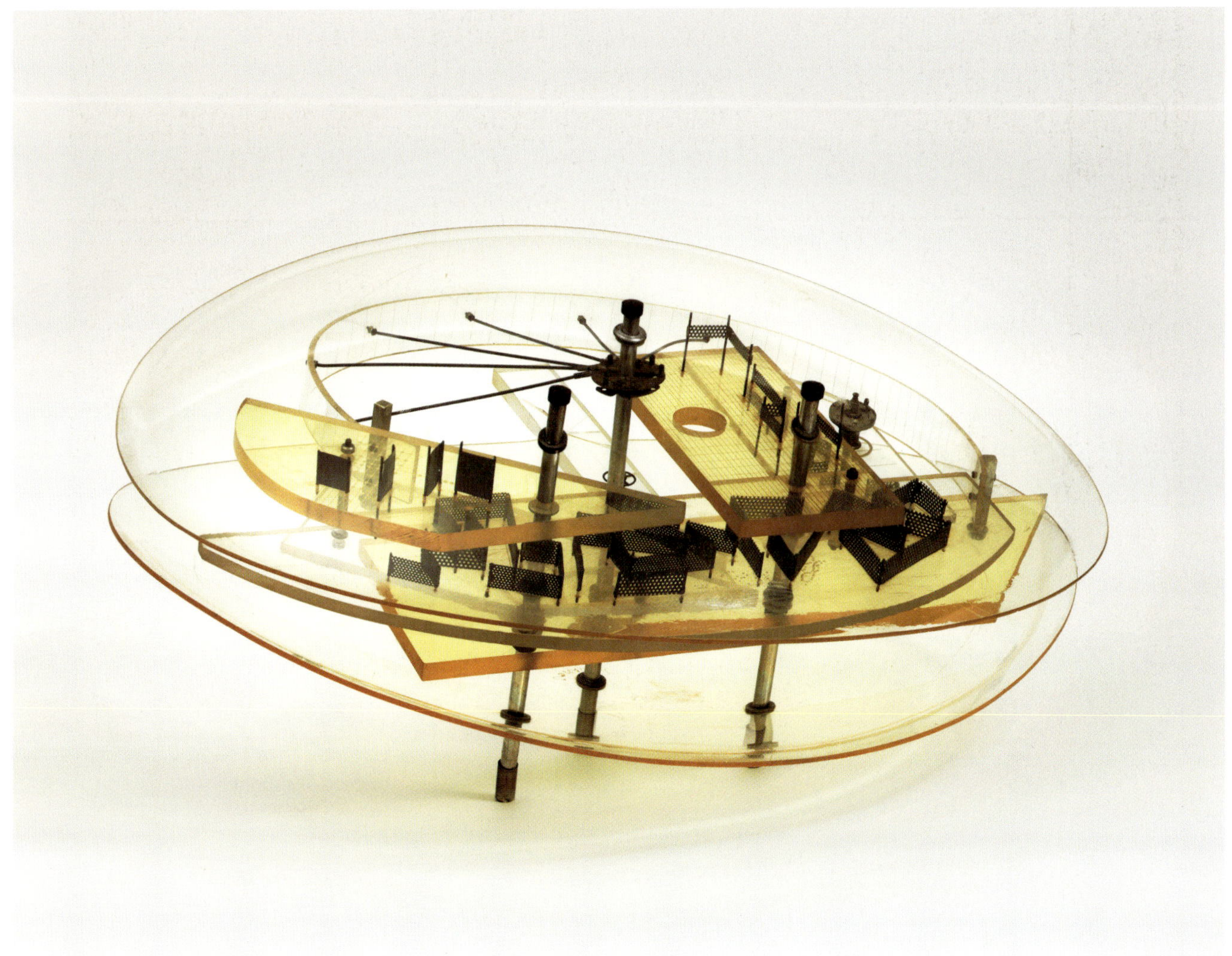

Spatiovore III, 1959
Plexiglas, aluminium, metal and wooden base,
24.7 x 55.8 x 41 cm
collection Stedelijk Museum Amsterdam

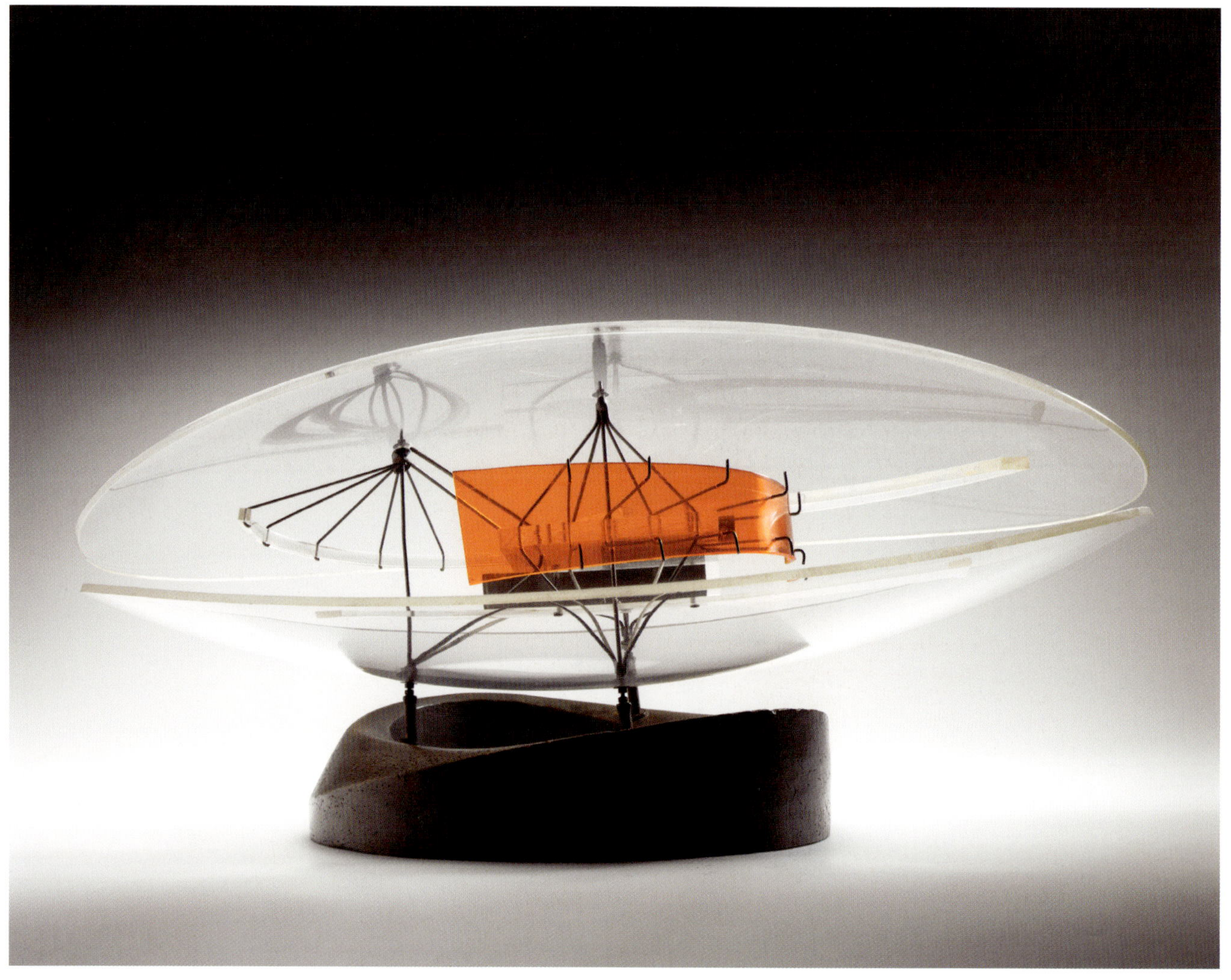

Paysage lunaire (Lunar Landscape), 1956
oil on linen, 119 x 99.5 cm
Rabo Art Collection, Utrecht

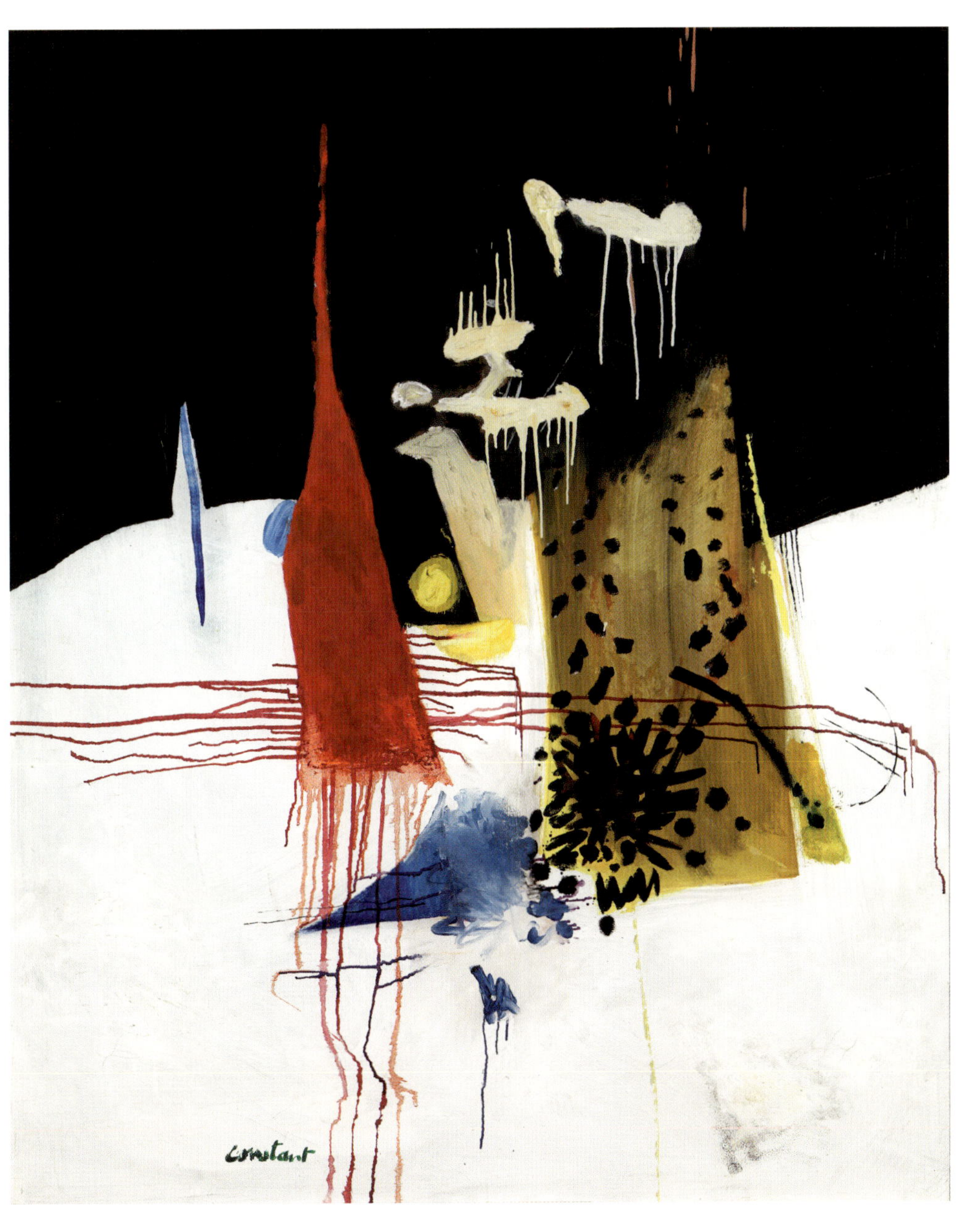

Ronde vorm met drie gaatjes
(Round Shape with Three Holes), 1961
edition of 20, dry point, 21.4 x 25 cm
collection Cobra Museum of Modern Art,
Amstelveen, gift of P. Mansaram

Ronde vorm (Round Shape), 1961
edition of 20, dry point, 22.2 x 27 cm
collection Cobra Museum for Modern Art,
Amstelveen, gift of P. Mansaram

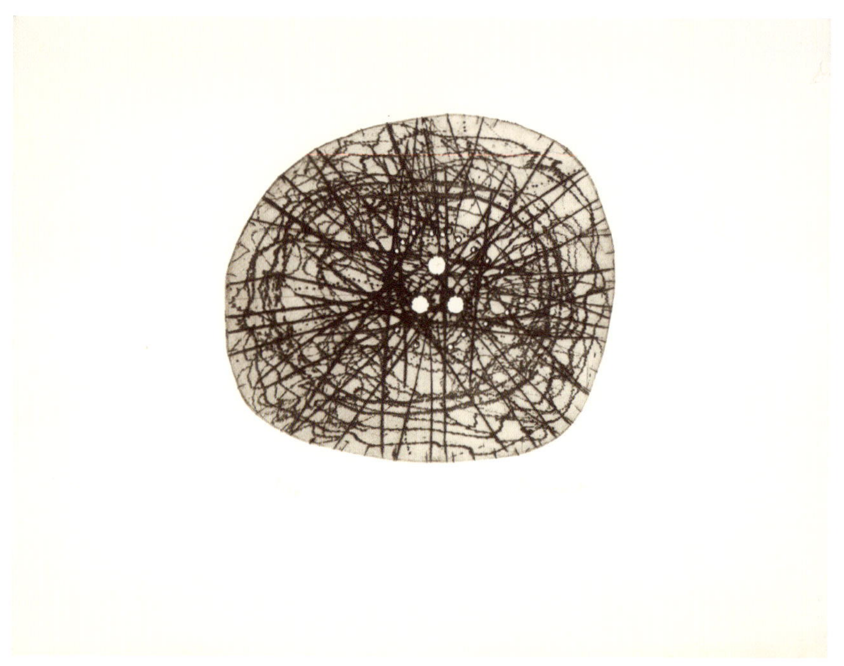

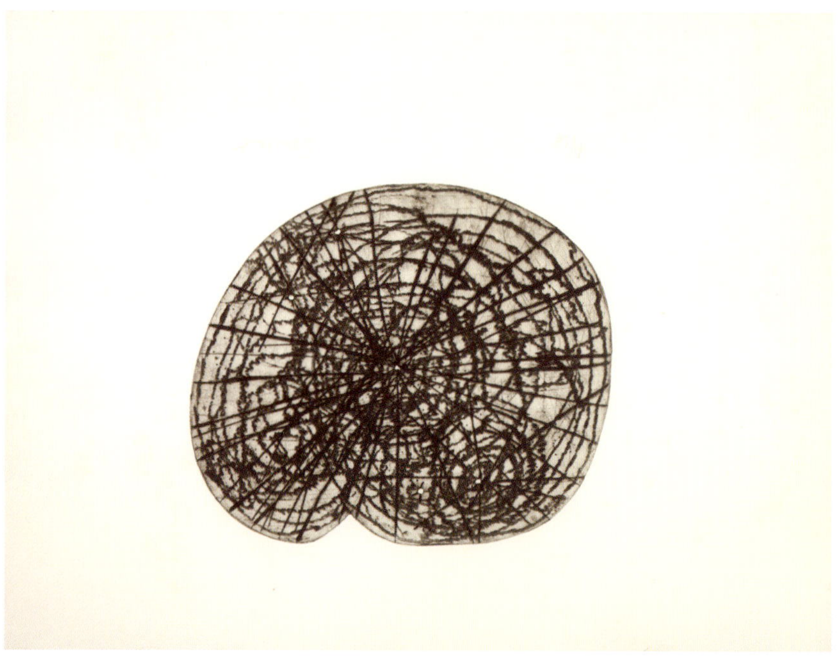

Divergerende stralen (Divergent Rays), 1961
edition of 20, dry point, 29.8 x 25 cm
collection Cobra Museum of Modern Art,
Amstelveen, gift of P. Mansaram

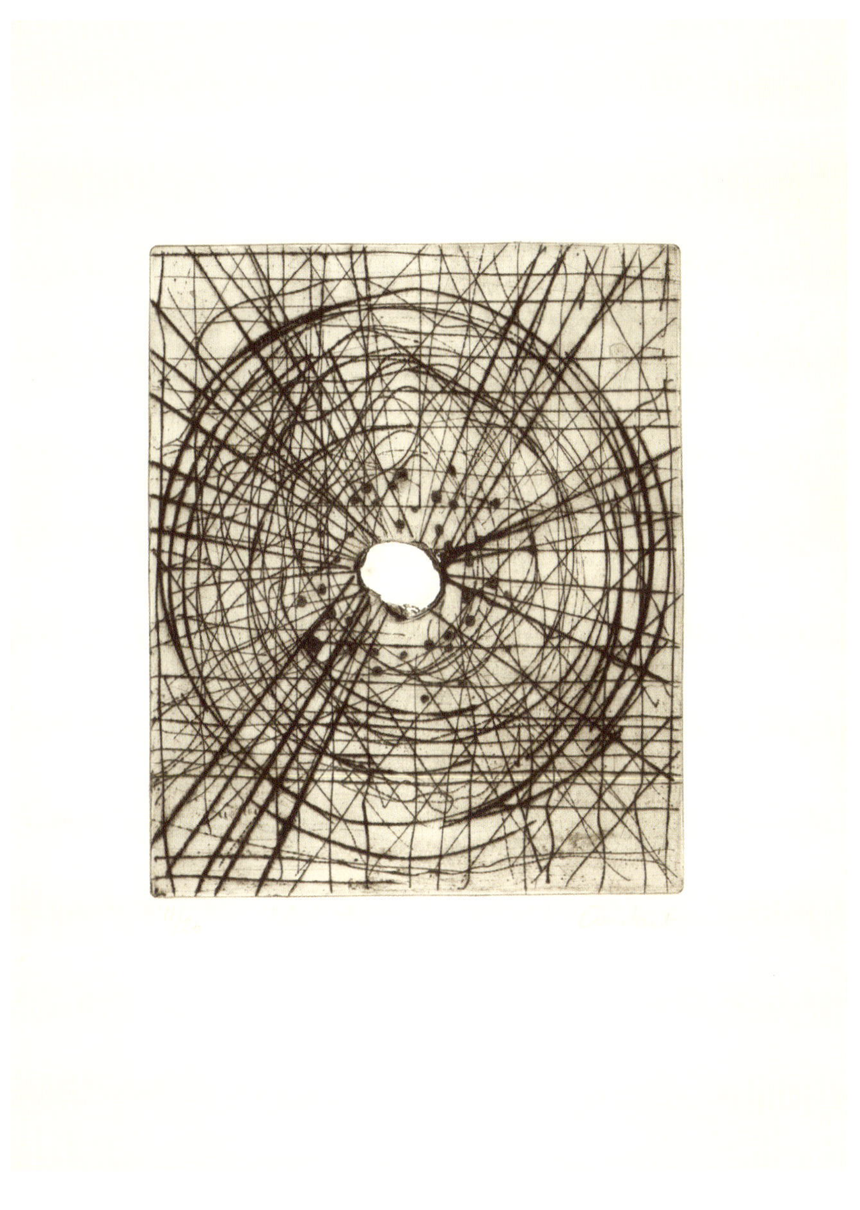

Turbulentie (Turbulence), 1961
edition of 20, dry point, 49.8 x 60 cm
collection Cobra Museum of Modern Art,
Amstelveen, gift of P. Mansaram

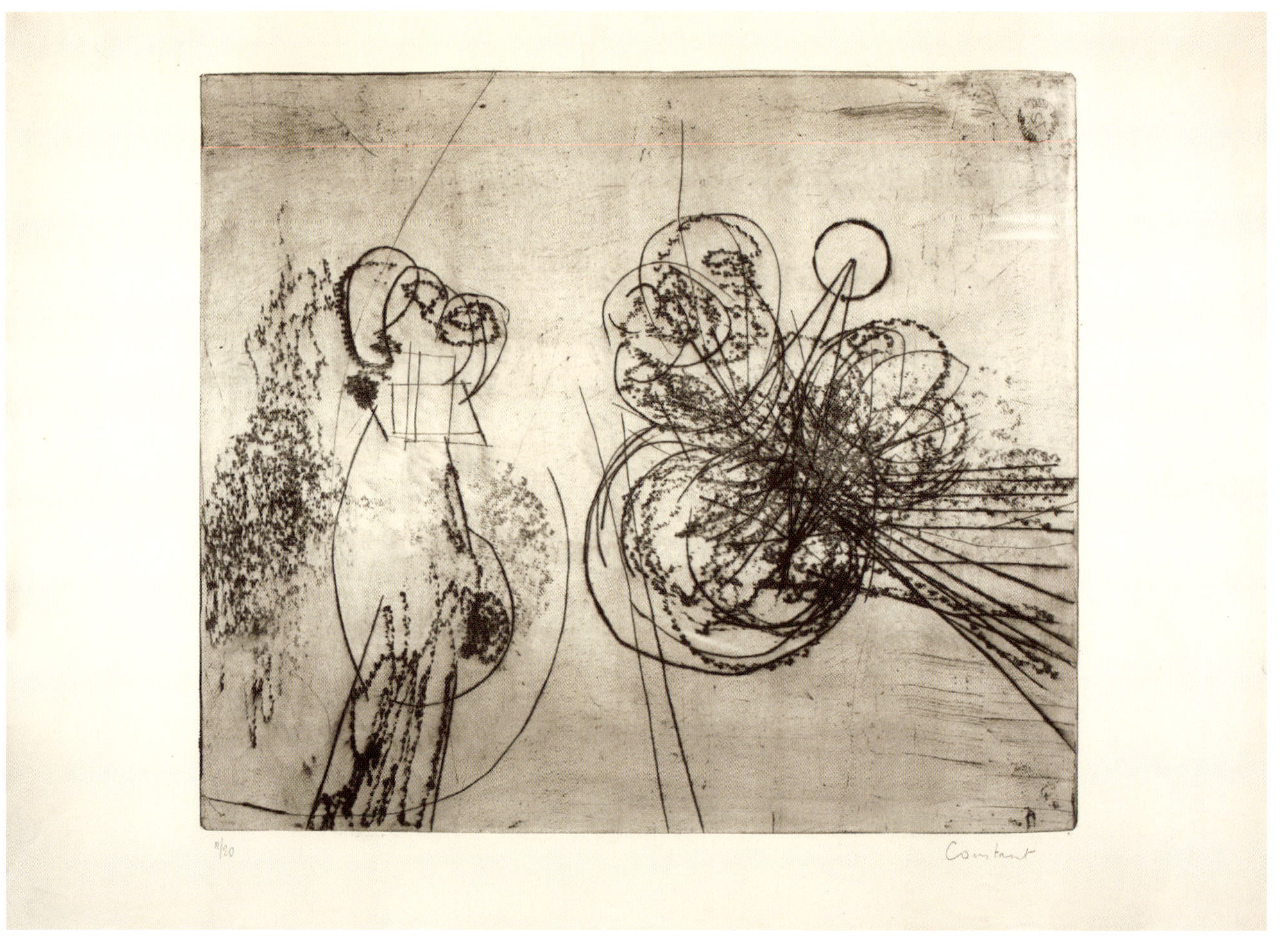

Kunstmatig landschap
(Artificial Landscape), 1961
edition of 20, dry point, 49.5 x 59.8 cm
collection Cobra Museum of Modern Art,
Amstelveen, gift of P. Mansaram

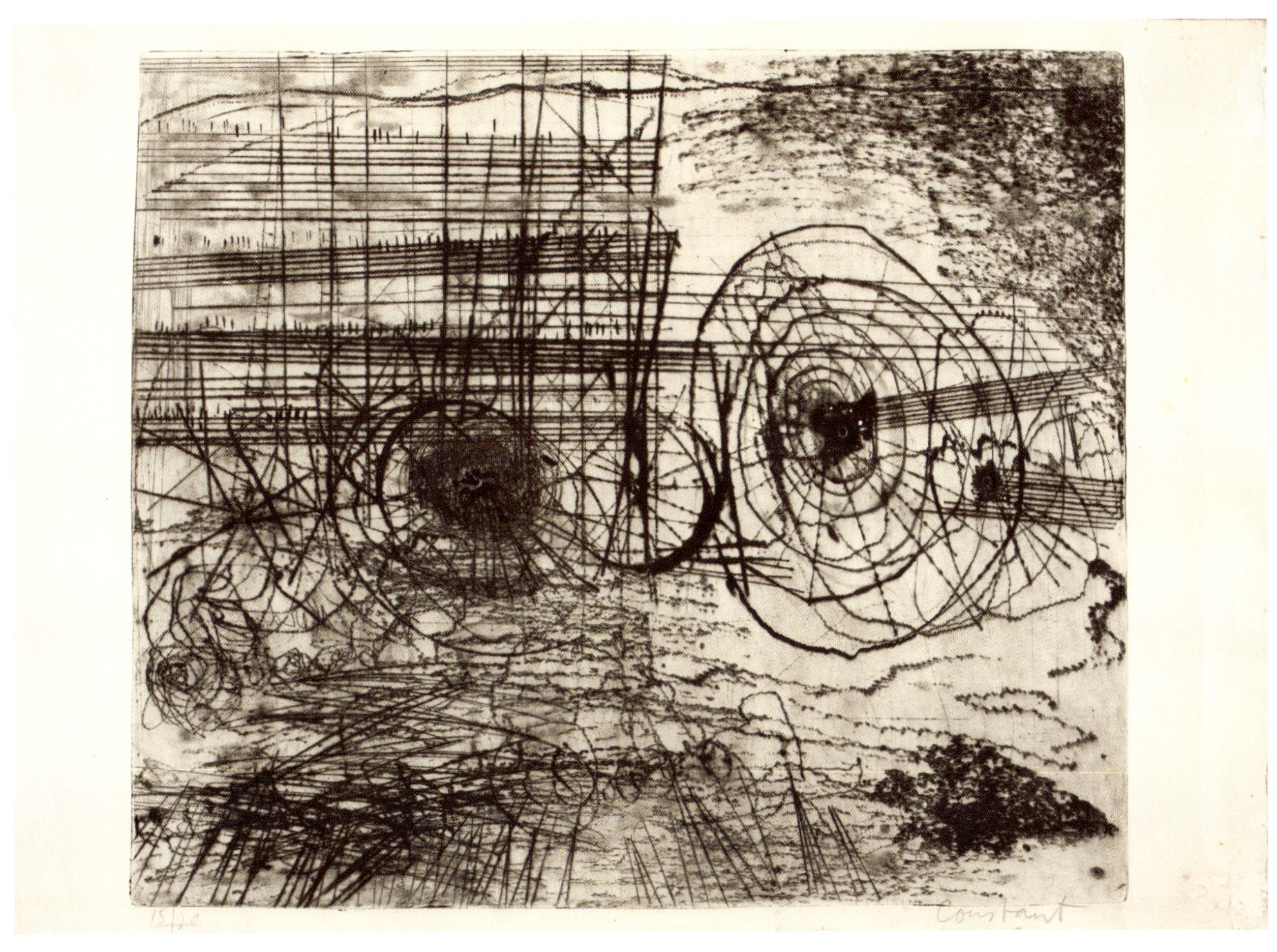

Landkaart (Map), 1961
edition of 20, dry point, 49.5 x 60 cm
collection Cobra Museum of Modern Art,
Amstelveen, gift of P. Mansaram

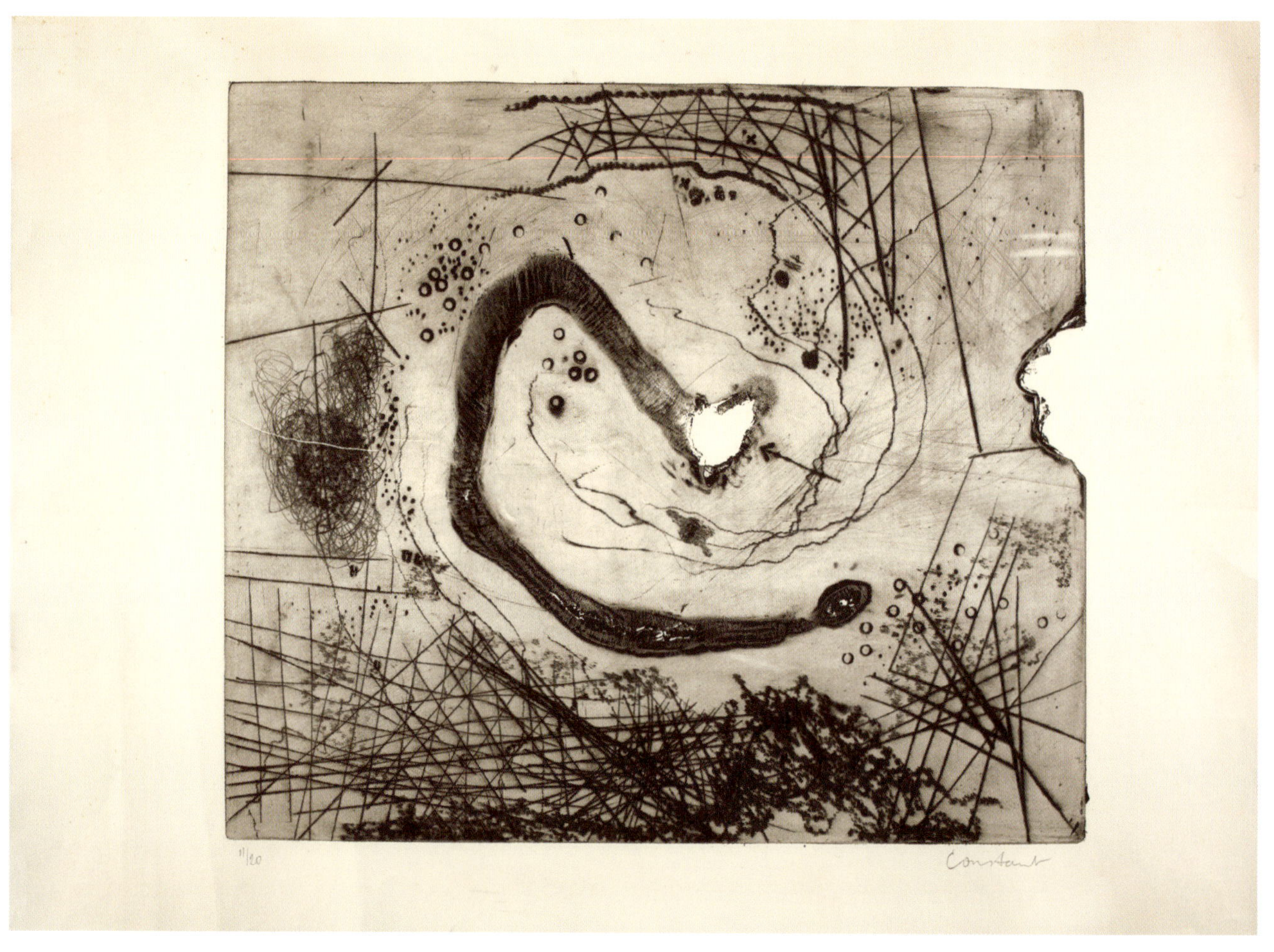

Gaten-ets (drie gaten)
(Holes etching [three holes]), 1961
edition of 20, dry point, 49.5 x 59.5 cm
collection Cobra Museum of Modern Art,
Amstelveen, gift of P. Mansaram

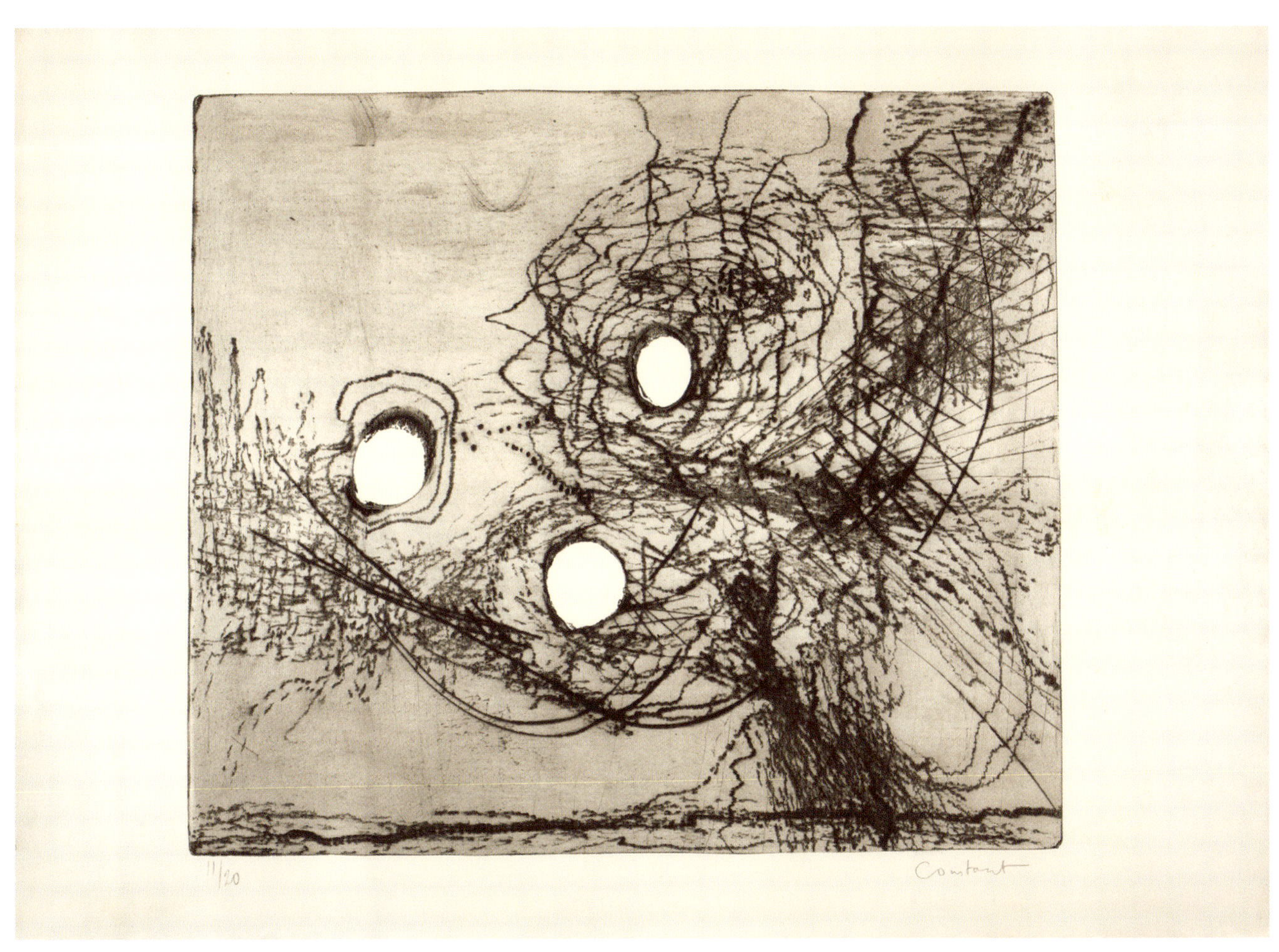

De zon (The Sun), 1956
oil on linen, 110.5 x 95.2 cm
collection Centraal Museum Utrecht

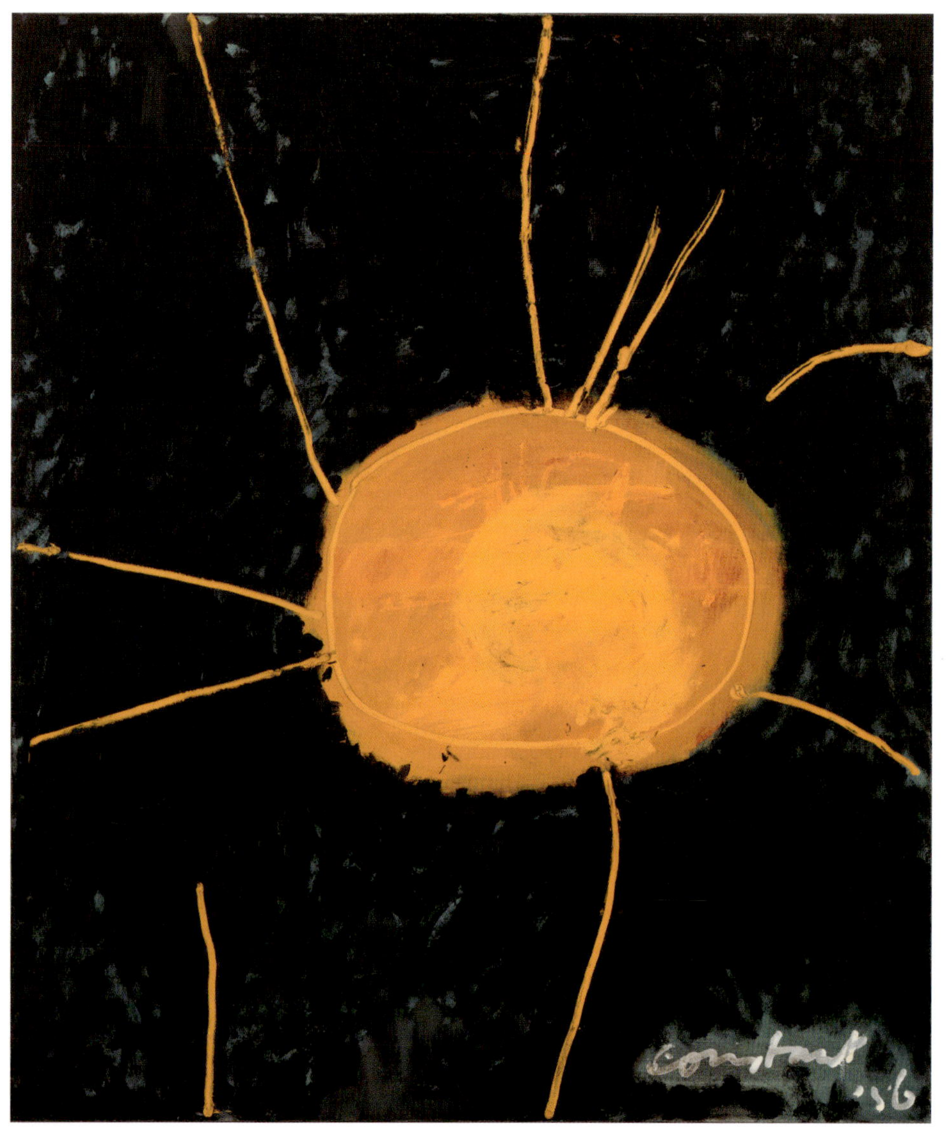

Constant soldering a three-dimensional construction in his studio, c. 1956. In the background, his sculpture *Observatorium* collection Fondation Constant

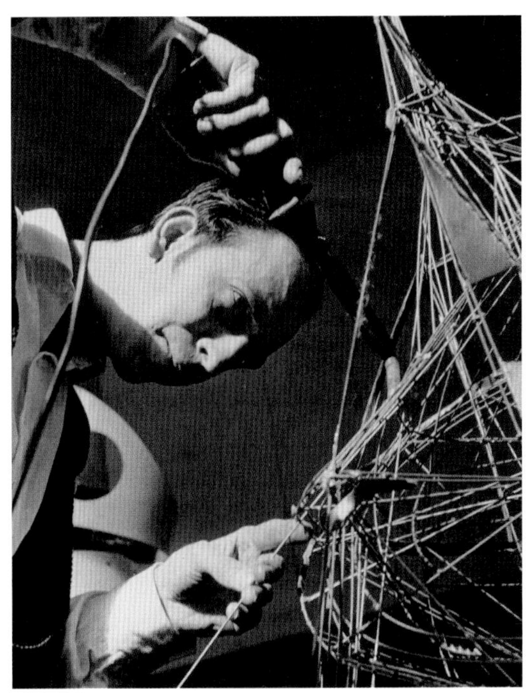

1956-1967
On the Way to *New Babylon*

The theme of space travel yielded a significant and impressive group of works, alongside his quest to design the human environment as a whole. Constant saw the urban network as an expression of collective creativity. Urbanism, in his eyes, could become a new total art, which would absorb all the old disciplines. The painting *Adieu la P.* hints at a farewell to painting (*Peinture*). Urbanism, for Constant, was not limited to spatial planning; it was an entirely new, all-encompassing art form whereby visual artists and engineers would work together on a new city of the future. The contours of *New Babylon* were already emerging in the second half of the 1950s, its broad outlines described by Constant in 1958 in his essay 'Our Ambition Lies in Ambiance' (p. 155).

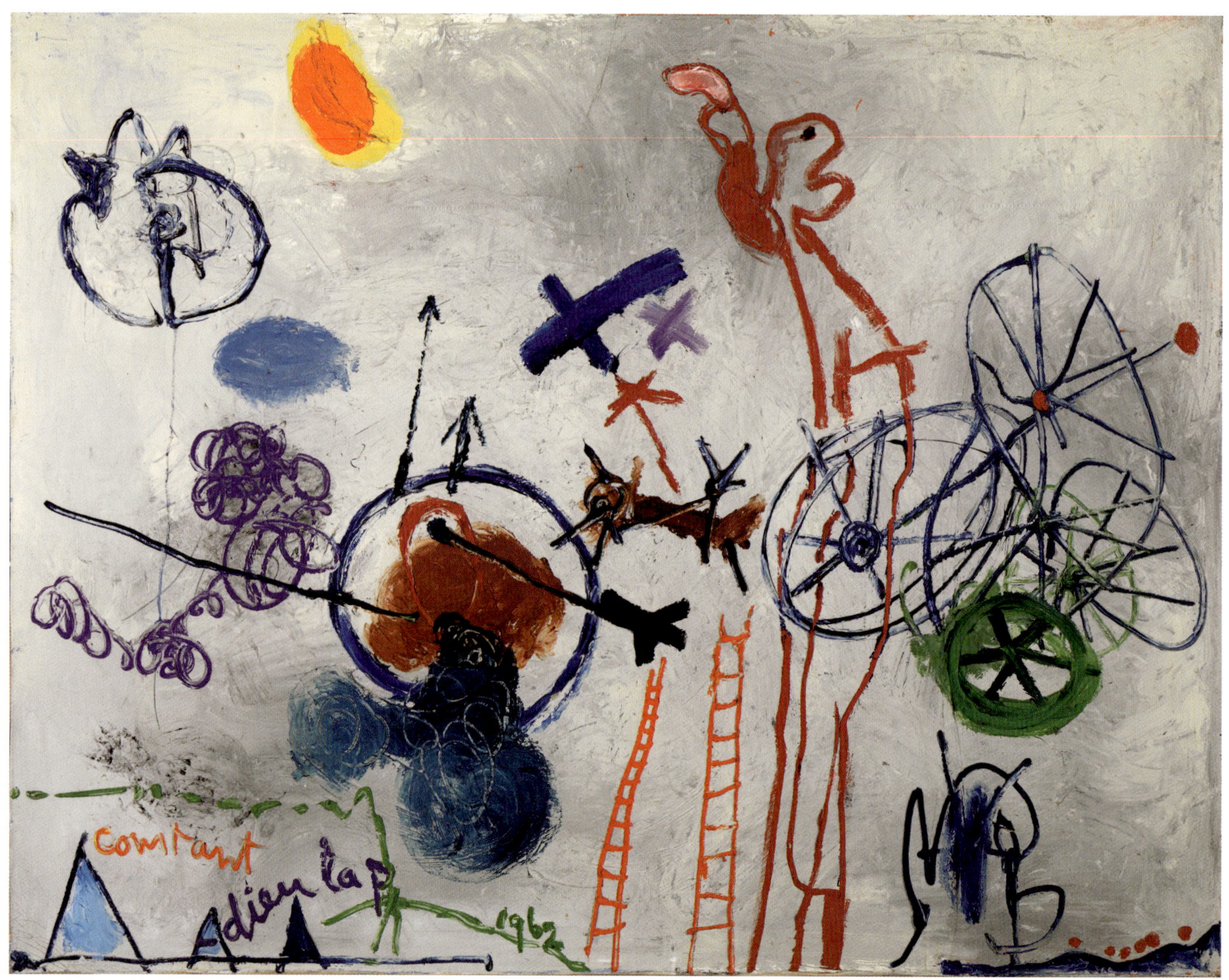

Adieu la P., 1962
oil on linen, 112.5 x 145.5 cm
collection Fondation Constant,
long-term loan to the Cobra Museum
of Modern Art, Amstelveen

Stofontwerp j (Fabric Design j), 1956
gouache on paper, 45.4 x 45.4 cm
collection Fondation Constant

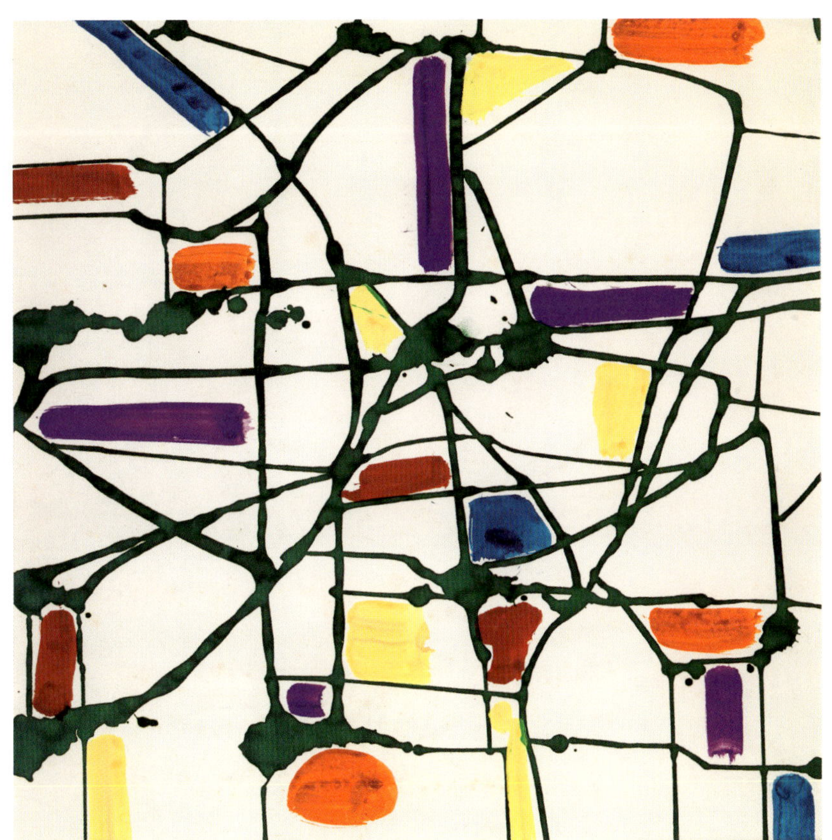

Stofontwerp I (Fabric Design I), 1956
gouache on paper, 43.5 x 51.8 cm
collection Fondation Constant

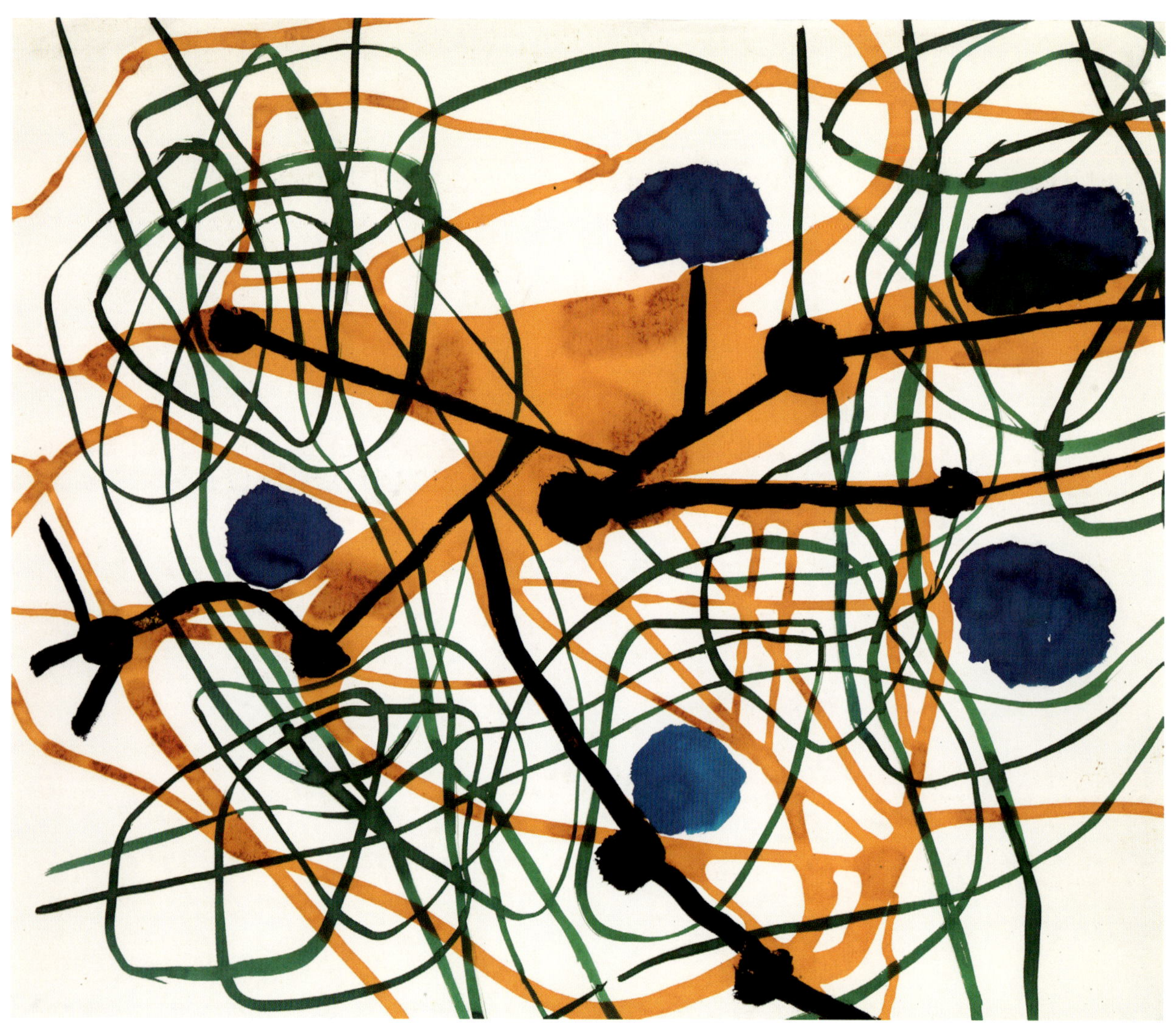

Stofontwerp k (Fabric Design k), 1956
gouache on paper, 36.3 x 44.7 cm
collection Fondation Constant

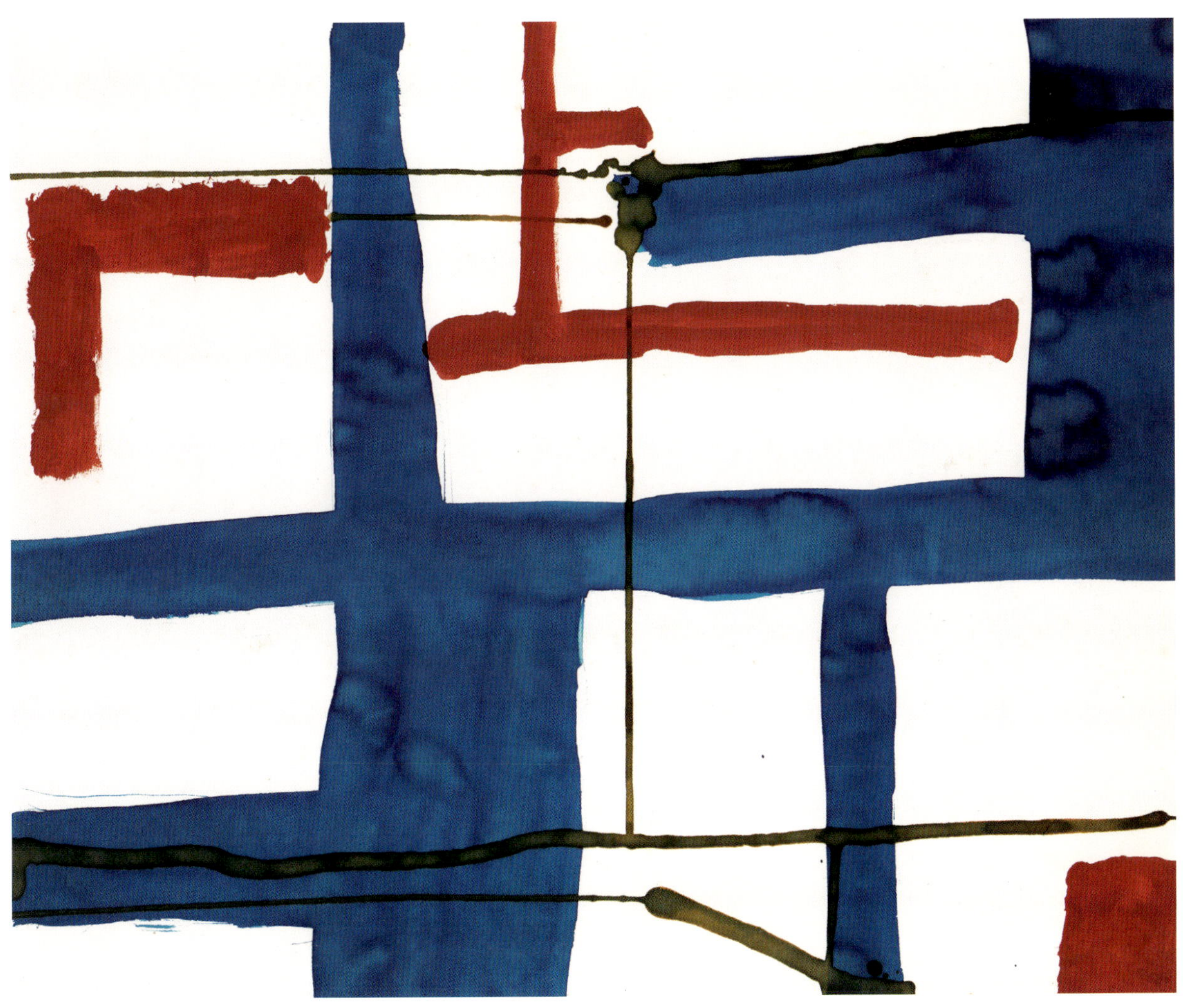

Zonder titel – Landschap met sectoren
(Untitled – Landscape with Sectors), 1953
oil on linen, 54 x 104 cm
collection Fondation Constant

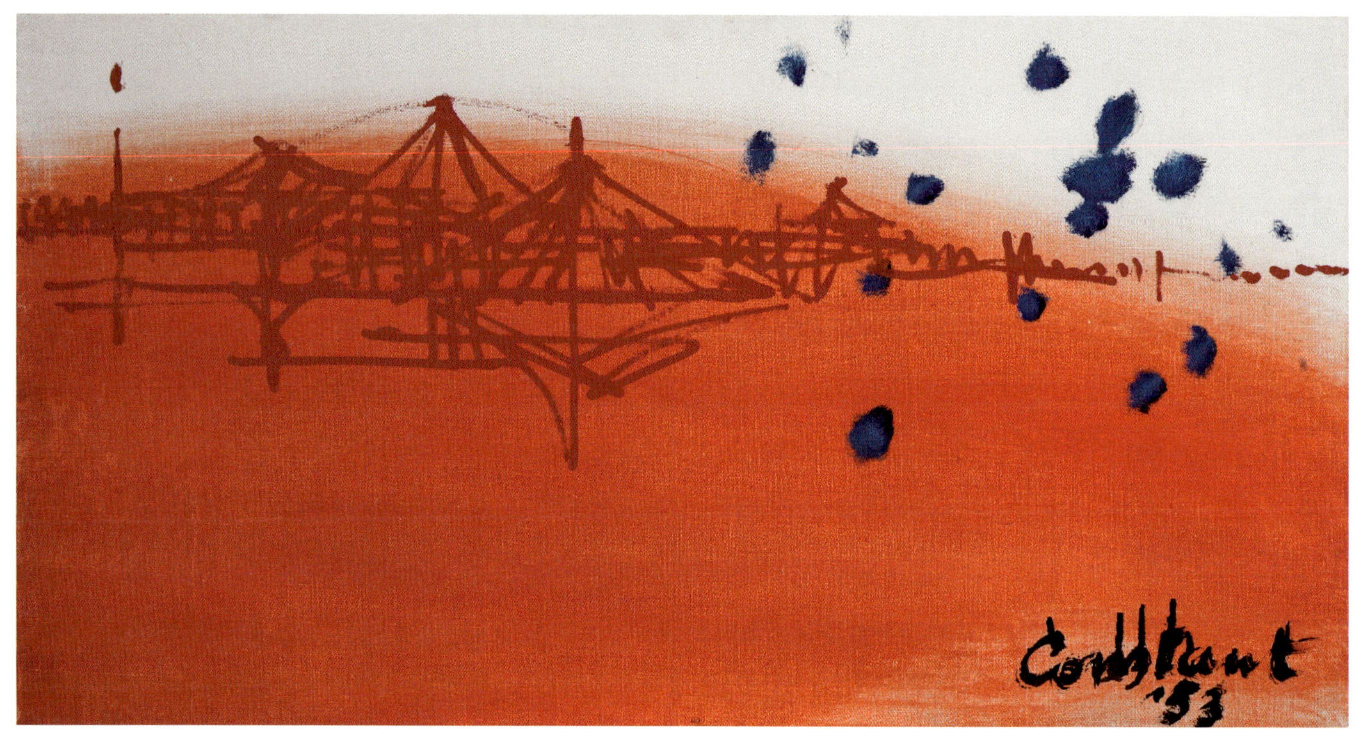

Stad (*Alba*) (City [Alba]), 1956
oil on linen, 60.5 x 80.5 cm
collection Fondation Constant

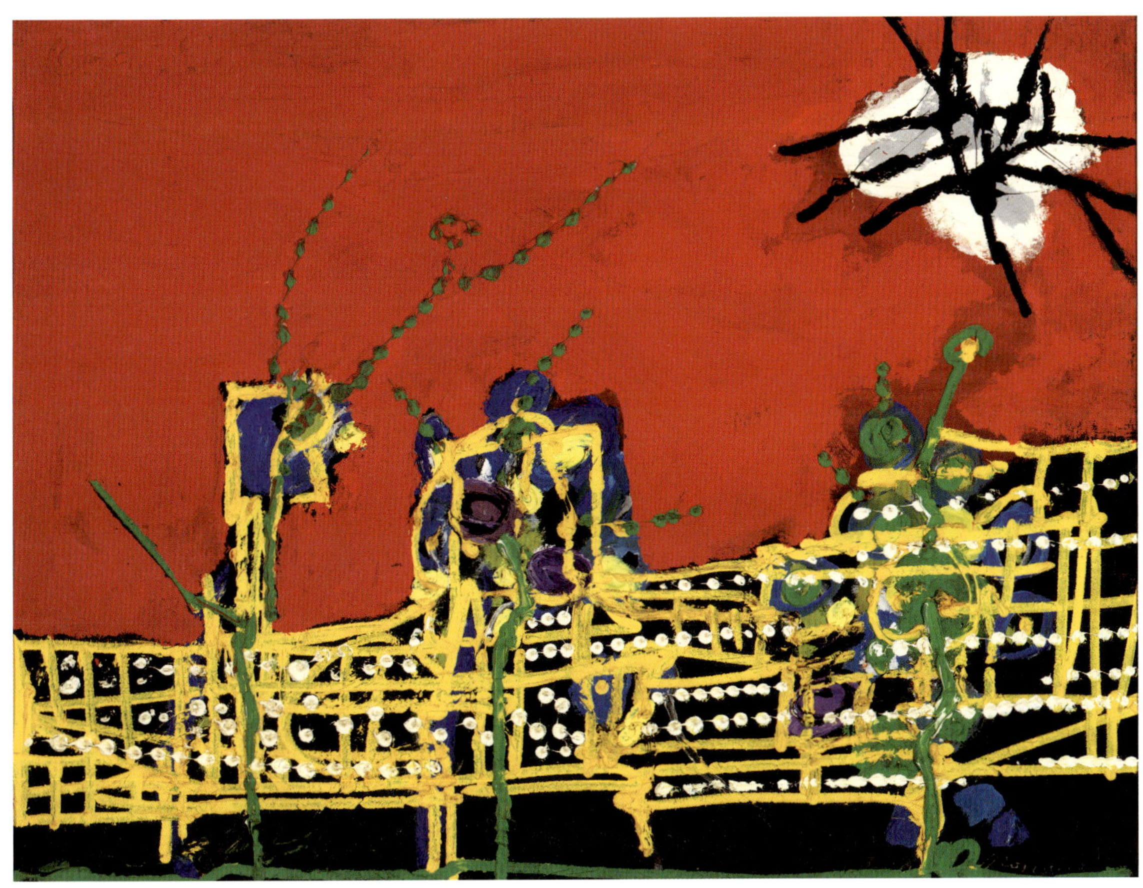

Twee Torens (Two Towers), 1959
steel wire and steel sheets coated with a silver paint,
plywood base with paint layer, 95 x 46 x 43.5 cm
collection Fondation Constant

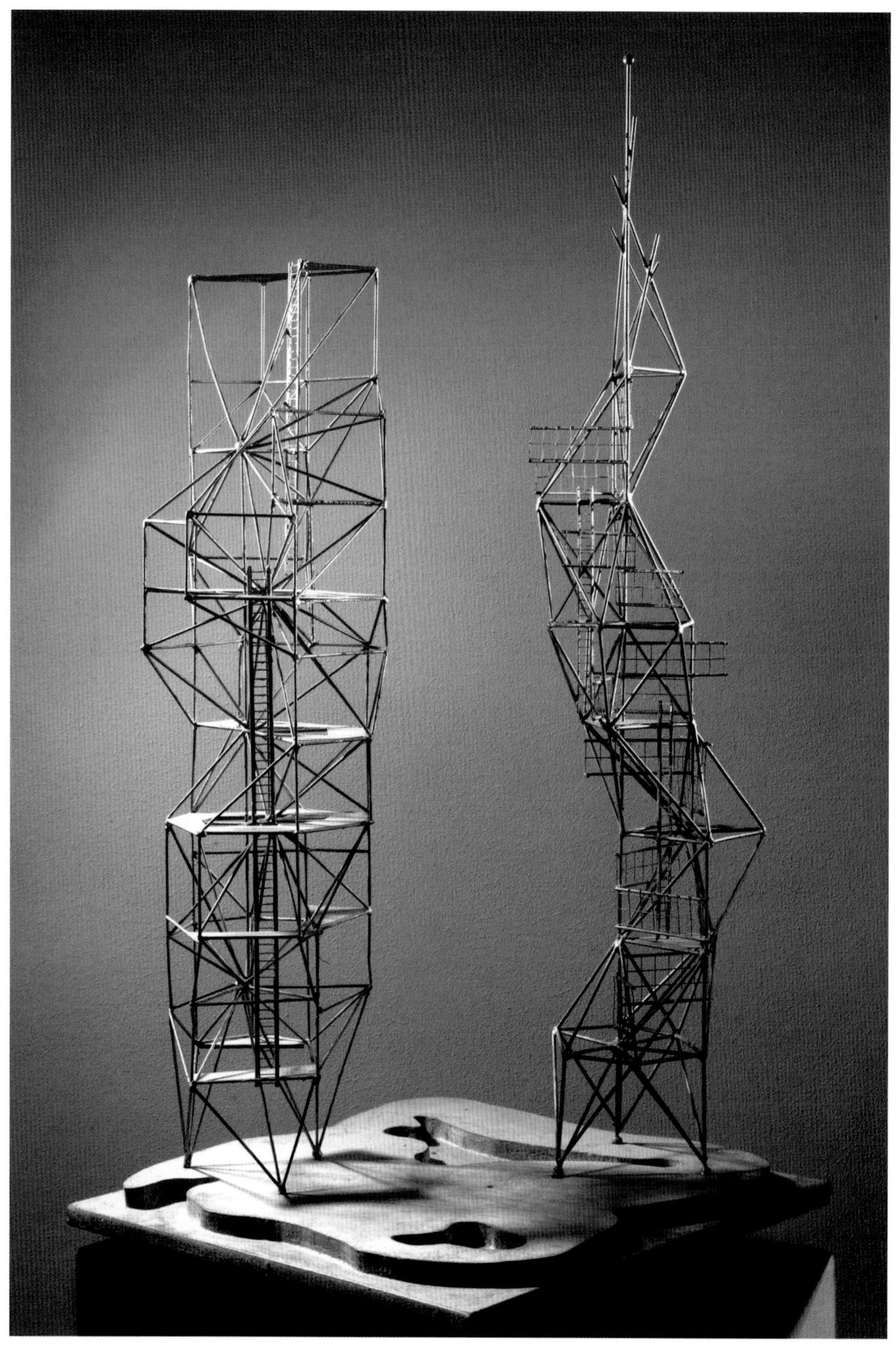

Hangende sector II (Hanging Sector II), 1960
Plexiglas, brass, iron wire, oil on wood and stone,
36 x 71 x 52 cm
Defares Collection

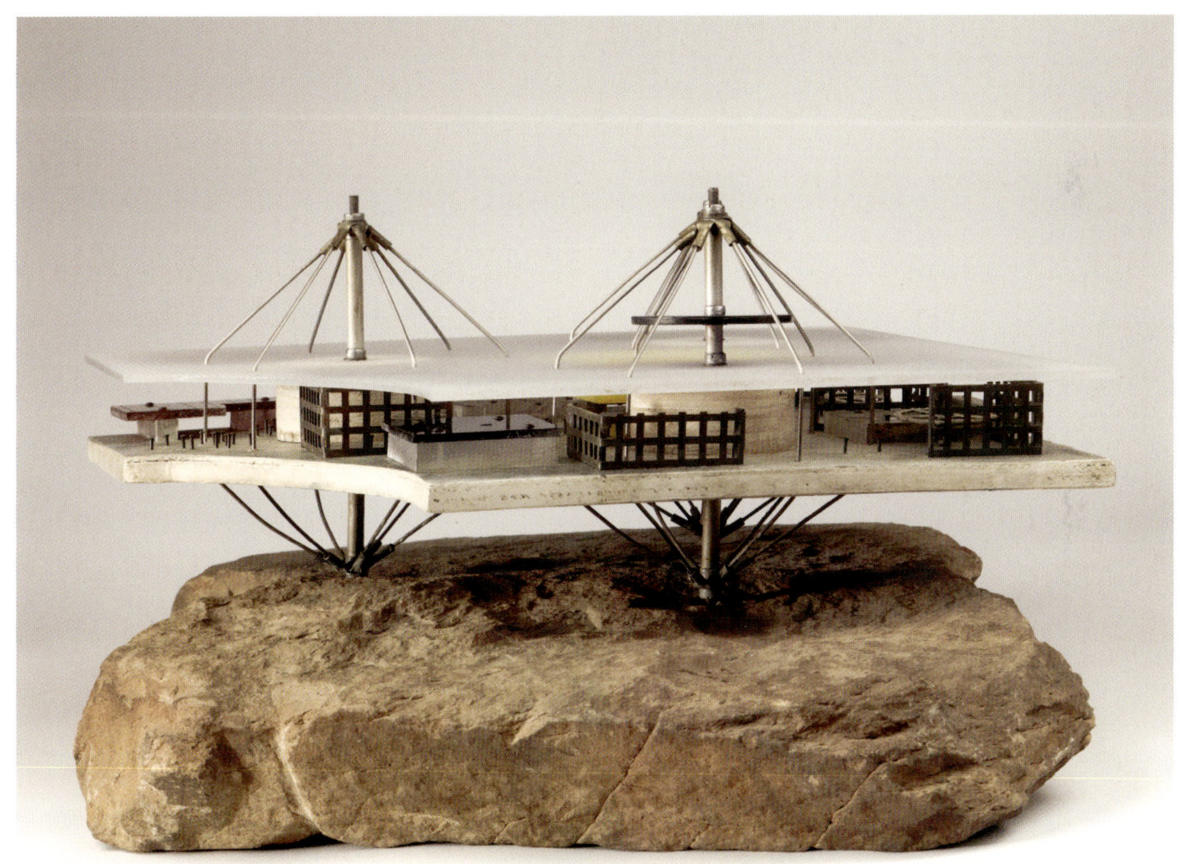

Grundriss von New Babylon über *Slotermeer*
(Ground Plan of New Babylon-Slotermeer), 1966
gelatin silver print on baryta paper and watercolour
on fibreboard, 100.5 x 100.2 cm
collection Fondation Constant, long-term loan
to the Cobra Museum of Modern Art, Amstelveen

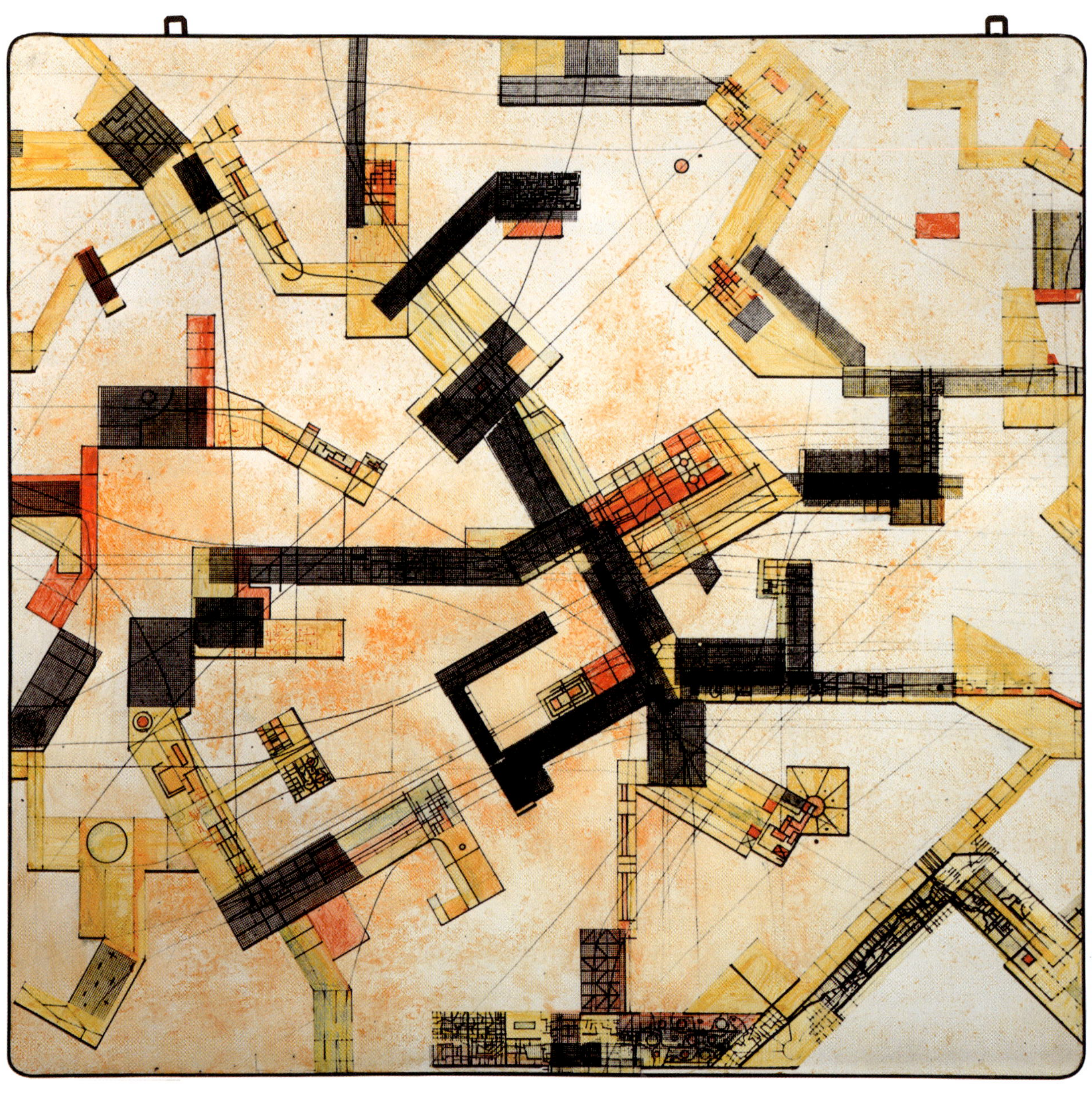

Schets voor een plattegrond (Sketch for a Map), 1963
Indian ink, watercolour and pencil on paper,
87.5 x 130.7 cm
collection Fondation Constant, long-term loan to
the Gemeentemuseum Den Haag, The Hague

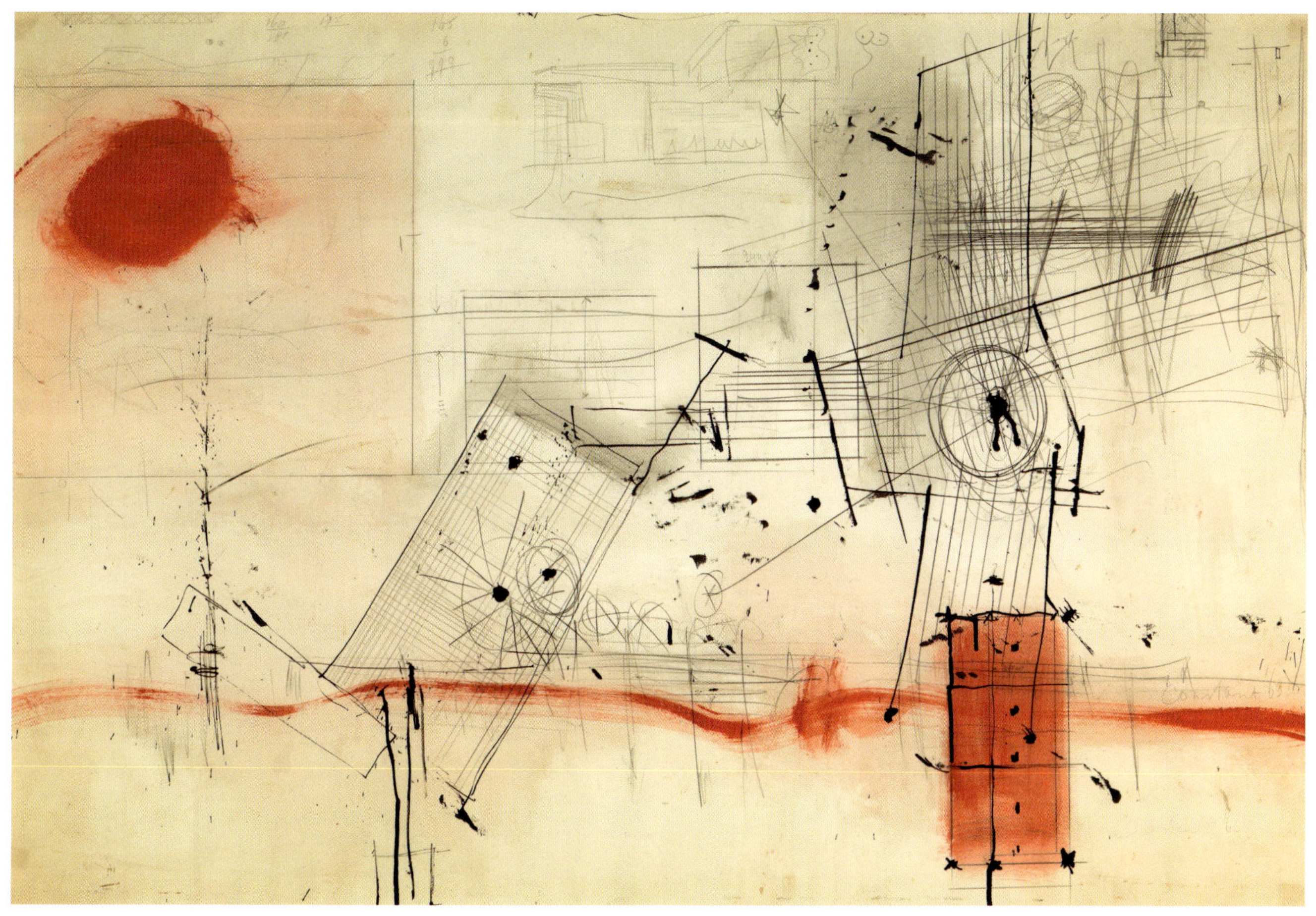

Eerste schets gedeelte New Babylon
(First sketch part New Babylon), 1958
coloured pencil and pencil on paper,
31 x 28.4 cm
collection Fondation Constant

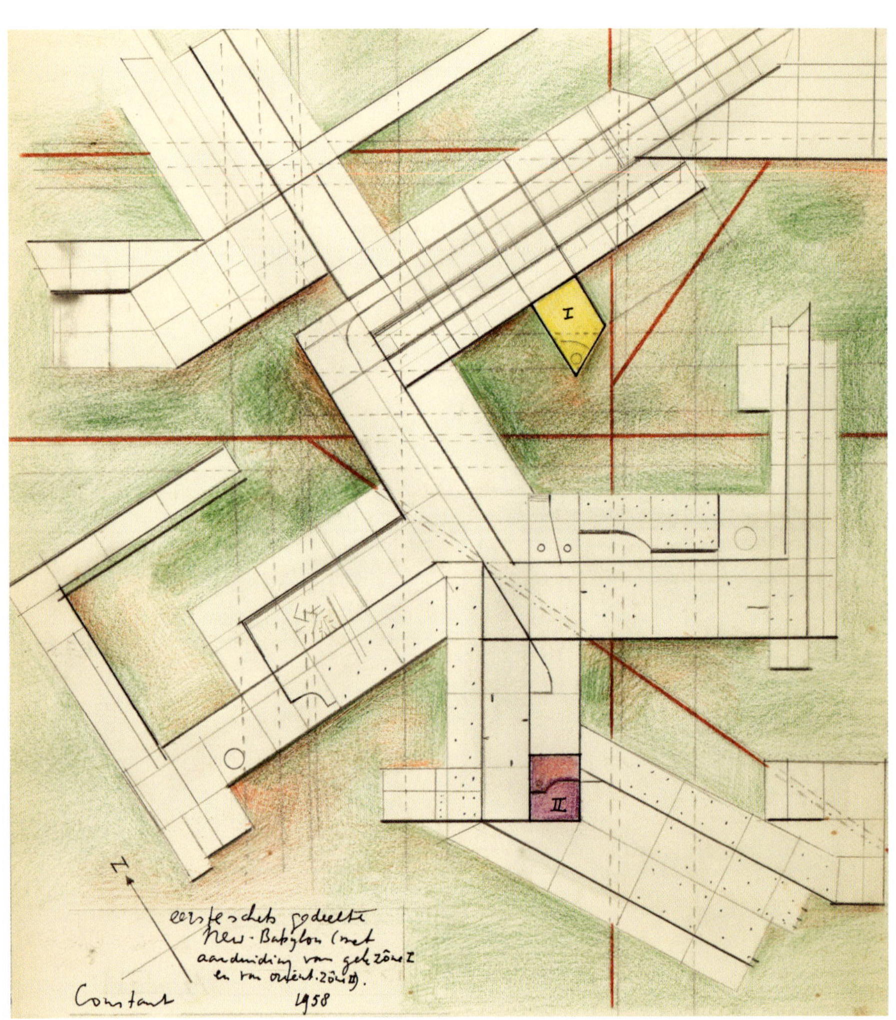

Don Juan in het labyrinth
(Don Juan in the Labyrinth), 1966
watercolour and pencil on paper, 89.1 x 92.9 cm
collection Fondation Constant

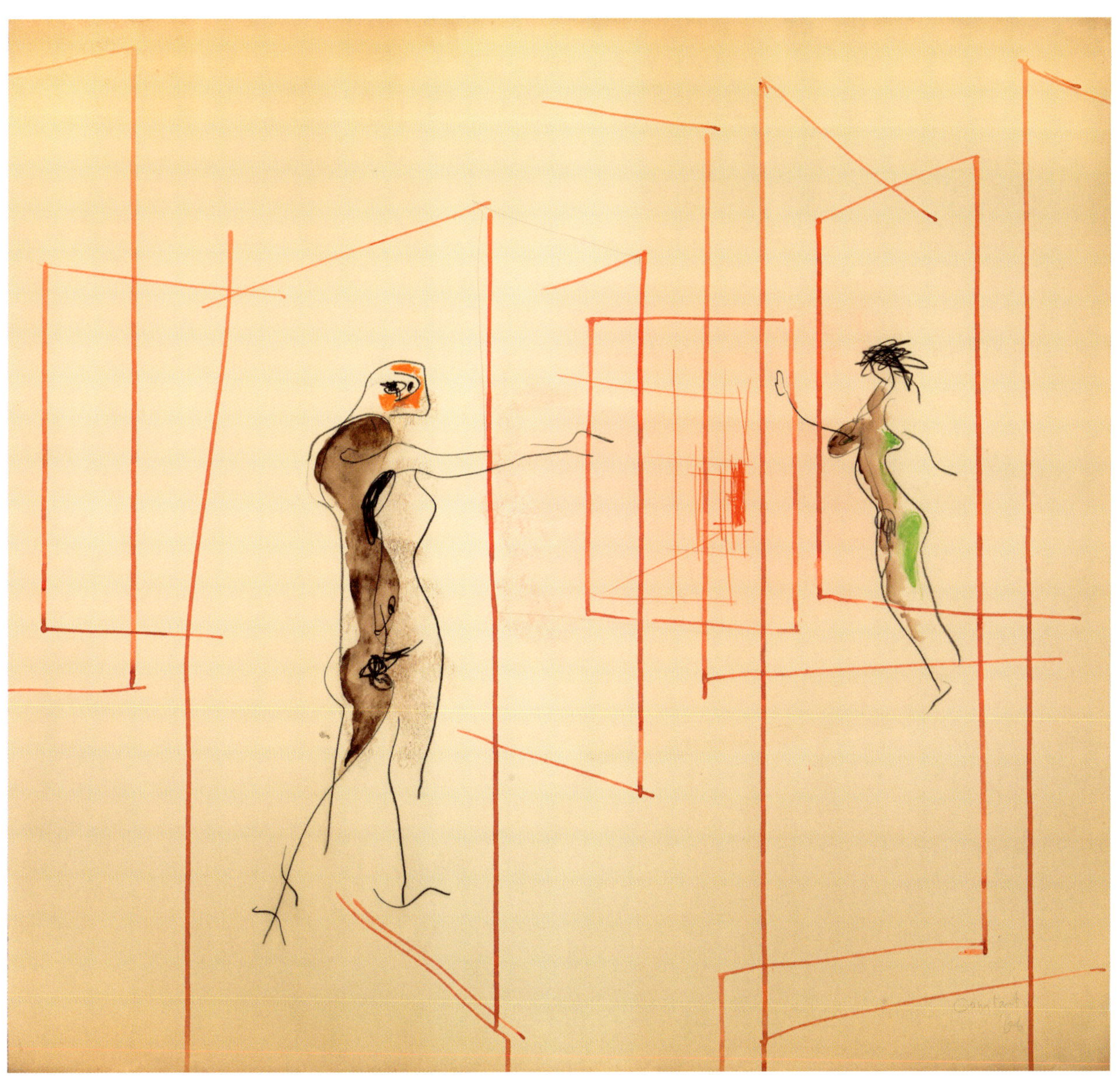

Figuren in een ruimte II
(Figures in a Space II), 1966
watercolour, gouache and pencil on paper,
83 x 136 cm
collection Fondation Constant

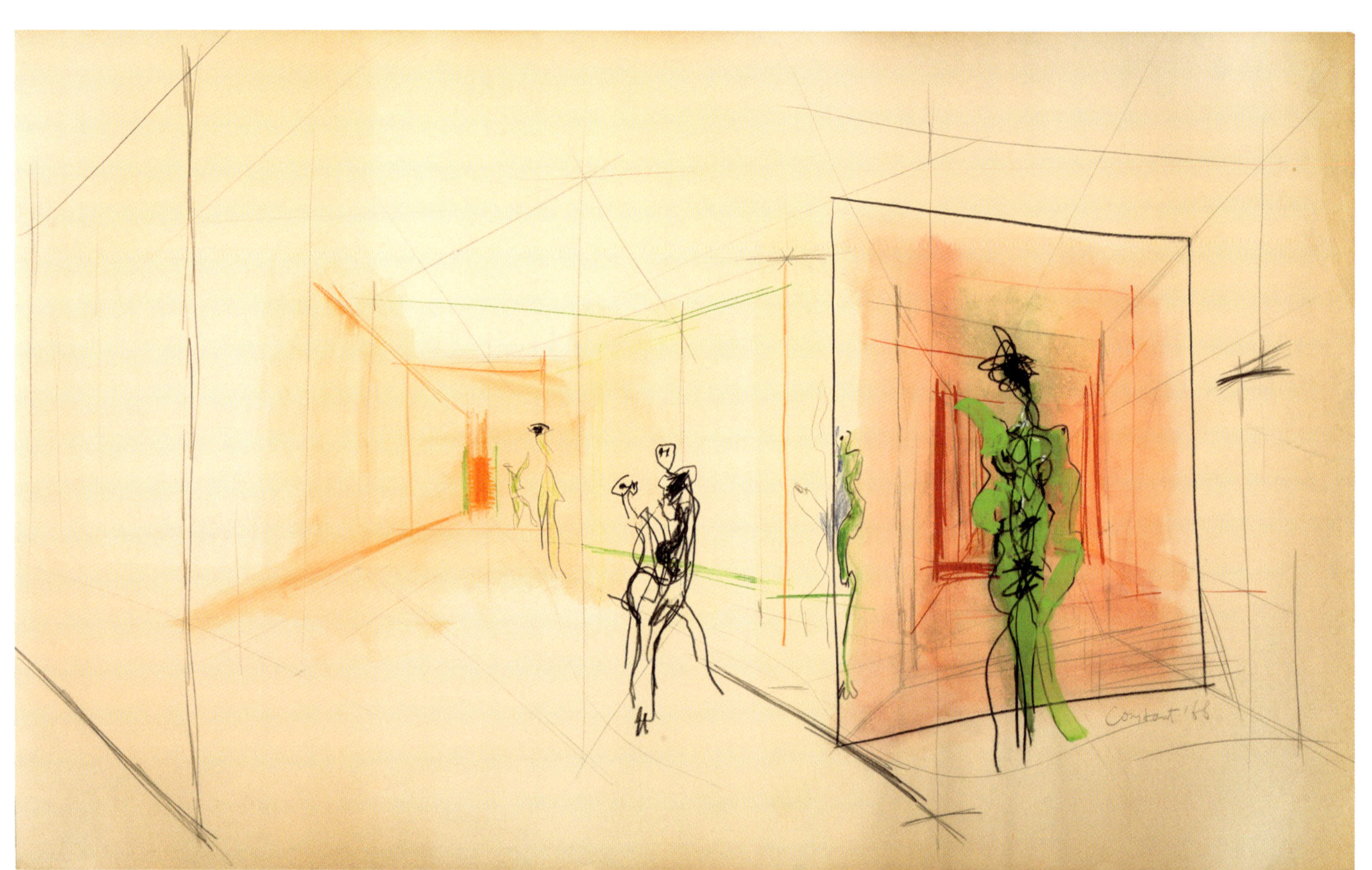

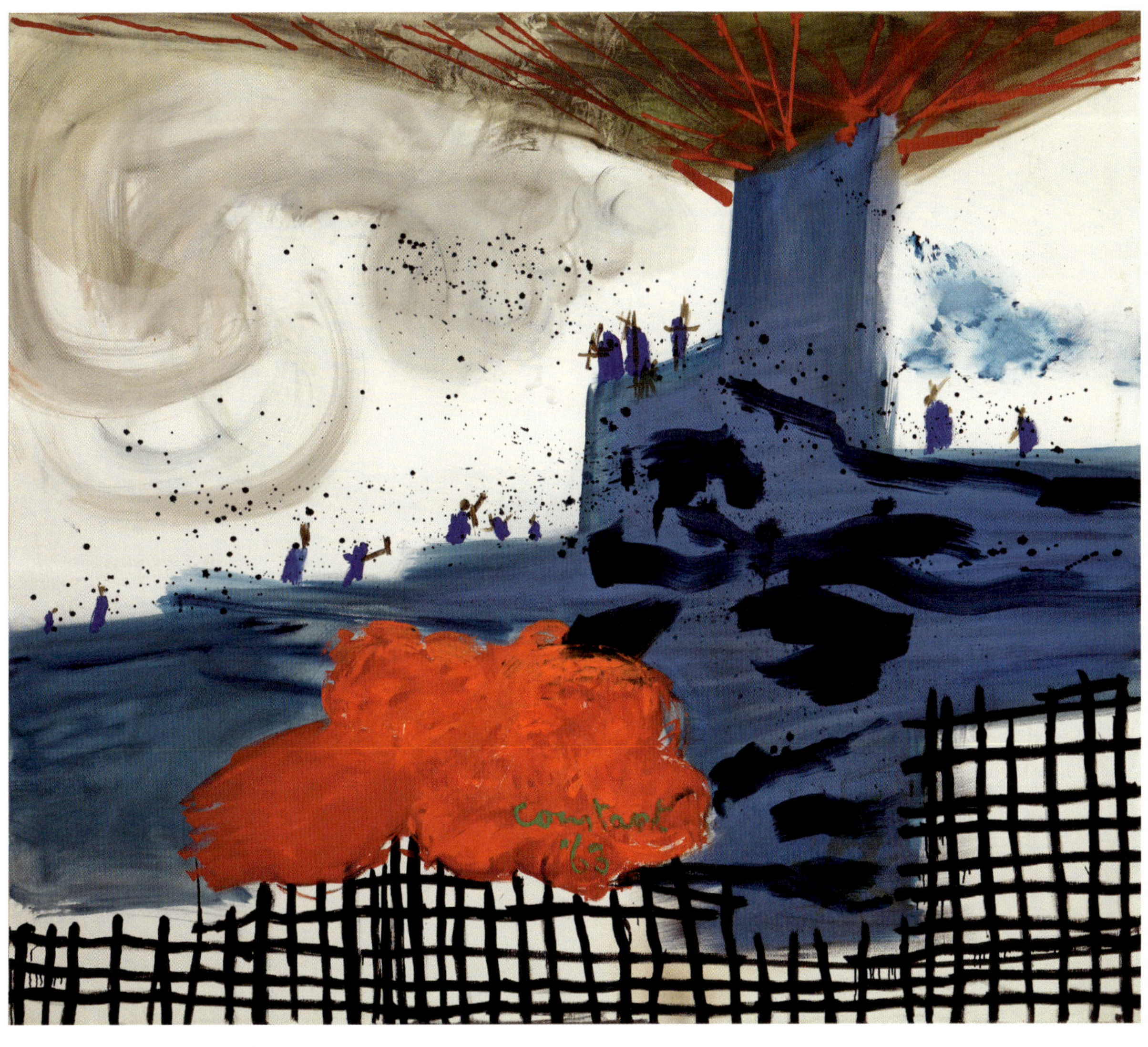

Groeten uit New Babylon
(Greetings from New Babylon), 1963
oil on linen, 159.5 x 184.8 cm
collection Cultural Heritage Agency of the Netherlands,
long-term loan to the Cobra Museum of Modern Art,
Amstelveen

Ladderlabyrinth (Ladder Labyrinth), 1967
Plexiglas, brass and wooden base,
71.5 x 96.x 86 cm
collection Lehmbruck Museum, Duisburg

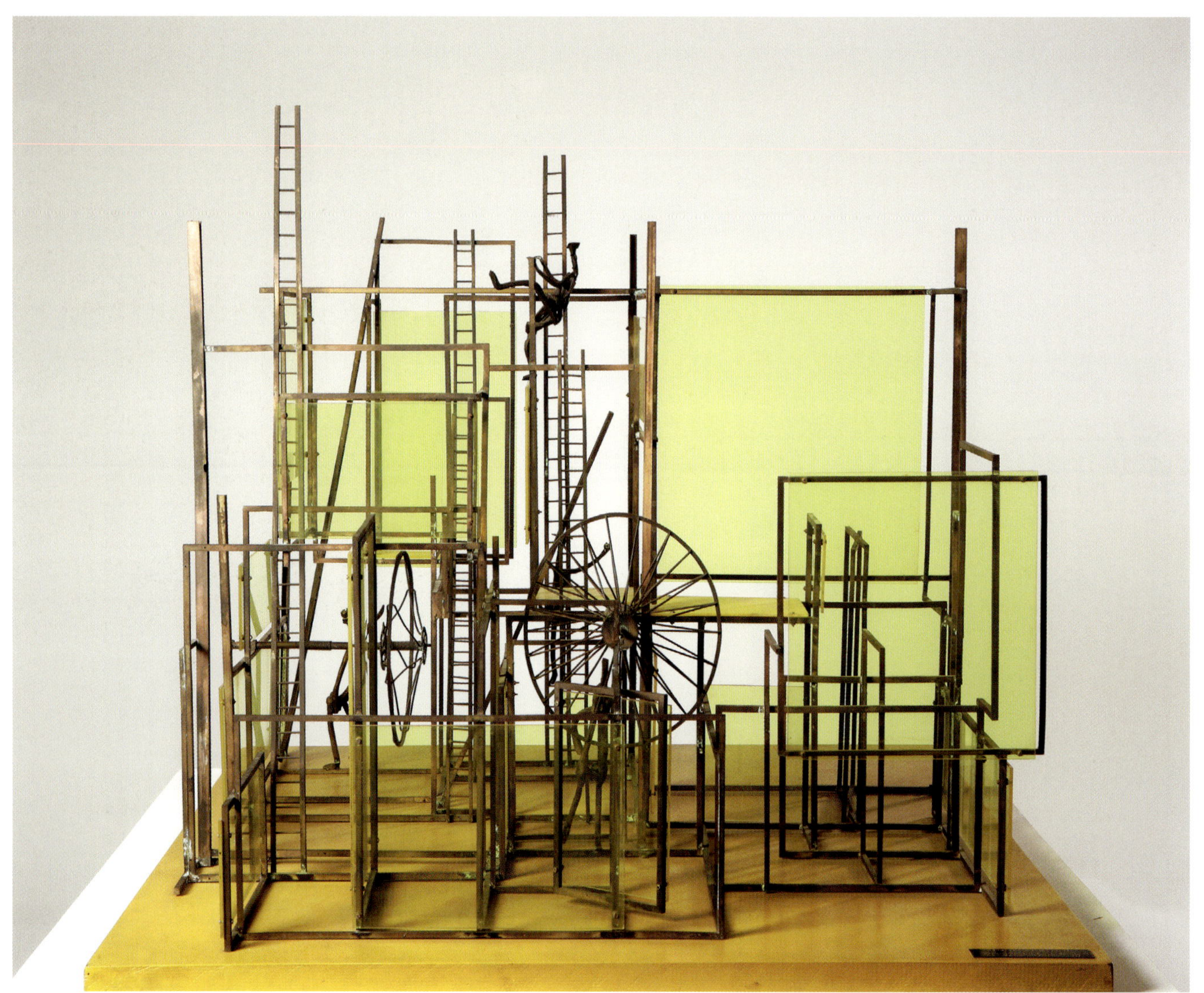

Constant and his son Victor with
Ladderlabyrinth (Ladder Labyrinth), c. 1966
collection Fondation Constant

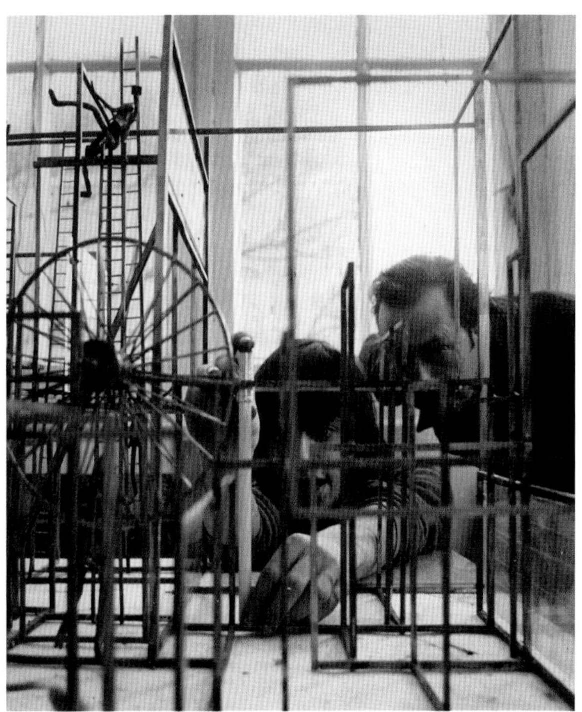

Constant
1920 - 2005

Trudy van der Horst

C'est notre désir qui fait la révolution[1]

On 8 November 1948, at the Café Le Notre Dame in Paris, six artists – Asger Jorn (Copenhagen), Christian Dotremont and Joseph Noiret (Brussels) and Constant Nieuwenhuys, Corneille and Karel Appel (Amsterdam) – established Cobra. The name is an acronym of the artists' home cities. On that November day the artists signed their manifesto, 'La cause était entendue' (The matter was settled), taking a stance against the earlier manifesto issued on 1 July 1947 by the French Revolutionary Surrealists, 'La cause est entendue' (The matter is settled), just one day after their conference had ended. For Constant, the main reason for breaking with them lay in the fact that the Belgian, Danish and Dutch groups associated art with political conviction, while the French had declined to do so. The Cobra movement would repeatedly inspire its members to new collective and creative expressions of their art.[2]

In autumn 1946 Constant met Danish artist Asger Jorn at a Joan Miró exhibition at Pierre Loeb's gallery in Paris, afterwards accompanying Jorn back to his hotel to see his paintings. Several hung in a dark room, pinned to the flowered wallpaper. Jorn's art had a profound impact on Constant, although, as with Munch, he found the colours harsh. At Café de Flore across the street Jorn introduced him to Alberto Giacometti, whose work Constant admired for the rest of his life, particularly his paintings. The encounter with Jorn was the start of a close friendship and collaboration. Jorn introduced Constant to his Danish experimentalist movement, Høst (and their magazine *Helhesten* [Hel Horse]). Together, Constant and Jorn started the theoretical preparations for a new, international avant-garde movement.

Like the Danes, Constant wanted to establish an experimental group in Holland, and sought to link it to the international avant-garde movement. His fellow students at the Rijksakademie, Hans Wiesman and David Kouwenaar, were not keen. David's younger brother, poet Gerrit Kouwenaar, who had known Constant for some time and was art editor at the *De Waarheid* daily newspaper from 1945 to 1950, did however join the group in 1948.[3] Constant was important to Gerrit Kouwenaar from a young age, as evidenced by his 1952 description of his first encounter with Constant in 1942: 'I believe I met him for the first time on the "Skinny Bridge"; it was lovely summer weather and there were *Schnellboote*[4] on the Amstel. Constant wore his hair fairly long and had a melancholy moustache. He was wearing a curious purplish suit that was too big for him, and big high-top shoes on his bare feet, like some of the gents in prints by Dubout. I admired him at once. In those days he lived in the Pijp district and he smoked a little red clay pipe with a grinning devil's face on the bowl....That was ten years ago. I still admire Constant. He now wears nice sneakers with white laces and is still a painter. His head pops out of all the paintings hanging on the wall here.'[5]

Karel Appel and Corneille visited Constant for the first time in late 1947. The Experimental Group in Holland was established at Constant's

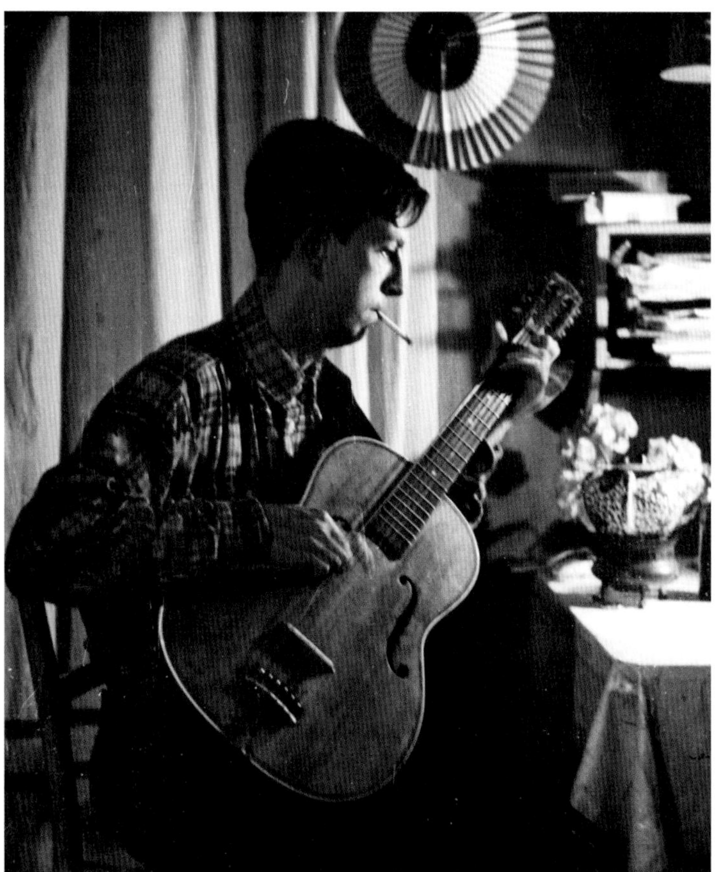

[1] Constant playing the guitar in his studio, Henri Polaklaan 25 in Amsterdam, c. 1949
collection Fondation Constant

home on 16 July 1948, by which time the group had expanded to include Jan Nieuwenhuijs (Constant's brother), Anton Rooskens and Theo Wolvecamp. Eugène Brands joined a month later, quickly followed by Dutch poets Jan Elburg, Gerrit Kouwenaar and Lucebert (pseudonym of Lubertus Jacobus Swaanswijk). The members of the group met regularly at their studio, showed their latest work, read their poems and commented on one another's work. At these meetings they often dressed up and played gramophone records or live music. Constant was a fine singer and a talented guitarist with an extensive repertoire, including classical music, French chansons and Spanish Flamenco improvisations [fig. 1].[6]

The first edition of the journal *Reflex* published by the Dutch Experimental Group appeared in September 1948. It contained poems by Elburg and Corneille, an account of what the group stood for written by Brands, and four original lithographs by Constant, Corneille, Appel and Jan Nieuwenhuijs. The greater part of this first edition was devoted to the manifesto Constant had previously written and which only he had signed. The manifesto called on artists to develop a revolutionary attitude, to renounce style and aesthetics and to strive for collective art. The artistic method, it argued, should be based on experiential (*expérience*) and experimental exploration. The second and final edition of *Reflex* was published in February 1949.

The first two issues of *Cobra* were published in March 1949. Issue 4, by the Dutch Experimental Group, served as the catalogue for the major international exhibition of experimental art at the Stedelijk Museum Amsterdam that ran from 3 to 28 November 1949 [fig. 2]. Constant wrote one of his most beautiful and militant pieces for the issue: 'C'est notre désir qui fait la révolution' ('It Is Our Desire That Makes Revolution'). The following quotation illustrates the beauty and passion of the piece: 'Creating means making something hitherto unknown, and the unknown strikes fear in the hearts of people who believe they have something to preserve or to protect. We, however, who have nothing to lose but our chains, are not afraid of the adventure. The only risk we run consists in the loss of a rather sterile virginity, the virginity of abstracts. We must soil the virginal purity of Mondrian, be it merely with our misery. Is misery not preferable to death, at least for those who are strong enough to fight?'[7]

Architect Aldo van Eyck, who had already been in contact with the Experimental Group in Holland for some time, was asked to design the layout of the exhibition. Van Eyck had a revolutionary way

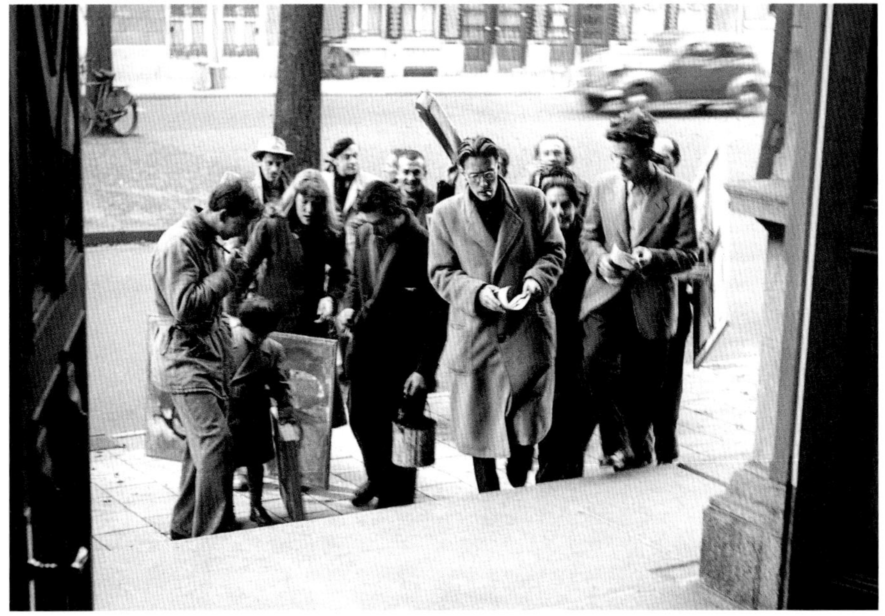

[2] The Experimental artists with their work on the stairs of Stedelijk Museum Amsterdam at the opening of the 'International Exhibition of Experimental Art', 3 November 1949
From left to right: Constant, his son Victor, Eugène Brands, Tony Appel, Anton Rooskens, Karel Appel, Corneille, Jacques Doucet, Gerrit Kouwenaar, Theo Wolvecamp, Lucebert and Jan Elburg
collection Fondation Constant

1 Constant, 'C'est notre désir qui fait la révolution', in *Cobra* no. 4 (November 1949), 3-4. A translation of this text can be found in the chapter 'Constant's Writings'.

2 Willemijn Stokvis, *Cobra. Geschiedenis, voorspel en betekenis van een beweging in de kunst van na de Tweede Wereldoorlog*, Amsterdam: De Bezige Bij, 1980, 80-82; reworked edition of a PhD thesis from Utrecht University, 1973.

3 Poets Gerrit Kouwenaar, Jan Elburg and Lucebert were members of the Dutch Experimental Group and the Cobra group, and participated in the Cobra exhibition (of international experimental artists) at the Stedelijk Museum Amsterdam from 3 - 28 November 1949. A short time later the poets formed their own literary movement (the *Vijftigers*), which Hugo Claus, Remco Campert and Hans Andreus also joined.

4 German navy torpedo boat.

5 Opening speech by Gerrit Kouwenaar at Constant's exhibition at Galerie Le Canard, Amsterdam, 26 January 1952.

6 While attending the Jesuit St Ignatius secondary school in Amsterdam Constant was selected for the Gregorian church choir, where he learned to sight-read music. He had perfect pitch and later sang and played by ear. From a young age Constant played mandolin, violin and guitar. At the age of 45 he learned to play cymbal from Hungarian cymbalist Jani Horváth.

7 Constant, 'C'est notre désir qui fait la révolution', in *Cobra* no. 4, reprinted in Christian Dotremont et al., *Cobra 1948-1957*, Paris: Éditions Jean-Michel Place, 1980, 3-4. A translation of this text can be found in the chapter 'Constant's Writings'.

of looking at things: he regarded the walls and floors of the halls as an empty canvas on which he would make a composition with the works of art. Three large paintings produced on site – by Constant (*Barricade*) [fig. 3], Brands (*Neergeschreven drift*; Passion written down), and Appel (*Mens en dieren*; Man and animals) – would provide powerful accents.

For the Dutch poets, Van Eyck provided a small room painted completely black with a large cage made of black slats in the centre. The room was sparsely lit, giving the space a mysterious atmosphere. The exhibition was challenging and revolutionary. A riot broke out on 5 November 1949, during an experimental literature recital. Dotremont was giving a long speech in French in which the word *Soviétique* occurred several times. Someone loudly pointed out that he was in Amsterdam not Paris. Van Eyck and Constant removed the heckler from the room. This sparked a tumultuous brawl, prompting the poets Elburg, Kouwenaar and Lucebert, along with the painters Brands, Rooskens and Wolvecamp, to sign a communiqué stating that they did not endorse the tenor of Dotremont's speech and that as a result of the incident they were leaving the Experimental Group in Holland. This was followed by a plethora of newspaper articles lambasting the exhibition and the policy pursued by Willem Sandberg (then director of the Stedelijk Museum Amsterdam). The exhibition subsequently drew huge numbers of visitors.

A dramatic change occurred in Constant's private life in May 1949, while he and his family were staying with Jorn in the latter's cottage on the Danish island of Bornholm. Suddenly his wife Matie left with Jorn, taking their two daughters, Martha (b. 1946) and Olga (b. 1948), with her. She left their son, Victor (b. 1944), behind with Constant. The friendship with Jorn was badly damaged.

In September 1950 Constant and Victor departed for Paris with Corneille and Appel. They found a studio in rue Santeuil, which Constant deemed unsuitable for his young son because of the lack of sanitary facilities. Constant and Victor moved into a *chambre de bonne* in rue Pigalle, where they

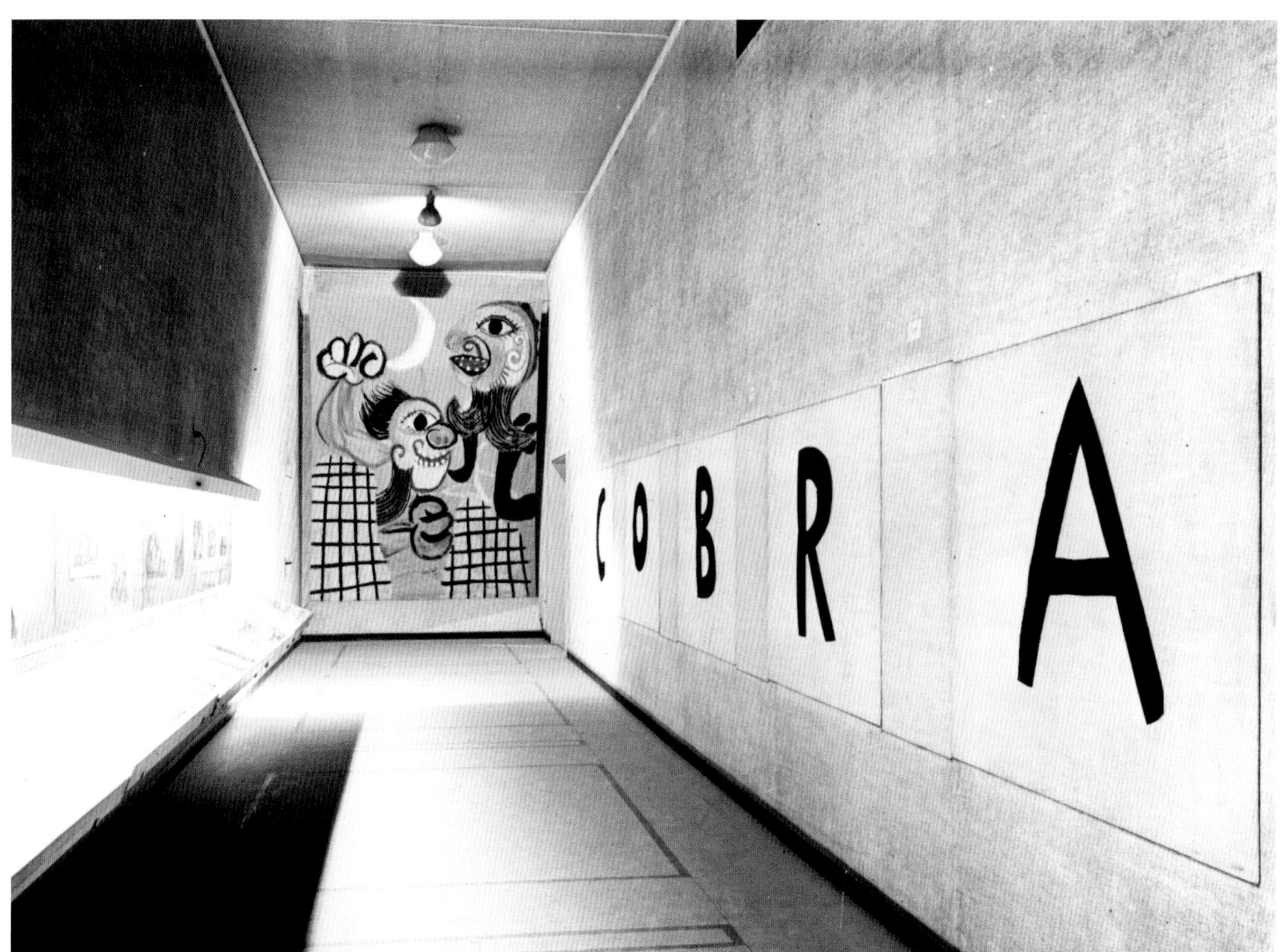

[3] *Barricade*, 1949, at the entrance of the 'International Exhibition of Experimental Art' at the Stedelijk Museum Amsterdam, 1949
collection Fondation Constant

lived among a hospitable community of prostitutes. He earned a small income as a busker, with Victor passing round the hat to collect the money. Appel and Corneille wanted to make a name for themselves and sell their work as quickly as possible. They regarded a child as an encumbrance. The three soon parted company. Constant regularly visited other artists and Cobra members living in Paris, including the English artist Stephen Gilbert and Japanese-American sculptor Shinkichi Tajiri.

In Paris Constant depicted his experiences during the Second World War in a series of paintings, rendered all the more topical by the Korean War and a brief stay in Frankfurt, where an exhibition of his work opened at Zimmergalerie Franck on 15 March 1951. Walking Victor to school every day in Frankfurt, Constant took a path across the *Trümmerhaufen* – bare patches of land strewn with ruined gable ends, rubble and stone. This desolate landscape was to recur for many years in two series of paintings: *Terre brulée* (Scorched Earth) and *Terrain vague* (Wasteland).

The Cobra movement finally disintegrated completely when both Jorn and Dotremont were admitted to a sanatorium with tuberculosis. The decision was taken to disband the movement, with a final international exhibition of experimental art at the Palais des Beaux Arts in Liège from 6 October to 6 November 1951. The final Cobra bulletin, number 10, was published in time for the exhibition. Five of Constant's 'war paintings' were shown, including *L'Incendie* (Fire, 1950), and a portfolio of five gouaches entitled *L'Imagination effrayante* (Terrifying Imagination, 1951) (p. 43 and 32). Writing in 1952, Kouwenaar described the war paintings thus, 'He paints war, he *makes* war – the war that still resides in newspaper columns; he makes it real, and he warns us. He is fighting in that rubble *himself*, and our head lies there like some laughable rutabaga.'[8]

Radical Change

The year 1952 was a turning point in Constant's artistic and intellectual development. Until then, Constant had shown little interest in abstract art. Looking back in 1981, he said, 'I just needed to jump the fence and potter around in that cold abstraction, because I realized that, while we had been busy with Cobra, all around us entire neighbourhoods had been built that were part of that 'abstraction froide': straight lines, steel frames, huge concrete surfaces. I wanted to explore that terrain for myself, in an aesthetic sense. That eventually brought me to *New Babylon*.'[9]

Though Paris was still the centre of the art world, in November 1952 Constant decided to pay a working visit to London. There he visited the studios of Herbert Read and Henry Moore, organized by the British Council. He also travelled to St. Ives (Cornwall) to visit Ben Nicholson and Barbara Hepworth. He discovered that the best painters there were William Scott and Victor Pasmore, who had been somewhat sidelined by the British Council. Scott, whom he had met in Paris, turned out to be a highly talented painter deserving of greater recognition. However, the British Council was anti-French and believed that the 'British spirit' was better suited to Surrealism. Surrealists like Francis Bacon, Roland Penrose and Graham Sutherland were much admired in Britain.[10]

Surrounded by the devastation of the Blitz in London, Constant began to think about the city as the stage setting of everyday life. The problems Constant faced were made clear in a letter to collector Martin Visser in which he argued forcefully against Visser's conclusion that the experimentals were past their prime: 'I myself regard the "experimental" period as precisely what the name suggests: my initiation into the problems of contemporary painting, immediately following a period of study that can be regarded as an initiation into the general problems of painting. No one jumps right into such a complex problem as modern plasticity, and all modern painters have had their experimental period before arriving

8 Kouwenaar, op. cit. (note 5).

9 Freddy de Vree, *Constant* (*Kunstpocket*, ser. 2, no. 10), Scheldenrode: Albert van Wiemeersch, 1983, 33.

10 As Constant wrote in a letter from London to collector Martin Visser, dated 10 November 1952 (Graham Birtwistle Archive).

at a solution to the problems. Such an experimental period is important only in the case of those characters who, in that period, display the features (difficult to identify at the beginning) typical of their later style. There is for example little difference to be discerned between an early Van der Leck and an early Chris Beekman, though the former later turned out to be important while the latter did not, and as a result their early experimental works are equal in value ... What applies to painters also applies to collectors: do not stop at your own discoveries, have the courage to strive for something more, indeed to renounce them if necessary.... We live in a revolutionary age, and though the past has borne some lovely fruit, the demands of a new spatiality present painters with a challenge they cannot simply ignore ... Mondrian painted for the whole of society, and that is why his work has such a huge impact extending far beyond painting. The same applies to Matisse who, less rationally and more intuitively, addressed the same problems. They are the forerunners of the new school, who develop and exploit the power of the plane as colour.'[11]

In London Constant contemplated the relationship between life's activities and the living environment and considered how he could contribute to the reconstruction of post-war Europe. He wondered how art might help to intensify all aspects of life. His time in London made him realize the impact that the built environment has on people (he saw that existing architecture – a dull way of building – created little room for people to develop a creative and playful lifestyle). From now on he would focus increasingly on urban planning. In a subsequent letter to Visser he wrote: 'I believe the entire development of painting can be understood on the basis of the sensation of space. Do not take this too lightly: it is the materialization of our entire spiritual existence, the projection of our individuality as humans relative to the "world" of nature.'[12]

Back in Amsterdam, Constant studied his friend Aldo van Eyck's books on architecture. He turned to abstraction, making paintings, collages and reliefs featuring interlocking planes of colour, like *Compositie in zwart en wit* (Composition in Black and White, 1953*), Zwart, rood, groen* (Black, Red, Green, 1953) and compositions like *Variations rythmiques* (Rhythmic Variations, 1953) (p. 64 and 71), which showed an affinity with (Russian) Constructivism. In 1953 he produced a relief, *Compositie met blauwe en witte blokjes* (Composition with Blue and White Cubes), adding another dimension to the two-dimensional painting [fig. 4].

In 1999, art historian Benjamin H.D. Buchloh interviewed Constant at a symposium accompanying an exhibition of his work in New York [fig. 5]. Buchloh identified a similarity between Constant's reliefs and Piet Mondrian's *Victory Boogie Woogie*, but Constant vehemently rejected this notion. His reliefs were created with an entirely different purpose than Mondrian's paintings.
The reliefs illustrated his ideas about architecture and urbanism. He experimented with what he had learned from Van Eyck's books. Buchloh concluded that no other Cobra artist had ever effected such a radical change in his work.[13]

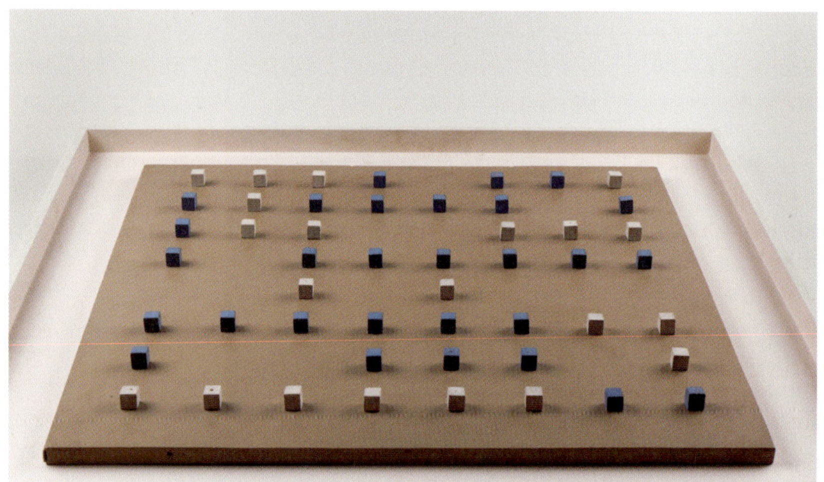

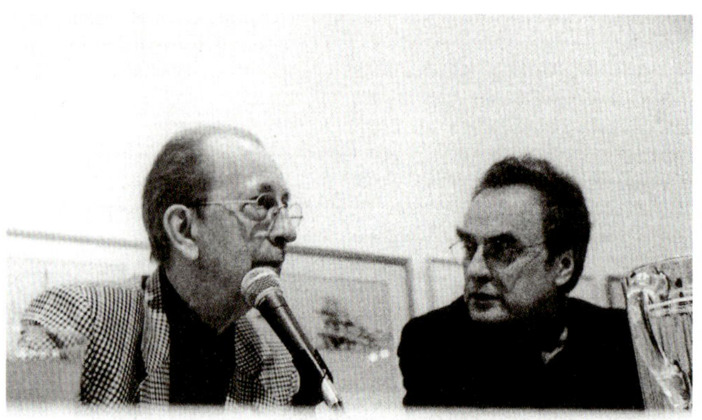

[4] *Compositie met blauwe en witte blokjes* (Composition with Blue and White Cubes), 1953
model in wood and paint, 60 x 59.8 x 4.5 cm
collection Kröller-Müller Museum, Otterlo

[5] Constant being interviewed by Benjamin Buchloh at the Symposium to accompany the exhibition 'Another City for Another Life. Constant's New Babylon', The Drawing Center, New York, 30 December 1999
collection Fondation Constant

'Spatial Colorism' and 'synthesis of arts'

In order to break with the political power structure and the monotony of post-war urban planning, Constant campaigned for a 'synthesis of arts'. During this period, he sought out like-minded professionals, such as the architects of the Congrès Internationaux d'architecture Moderne (CIAM); became an active member of the Liga Nieuw Beelden (League for New Representation), established on 24 January 1955; and collaborated with architects 'and other (plastic) artists'.

In 1952, Van Eyck got Constant involved in an experiment for the exhibition 'Mens en Huis' (Man and home) at the Stedelijk Museum Amsterdam.[14] The walls, floors and ceilings in the 'space' were painted half purple, half blue. Van Eyck designed a bench, realized in rough wood. Constant created a mural for one wall [fig. 6]. On the opposite wall, lines of poetry by Lucebert were applied in vermillion . The exhibition catalogue referred to the design of *een ruimte in kleur* (A Space in Colour) as an example of collaboration between architect, painter and poet.[15] This clearly linked the 'experiment' to the debate on a potential 'new synthesis'.[16] Since colour played a passive role in modern architecture, Van Eyck and Constant called for a synthesis of colour and form in architecture in order to make it more interesting and suggestive and thus stimulate people's creativity.

In June 1953 Van Eyck and Constant took their experiment a step further with colour illustrations in the portfolio *Voor een spatiaal colorisme* (For A Spatial Colorism). Van Eyck wrote the introduction, and on the final three pages there was a text by Constant about the importance of synthesizing form and colour to create an entirely new plastic art.[17] In order to achieve this, architecture and painting would not be merged, as in the Baroque period. Instead, a synthesis of the two art forms would be created: a plastic reality organized at a higher level. In 1960 Van Eyck and Constant received the Sikkens Prize for their manifesto 'Spatial Colorism' and the demonstration of their ideas at the exhibition in the Amsterdam Stedelijk Museum.

In February 1954 Constant designed a model interior for the Bijenkorf department store in Amsterdam, together with architect Gerrit Rietveld. Martin Visser, head of the Bijenkorf's furniture department, asked Rietveld to design a stand for the 'Kleurenharmonie in uw woning' ('Colour harmony in your home') event, showing how to make maximum use of minimum space. Rietveld invited Constant to design a colour scheme for the space. He designed a scheme

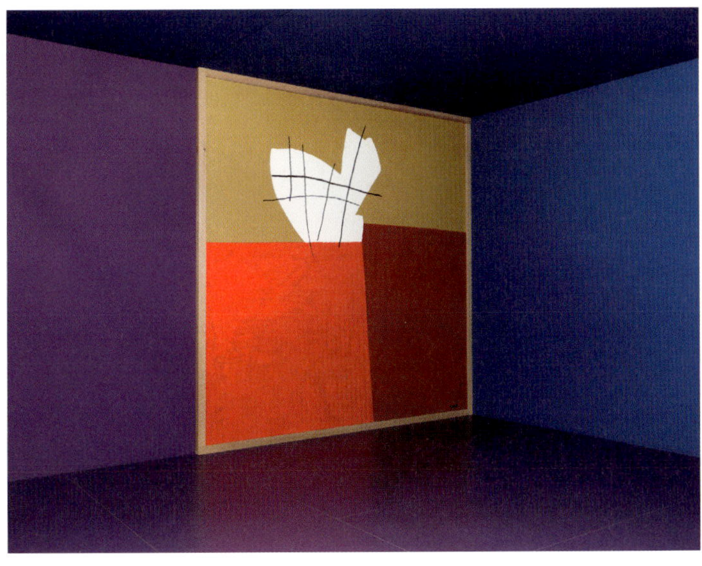

[6] Reconstruction of *een ruimte in kleur* (A Space in Colour), 1952 with the mural by Constant, at the exhibition 'Constant. Nueva Babilonia', Museo Nacional Centro de Arte Reina Sofía, Madrid, 20 October 2015-29 February 2016 collection Fondation Constant

11 Letter of 15 January 1953 to Martin Visser, from London (Graham Birtwistle Archive).

12 Letter of 3 February 1953 to Martin Visser, from London (Graham Birtwistle Archive).

13 Catherine de Zegher and Mark Wigley (eds.), *The Activist Drawing: Retracing Situationist Architectures from Constant's New Babylon to Beyond*, New York: The Drawing Center, 2001, 17-18.

14 From 21 November 1952-5 January 1953.

15 Referred to by Aldo van Eyck in *Forum* 1953, no. 3 and in later publications on his work by Francis Strauven as 'a space bounded by colour'.

16 Marcel Hummelink, *Après nous la liberté: Constant en de artistieke avant-garde in de jaren 1946-1960*, Amsterdam: self-published, 2003, 130.

17 Constant, 'Spatiaal colorisme', in Constant and Aldo van Eyck, *Voor een spatiaal colorisme*, Amsterdam 1953, 6-7. A translation of this text can be found in the chapter 'Constant's Writings'.

consisting of several large colour planes.

From 1951 to 1955 Constant and Gilbert collaborated closely on spatial experiments. The two artists engaged in a profound theoretical debate. In 1954 they established Néovision, together with the Hungarian-French sculptor Nicolas Schöffer. Gilbert and Schöffer challenged Constant to create three-dimensional sculptures. This gave rise to *Construction aux plans transparents* (Construction with Transparent Planes, 1954), *Constructie met gekleurde vlakken/Constructie met rechthoekige vlakken* (Construction with Coloured Planes/ Construction with Rectangular Planes, 1954) (p. 70 and 69), and the 16-metre-tall structure *Monument for Reconstruction* (1955, fig. 7), for the 'E55' exhibition (National Energy Manifestation) in Rotterdam, in which the rectangular forms preferred by Schöffer and Gilbert were visible. Constant soon replaced them with curved forms. He became convinced that constructions based on 'l'infinie des paraboles' (the infinity of the parabola) had a stronger impact on the surrounding space than structures based on the closed form of a box.[18]

Shortly before the establishment of the Liga Nieuw Beelden, Constant worked with Anton Rooskens on a model commissioned by Sonia Gaskell for a Dutch National Ballet 'experimental' performance of *The Trial* (of Franz Kafka), with choreography by Jaap Flier to music by Jan Mul (p. 84). The ballet premiered on 20 January 1955 at the Koninklijke Schouwburg in The Hague.

Though the Liga Nieuw Beelden did not give Constant the synthesis of arts he sought, it did provide an opportunity to exhibit his work and acquire commissions from public bodies. These included designs for two concrete play sculptures and a mobile construction, a commission from the staff of the Gemeentelijke Woningdienst, Amsterdam (Amsterdam Municipal Housing Service).[19] In 1955 furniture manufacturers 't Spectrum started producing a 1953 design, the *IJhorst* table (p. 85) and textile manufacturer Stoomweverij Nijverheid in Enschede commissioned Constant to produce fabric designs for both clothing and curtains (p. 87-90).

The Dutch pavilion at the Venice Biennale in 1956 featured work by Constant, André Volten and Bart van der Leck. Contrary to the artists' wish for their art to be associated with their views on the synthesis of arts, it was instead referred to as 'architectonically abstract'.[20]

Constant's attempts to achieve a true synthesis of the plastic arts failed for lack of funding and due to a change of heart in those who had previously espoused the same views.

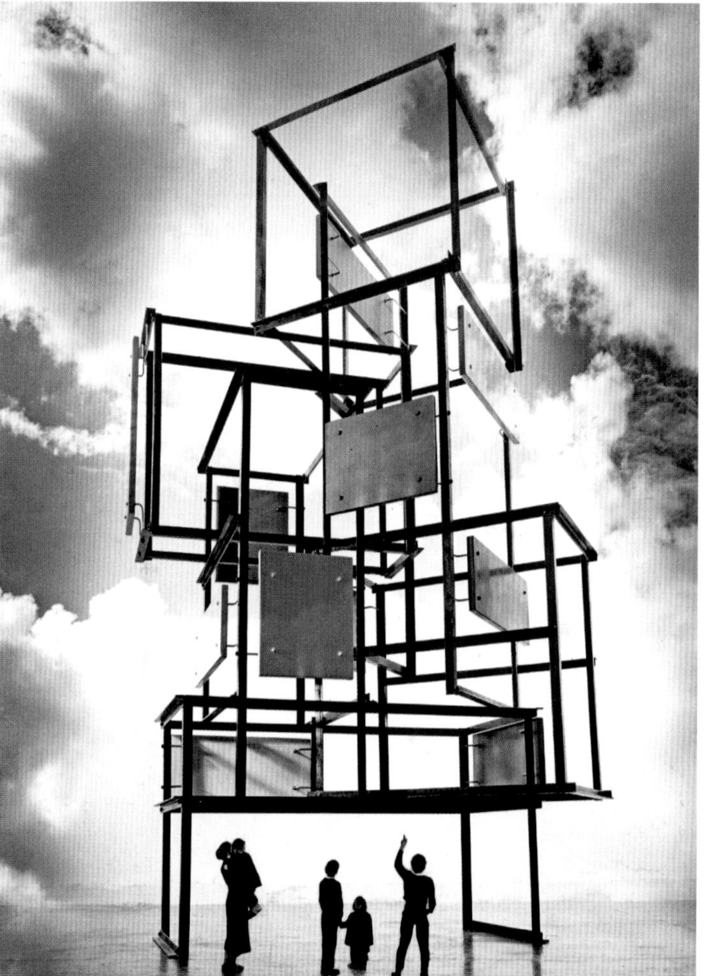

[7] Design for *Monument voor de wederopbouw* (Monument for the Reconstruction, 1955) for the 'E55' Manifestation in Rotterdam collection Fondation Constant

Demain la poésie logera la vie:[21] prelude to *New Babylon*[21]

Even though, from Constant's perspective his friendship with Jorn had cooled considerably, they continued to correspond. In 1953 Jorn visited Constant's studio in Amsterdam. On seeing *Reeks van 6 gekleurde vlakken* (Series of 6 Coloured Planes, fig. 8), which Constant had created by spraying car paint onto steel plates,[22] his only comment was 'merde'. Jorn believed that Constant was betraying himself as a painter. Despite their difference of opinion on the relationship between 'free' and 'applied' arts and the link between technology and aesthetics, Constant and Jorn were united in their fight against functionalist architecture and design. Whereas Constant called for art to fulfil a societal role in promoting a creative way of life, Jorn thought art should be practised in total freedom. Nevertheless, in July 1956 Constant decided to work with Jorn in the Mouvement International pour un Bauhaus Imaginiste contre un Bauhaus Imaginaire (M.I.B.I.), established by Jorn in 1954. They both went on to become members of the Situationist International.

In the 1956 article 'Le technicisme',[23] Constant highlighted the huge gap that had emerged between the fine arts and architecture and design, because visual artists never considered the aesthetic potential of 'modern' materials such as metal, concrete, Plexiglas and plastic. As a result, most industrial products were poorly designed, and art was used only decoratively in the built environment. He argued for a new aesthetic that he called *technicisme*. This was to be based on the constructive properties of the materials that technological progress had given us and that were being used on a large scale in industry and in construction. Jorn, on the other hand, saw a 'complementary contrast' between aesthetics and technology.[24]

Jorn invited Constant to a conference on 'Industry and Fine Arts' in Alba (Piedmont) from 2 to 8 September 1956. Constant was to attend as a specialist on architecture. He wrote a lecture, 'Demain la poésie logera la vie' ('Tomorrow, Life Will Reside in Poetry'), in which he argued for the most complete art that will be 'at once lyrical in its means and social in its very nature'.[25]

The experimental laboratory in Alba was run by two painters, Pinot Gallizio and Piero Simondo. They offered Constant space to live and work there, allowing him to stay for a few months.

When he saw the desolate place where gypsies

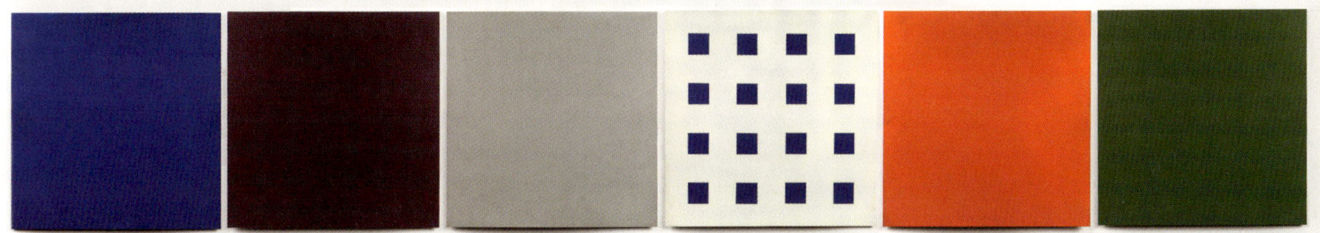

[8] *Reeks van 6 gekleurde vlakken* (Series of 6 Coloured Planes), 1953
car paint on steel sheet, 61.5 x 61.5 x 2.7 cm each
collection Gemeentemuseum Den Haag, The Hague

18 Hummelink, op. cit (note 16), 188.

19 The mobile construction *Draaibare constructie* (Pivotting Construction, 1956), currently part of the collection of the Stedelijk Museum Amsterdam, has been severely damaged from being relocated several times. The possibility of making a reconstruction based on the scale model is being considered.

20 See André Volten and Charles Karsten, 'Biënnale van Venetië 1956', *Liga-Bulletin*, August 1956, 3-4.

21 Constant, 'Demain la poésie logera la vie' ('Tomorrow Life will Reside in Poetry'), written in Paris on 19 August 1956, as a lecture to be held at the First World Congress of Free Artists, Alba, 2-8 September 1956. A translation of this text can be found in the chapter 'Constant's Writings'.

22 These are in Gemeentemuseum Den Haag's collection. The steel plates have rusted, however, and they could be photographed in early 2015 because of their poor condition. The paintings were restored in 2015 and will appear in the exhibition 'Constant. New Babylon' at Gemeentemuseum Den Haag in 2016.

23 Constant, 'Le technicisme', unpublished text, July 1956. A translation of this text can be found in the chapter 'Constant's Writings'.

24 Hummelink, op. cit. (note 16), 227.

25 Mark Wigley, *Constant's New Babylon: The Hyper-Architecture of Desire* (Rotterdam: 010 Publishers, 1998), 78.

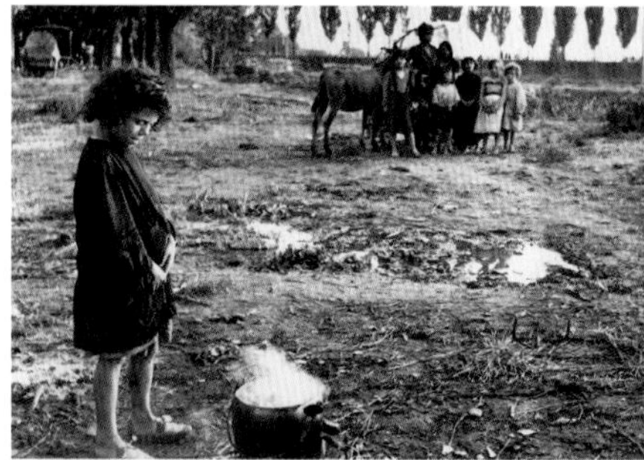

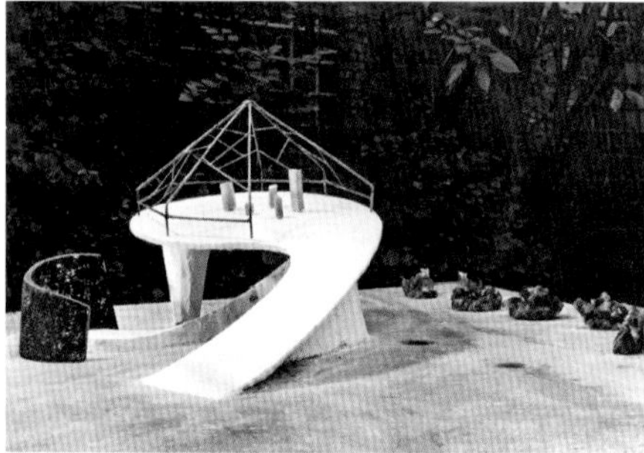

[9] Gypsies, camping on the banks of the Tanaro River in Alba, 1956

[10] Design for *Pavilion for the Milan Triennale in 1957*, 1956 collection Fondation Constant

camped on the banks of the Tanaro River [fig. 9], Constant conceived the idea of a permanent gypsy camp for Alba, for which he constructed a model consisting of collective lodgings made up of movable elements beneath a shelter – a nomadic camp on a global scale. However, the local council refused to fund the development. In 1956 Constant made a second model for a pavilion at the Milan Triennale [fig. 10]. These designs were followed by the model *Ambiance de jeu* (1956), which marked the start of the later *New Babylon* series.

Guy Debord – writer, filmmaker and strategic activist, founder of the Lettrist International in 1952 – visited Constant in Alba in December 1956 [fig. 11]. Since 1954 his group had been campaigning against functionalist architecture in its newsletter *Potlatch*. From the moment he met Constant, Debord wanted to found a more radical group. They were both convinced that art and modern technology should be integrated into a new, 'unitary' form of urban planning. In their eyes, the city was both the matrix for and the result of people's feelings and behaviour. The Situationist International came into being in Cosio di Arroscia, Italy, in July 1957. The second edition of their bulletin, entitled *Internationale Situationniste*, clearly stated their opposition to independent art and applied art. Art should be used to construct living environments. Nevertheless, Constant still had serious objections that prevented him from joining. The Situationist International was no different from the Cobra movement, since it consisted mainly of painters in search of individual recognition. Constant regarded painting as an outmoded individualistic form of art.

Constant did not become an active member of the Situationist International until June 1958, by which time his objections had been laid to rest, as everyone in the movement had clearly expressed their support for the 'unitary urbanism' that Constant and Debord defined as the 'ceaseless, complex activity that aims consciously to recreate man's environment in accordance with the most progressive ideas in all areas'.[26] An intense correspondence immediately commenced between Debord and Constant and continued until Constant left the movement in August 1960.
In explanation of his decision to leave, he said that the Situationist International did not go far enough in extrapolating consequences and was still too much a grouping of painters. During his time as a member, Constant wrote many articles for *Internationale Situationniste*, and two of his models appeared in the bulletin: *Ambiance d'une ville future* (1958), [fig. 12] and *Gele Sector* (Yellow Sector, 1958).

In early 1960 Guy Debord dubbed Constant's designs for a new urban environment *New Babylon*. Constant considered the name most apposite. To him, 'Babylon' was highly suggestive of human hubris, of unchristian morals, unprecedented wealth and fantastical ways of living, which were all very much in keeping with his project. And the English 'New' was more appropriate than the Dutch 'Nieuw', since this was a global project.[27]

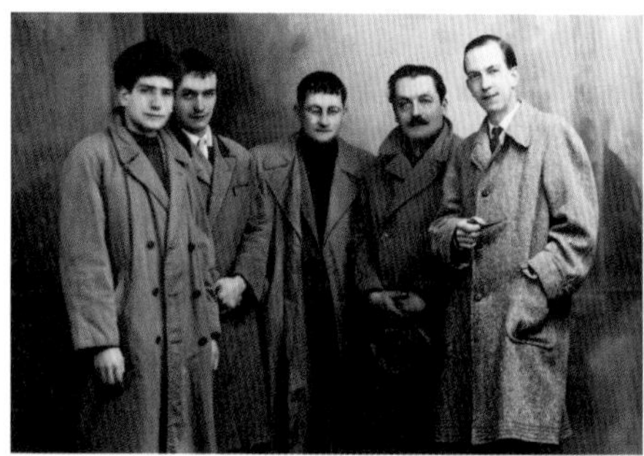

[11] From left to right: Walter Olmo, Piero Simondo, Guy Debord, Pinot Gallizio and Constant in Alba, December 1955 collection Fondation Constant

His active participation in the Situationist International did not bring about the synthesis of arts that Constant had hoped to realize. Two Dutch architects introduced by Constant in 1959, Har Oudejans and Ton Alberts, were excommunicated by Debord in 1960 for producing a design for a church. Constant and Jorn both left the movement of their own accord, albeit at different times. They were the only ones not to be excommunicated by Debord.

Space as a Playing Field

In the mid 1950s, the United States and the Soviet Union launched satellites and began exploring space. Political tensions between East and West led to a race to conquer space. Constant saw space as a new playing field.

In 1955 he made two sculptures, *Observatorium* (Observatory, p. 79) and *Planetarium*, using modern materials such as Plexiglas, aluminium and metal, whose titles refer to solar systems and the observation of galaxies. In the years that followed, his constructions were given titles combining the concepts of *space* and *play*, as in *Ruimtecircus* (Space Circus), *Lijn zonder einde* (Infinite Line) (p. 94 and 99) and *Zonneschip* (Sun Vessel). The various constructions titled *Nébulose mécanique* referred to heavenly bodies (p. 98 and 100). *Départ pour l'espace* (Departure for Space) referred to the launching of *Sputnik 1* by the Soviets on 4 October 1957. Initially, the model *Spatiovore* was called *Concert Hall for Electronic Music*.[28] The platform in the construction, which resembles a lunar landscape, lent itself more to a name like *Spatiovore* [fig. 13]. Constant made several versions of *Spatiovore*: he placed one on a milliners's hat block he had purchased on Waterlooplein (p. 106, 107, 108). Constant ingeniously managed to combine the poetic unity of colour and space he regarded as so important with his preference for curves. In the designs of spatial constructions, he combined Plexiglas with metal spokes and copper wire. He managed to bend Plexiglas into three-dimensional shapes in such a way as to obtain the optimum interplay of light and colour. He scratched lines in the Plexiglas and skilfully allowed ink to run into the scratches [fig. 14]. The play of colour and lines thus created gave his constructions an extra dynamism.

In this period Constant painted *De zon* (The Sun, 1956), *Paysage lunaire* (Lunar Landscape, 1956), *Sterrenbeeld* (Constellation, 1956) and *De grote beer* (Ursa Major, 1956). He transformed panels with oil paints, scratched lines and holes to create artistic space landscapes to which he gave names like *Kosmisch landschap* (Cosmic Landscape, 1956), *Ruimtelandschap* (Space Landscape, 1957), *Voyage dans l'espace* (Space Travel, 1957) and *Structures dans l'espace* (Structures in Space, 1958) (p. 102, 103, 104, 105).

In 1958 Constant collaborated with the American experimental filmmaker and photographer Hy (Hyman) Hirsch on an abstract film, *Gyromorphosis*. His spatial constructions were shown, dynamically and playfully interacting with the improvised sounds of jazz music, in a fascinating performance featuring sound, space and light.

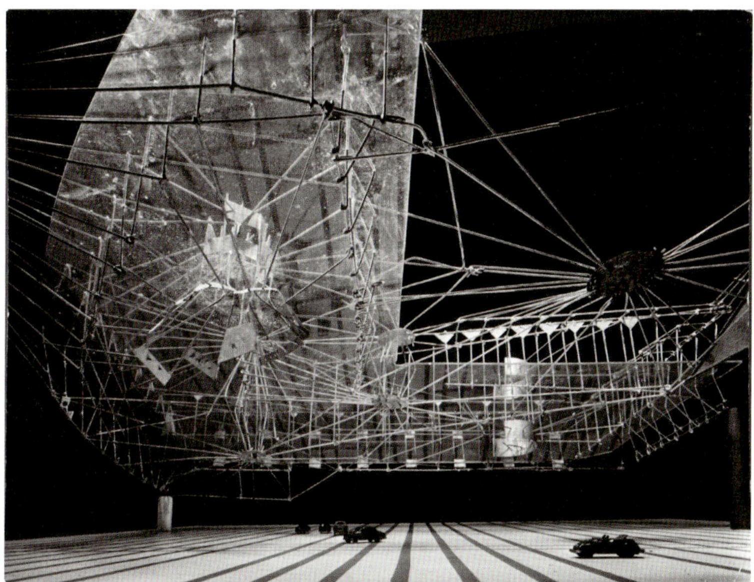

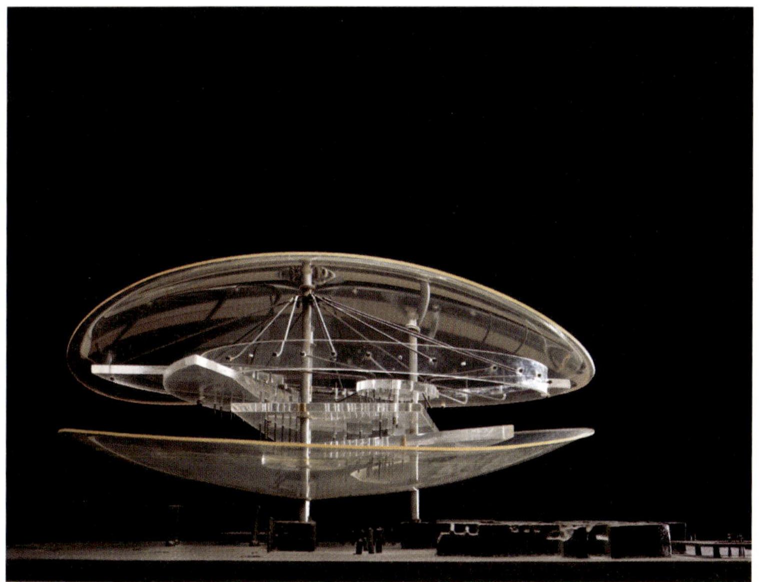

26 Constant and Guy Ernest Debord, 'La déclaration d'Amsterdam', *Internationale Situationniste*, no. 2 (December 1958), 31.

27 L.J. Locher and Constant, *New Babylon*, exh. cat. The Hague (Haags Gemeentemuseum) 15 June - 1 September 1974) 12.

28 In *Catalogo della XXXIII Esposizione Biennale Internazionale d'Arte Venezia* (1966), 193.

[12] *Ambiance d'une ville future*, 1958
photograph on panel, 75 x 107.5 cm
collection Fondation Constant, long-term loan to the Stedelijk Museum Schiedam

[13] *Spatiovore*, 1960
Plexiglas, metal, wood and paint, 35 x 89.7 x 64 cm
collection Centre national d'art et de culture Georges-Pompidou, Paris

I Am a Utopien: Practice and Conclusion of *New Babylon*

Constant continued experimenting with ways of visualizing the idea of 'unitary urbanism'. From 1960 to 1969, he was hugely productive and publicly active, working on models, paintings, watercolours, gouaches, collages, drawings and geographical maps. He wrote numerous articles that can be regarded as works of cultural philosophy, in order to provide a theoretical foundation for *New Babylon*. The enormous international interest in *New Babylon* took him all around Europe. He showed his work at 23 exhibitions, presented lectures with slide shows and gave interviews. He worked with a range of artists and craftsmen on industrial and municipal commissions.

In 1969 Constant stopped working on the models. He explained why in the 1965 article 'De dialektiek van het experiment' ('The Dialectic of the Experiment'), in which he stated that although he could visualize unitary urbanism, the situation in which we lived differed fundamentally from the social situation essential for the achievement of such a revolutionary programme.[29] As a result, unitary urbanism was limited to isolated experiments and degenerated into a mere exercise. The creative process shifted from reality to a conception thereof. Culture became 'utopian'. The *New Babylon* plan has to be seen in this light.

Constant wanted to work on feasible projects. He did not want to become a *utopiste*, one who explores impossibilities. Henri Lefebvre called him a *utopien*: one who realizes possibilities.[30]

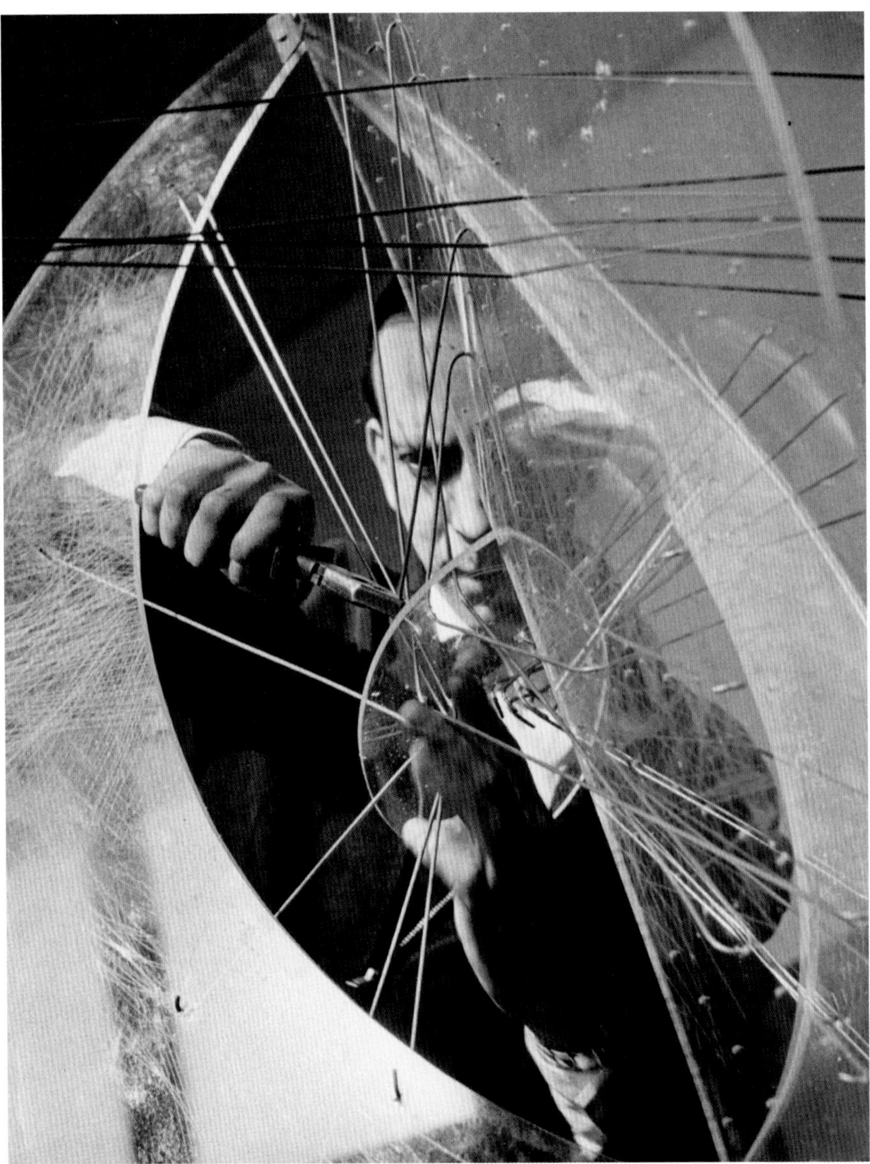

[14] Constant working on Eivormige constructive (Ovoid Construction), 1957 collection Fondation Constant

Officially, the *New Babylon* period lasts from 1956 to 1974, though it was not called *New Babylon* until 1960. Constant's environment-oriented engagement placed him in the modernist avant-garde tradition, particularly Constructivism. However, for Constant form was not determined by ideology; it was discovered through experience and experiment.

Colorism

From 1969 to 2005 Constant continued his colorist experiments on a two-dimensional surface, following such great predecessors as Tiziano Vecellio, Eugène Delacroix and Paul Cézanne. Until well into the 1980s, Constant's paintings combined architectural compositions with colorism [fig. 15]. He described Cézanne's colorism in *À propos de Cézanne*.[31] Constant took Cézanne's colorism further, creating space and depth without any line work at all, using only colour, as in *Les baigneurs* (The Bathers, 2002) [fig. 16].[32]

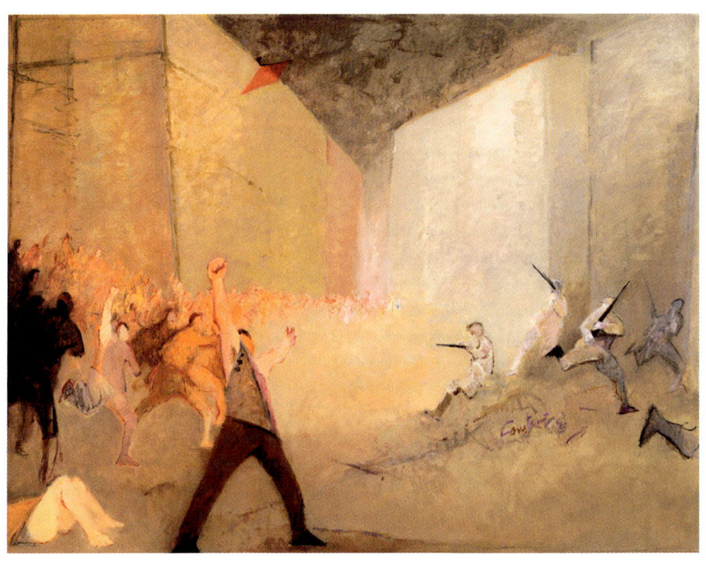

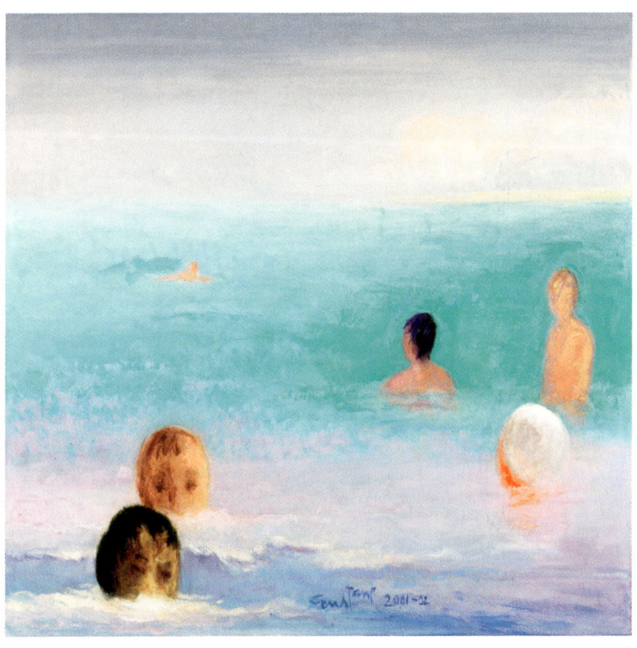

[15] *L'Insurrection* (The Revolt),1985
oil on linen, 148 x 198 cm
collection Fondation Constant, long-term loan to the Stedelijk Museum Schiedam

[16] *Les baigneurs* (The Bathers) 2002
oil on linen, 163 x 170 cm
collection Fondation Constant, long-term loan to the Stedelijk Museum Schiedam

29 Constant, 'De dialektiek van het experiment', in exh. cat. *Constant* The Hague (Haags Gemeentemuseum) 1 October-21 November 1965).
A translation of this text can be found in the chapter 'Constant's Writings'.

30 Henri Lefebvre defined the difference between utopiste and utopien thus: 'Il faut distinguer des utopiens, autrement dit l'utopie abstraite de l'utopie concrète… La pensée utopiste explore l'impossible; la pensée utopienne dégage le possible.' Quoted in Jean-Clarence Lambert, *Constant: Art et utopie*, Paris: Éditions Cercle d'Art, 1997, 7.

31 Constant, *À propos de Cézanne: Aantekeningen naar aanleiding van de tentoonstelling: 'Cézanne: Les dernières années 1895-1906'*, Amsterdam: self-published, 100 signed and numbered copies, July 1985; exhibition at Grand Palais, Paris, 10 April-23 July 1978.

32 Trudy van der Horst, *Constant. De late periode*, Nijmegen: BnM uitgevers, 2008, 240-250.

De brand (Fire), 1987
oil on linen, 80 x 83 cm
collection Fondation Constant

In 1986, Adèle van Rijckevorsel, Constant's friend at the time, asked him whether he would still paint the Cobra painting *L'Incendie* (Fire, p. 43) in the same way. 'I'll show you' was his reply.

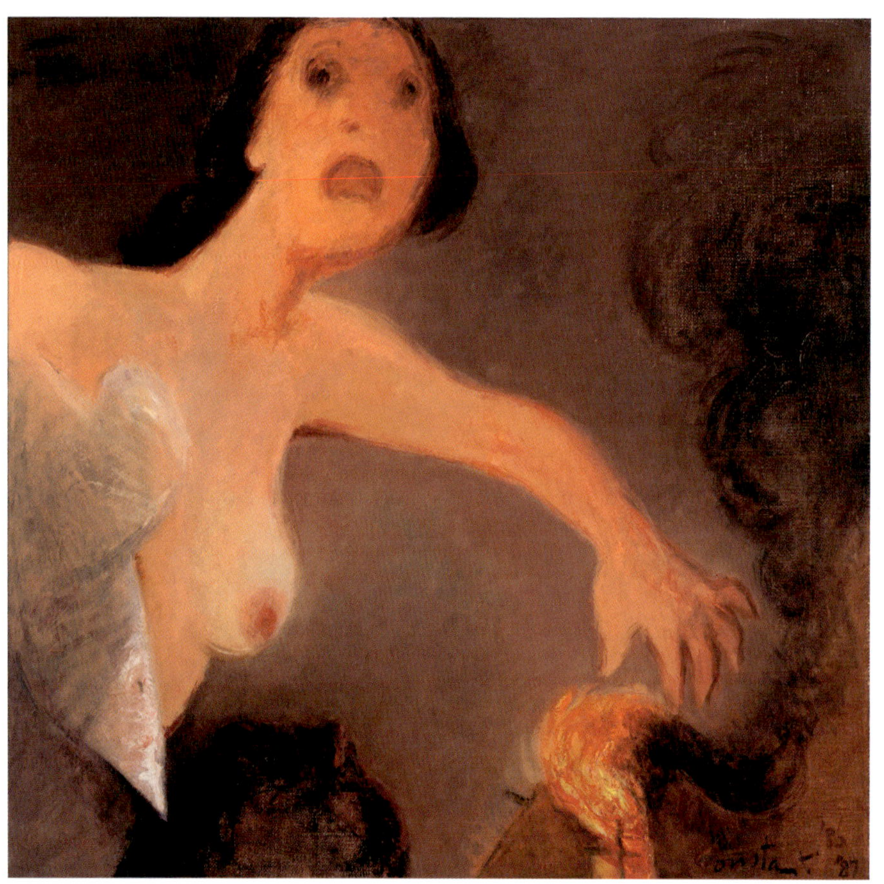

Constant's Writings

(a selection)

1

It Is Our Desire That Makes Revolution, 1949

This text, parts of which have often been quoted, appeared in 1949 in *Cobra* under the title 'C'est notre désir qui fait la révolution'. *Cobra* was the journal of the International Cobra Group, and its fourth issue, an edition of the Dutch Experimental Group in Holland, served as a catalogue for the great 'International Exhibition of Experimental Art' at the Stedelijk Museum in Amsterdam from 3 to 28 November 1949. Constant took a radical stand against Mondrian's geometric abstraction. The text was translated into Dutch with a view to being included in a collection of texts dating from 1945 to 1968, which was in fact never published

It Is Our Desire That Makes Revolution

'Die, ye old forms and ideas!
Slave-born, awake, awake!
The world is driven by new forces,
Desire has touched us!'

The International – in the Dutch version

For those who wish to learn about human desires, whether in the domain of art, the domain of sex, or any other domain, the experiment is an indispensable tool for gathering data on the objective and the source of our aspirations, on their possibilities and their limitations. One might wonder what purpose is served by following man from one extreme to the other, and being unafraid of flouting the norms set by ethics, by aesthetics, by philosophy in doing so. Why is it that we feel the need to break the bonds that have held us within a social system for dozens of centuries and thanks to which we have remained capable of thinking, of living, of creating? Does our culture no longer have a future, will it be impossible to satisfy our deepest desires within the confines of this culture?
In reality no human desire has ever been satisfied within the confines of this culture, no more in the case of a slave than in the case of a master, for all that the latter may have fancied himself happy in luxury and in a lust with which he believed he was exploiting all the creative potential of man to the full. So when we people of the twentieth century speak of human desire, we are actually speaking of something unknown. After all, all we know of that immeasurable realm of our actual desires is merely this: that all these desires converge into a single overriding desire for freedom. To gain access to this unknown world in which our desires can be satisfied, and in which all the cultural aspects of our lives as well as the relationships among all of our lives can acquire higher value, we must first liberate our social life – we consider this our first and most elementary task.

The only way to know thoroughly a desire is to satisfy it, and the satisfaction of our most essential desire is revolution. The true creative activity – the culture – of our time is based on revolution. Only through revolutionary activity can we learn about the desires that slumber within the human being of NOW, of 1949. No formulation can take the place of our revolutionary experience. Dialectical materialism has taught us that our consciousness is dependent on the social conditions we are living in. If, however, these conditions are such that satisfaction of our essential desires must be deemed impossible, we feel the need to explore that which we desire. This need gave birth to the experiment, the means to develop the knowledge of the desires that slumber within us.
The experiment, however, is not simply a means to expand our knowledge. From the moment we are forced to acknowledge that our needs are not compatible with the cultural norms that are meant to channel our desires, the experiment becomes the very prerequisite for knowledge.
One might then wonder what forms the basis of the experiment itself.

Since our desires are largely unknown to us, the experiment can have no other starting point than the knowledge present within us at any given time. What we know, at any moment, is the material with which we continue building. And with the new application of this material begins the phase in which we become able to cultivate new realms, realms we cannot yet imagine.
With these facts in mind, the artists of today have activated themselves to rediscover the creativity that has been suppressed and smothered since the beginning of our current culture. Creativity is the way to knowledge, the pre-eminent means to conquer our freedom, the best weapon of the revolution.

The current, individualistic culture has substituted artistic production for creativity. Yet what has been produced are merely the tragic symbols of impotence, the rare cries of desperation of a shackled individual, constrained by aesthetic taboos. Creating means making something hitherto unknown, and the unknown strikes fear in the hearts of people who believe they have something to preserve or to protect. We, however, who have nothing to lose but our chains, are not afraid of the adventure. The only risk we run consists of the loss of a rather sterile virginity, the virginity of abstracts. We must soil the virginal purity of Mondrian, be it merely with our misery. Is misery not preferable to death, at least for those who are strong enough to fight? The enemy has forced us to become partisans and to join the resistance, and while he may have discipline, we have courage, and in the end it is not discipline but courage that determines victory.
This is our answer to the abstract artists, whether they claim spontaneity or not. Their 'spontaneity' is that of a rebellious child, who does not know what it really wants, who wants to be free but is unable to achieve it outside the protection of its parents.
To be free one must be strong: freedom can only exist in creativity or in struggle, which actually share the same objective: the fulfilment of our life.

CREATIVITY IS WHAT LIFE DEMANDS OF US; BEAUTY IS LIFE.
So when we witness society turning against us and against our works, and accusing us of being 'undefinable' or 'incomprehensible', we reply:
1. That human beings in 1949 are incapable of understanding anything except the necessary struggle for their liberation.
2. That we do not seek to be 'understood' – we too want to be liberated – and that WE ARE COMPELLED TO EXPERIMENT BY THE SAME FORCES THAT FORCE THE WORLD TO FIGHT.
3. That we could not be creative in a world that is passive and that OUR CREATIVITY IS SUSTAINED BY THE CURRENT SOCIAL STRUGGLE.
4. And finally, that humanity, once it begins to live creatively, will automatically cease to need aesthetic or ethical norms, which have never been intended for anything other than to constrain creativity and which are now the cause of the general lack of understanding for our experiments.
Understanding, after all, is nothing more than recreating something based on a shared desire. Humanity, including us, is on a quest to explore its own desires. We shall reveal these desires by satisfying them.

'C'est notre désir qui fait la révolution', published in *Cobra, organe du front international des artistes expérimentaux d'avant-garde* [organ of the International Front of Avant-garde Experimental Artists], 4 November 1949, 3-4.

The typed manuscript in Dutch is in the Constant archive at the Netherlands Institute for Art History (RKD).

Spatial Colorism
(with remarks by Gerrit Rietveld), 1953

In 1953 Constant published, with architect Aldo van Eyck, the portfolio *Voor een spatiaal colorisme* (For A Spatial Colorism). In this publication they looked back on their collaboration on *een ruimte in kleur* (A Space in Colour), an environment for the home exhibition 'Mens en Huis' (Man and home) at the Stedelijk Museum Amsterdam. In the text Constant points out the relationship between colour and space, each inconceivable without the other. He pleads for an integrated approach through which a more highly organized plastic reality emerges. In order to achieve this, painters and architects work together as a team towards a common objective. Constant sent a copy of the portfolio to De Stijl architect Gerrit Rietveld, who annotated his manifesto with comments. These hitherto unpublished comments are included here in the form of footnotes.

Spatial Colorism
(with remarks by Gerrit Rietveld)

In a reaction to the 'building' of the nineteenth century, where form was often buried under decoration to such an extent as to render the content unrecognizable, the modern architect has ended up concentrating primarily on spatial form, regarding colour as secondary and making it subordinate to form.[R01]
The architect sees size, proportion and structure as the basic elements of 'pure' spatial form.[R02] It is chiefly these elements that underpin an architectural design in which space is conceived as colourless.[R03]

The execution of a design based primarily on form begins with a conflict: the conflict

---

Remarks on 'Spatial Colorism' by Gerrit Rietveld

R01: ? De Stijl!
R02: and material, at least if you regard it as equally distinct visually
R03: at any rate light and dark, or rather: lighter and less light
R04: colour and matter is a conflict too
R05: yes
R06 the architect must immediately determine light and less light in his design. the painter can if necessary

between idea and matter, between form and colour.[R04]
The architect is inclined to keep colour passive: he minimizes the number of colours and avoids intense colours. But colour is unavoidably introduced by way of material, finishing and furnishings.[R05]
Colour, added at a later stage, constitutes a random element as far as the design is concerned, and thus loses its constituent, constructive value for the spatial plasticity. As a consequence, colour's enormous space-creating potential is reduced to a matter of chance and because of this the spatial effect itself is always deficient.[R06]
Eliminating colour, which is just as important a determinant of space as architectural form, precludes unity of form and colour.
The realistic spatial conception is the conception of space in colour.[R07]

It goes without saying that the spatial use of colour has nothing to do with the use of colour for decorative or 'functional' purposes.

Nor can the use of colour as a means of correcting an impure size or form by means of optical illusion be counted as a plastic use of colour because in this instance form remains passive with respect to colour. Nonetheless, the use of colour as a corrective carries an implicit recognition of its three-dimensional qualities.[R08]
Spatial form and spatial colour can only form an indissoluble unity if they develop at the same time and in relation to one another.[R09]
What holds for painting on a flat surface also holds for the spatial conception of colour:
Colour is nothing but the colour of the form and form is nothing but the form of the colour.[R10]

So a spatial conception of colour entails more than the use of colour in the creation of architectural spatial effects. The absolute unity of form and colour, in other words the purely plastic use of colour, takes the architect into the domain of painting.[R11]
The result, however, is an architecture based on a visual reality in which form and colour are one, rather than on abstracted formal elements;[R12] and painting in which the colour is not used for personal expression but is systematically used for immediate plastic effect.

'Spatial colorism' is therefore[R13] a totally new plastic art with its own independent laws, and with a potential far outstripping that of both architecture and painting.[R14]
'Spatial colorism' elevates the schematic form to physical form and is for this reason an indispensable expressive factor in making human space in the broadest sense of universal human settlement.[R15+16]

Even the concept of colour plasticity familiar in painting acquires new meaning in space. The spatial conception of colour not only puts an end to centralized composition but also to the 'simultaneity' of colour effects:[R17] the experience of colour plastic will take place in time.[R18]

Moreover, the 'scale', the ratio of colour quantity to human dimensions, becomes crucially important when the closed character of the painting is replaced by the surrounding space.[R19]

The development of 'spatial colorism' as a spatial conception and the realization of space in colour, demands close contact between painters and architects. Furthermore, it is important that, rather than remaining specialists in their own carefully circumscribed field, they should work together as a 'team' in pursuit of a common goal.[R20]
This goal is not the amalgamation of architecture and painting,[R21] as in the Baroque, but a higher order of three-dimensional plastic reality that surpasses both and in which colour and spatiality are inconceivable one without the other.
'Spatial colorism' is not a theory but a practice.[R22]

'Spatiaal colorisme', published in: Constant and Aldo van Eyck, *Voor een spatiaal colorisme*, Amsterdam, 1953, 6-8.

---

turn this light and dark into colour contrasts
R07: yes, I think this is correct, although it's not a logical consequence of the above
R08: yes
R09: in terms of differences in lightness
R10: has a nice ring to it, but is meaningless
R11: this is completely wrong. nor should the painter encroach on the architect's domain, even when there are only two parties, let alone more
R12: read: space R
R13: why
R14: I don't begrudge the painter this illusion
R15: don't go too far – because what's being claimed here applies at best to the art of painting and to colour-space as art for art's sake (preferably uninhabited). When space is required to be a shelter and boundary and a backdrop for living, colour should not be seen as the be-all and end-all. The space must remain receptive
R16: The poorer the architecture the more colour is needed. if the balance between light and dark is good, it's best to leave the experience to the resident – I abandon the abstract view here because the final word is (not by chance) 'practice'
R17: it depends on how much you can absorb at once
R18: this too
R19: so why does the demonstration in the Stedelijk Museum include a centralized composition? The painter appears to derive great pleasure from it, and so do I
R20: nonsense and impossible. Besides, an architect would be overstepping the mark if [he] tried to impose his will on a painting
R21: aha
R22: agreed R

Art and Habitat, 1955

This text has its origin in a declaration of principles for the journal *Art et Habitat*, which Constant and Stephen Gilbert intended to devote to the 'synthesis of the arts' (1953). The journal was never published, however, and Constant revised and developed the text in 1955. In it he examines the conditions necessary for a fundamental transformation of both aesthetic and functional concepts, which will lead to a true integration of the arts. Constant argues that contemporary architecture is directed at rational and functional production. He accuses the free arts of remaining apart from the public sphere. A genuine integration of the arts involves an intensive collaboration between the architect and the visual artist. As a result of this close contact, space, form and colour achieve an unbreakable unity because they are created in interaction with one another.

ART AND HABITAT

1. AESTHETICS AND FUNCTION

It seems that a closer relationship than mere influence between the plastic arts and architecture would be desirable, a relationship that would go so far as to eliminate the limits of each specific art, finally arriving at a true integration of the arts. However, coming closer like this cannot take place without a fundamental change in aesthetic as well as functional concepts.
Examining the conditions that might lead to such change is the point of this study.
This direct influence of function becomes particularly significant when one starts to consider the relationship between the plastic arts and modern architecture.
The architect, preoccupied by his technical problems, which leave him little time to study and elaborate the plastic expression of his work, seems to be able to do little better than let himself be inspired by the plastic products of free art.
On the other hand, the plastic artist, painter or sculptor, refuses to sacrifice any part of his freedom of expression by being tied to a functional problem of housing – insofar as he would have been able to surmount the technical difficulties of such an activity, which would require lengthy study.
The result of this situation, in spite of all attempts to bring them together, is a growing distance between aesthetic creation and functional production. Consequently, architecture will never reach its full potential in terms of plasticity, and the free arts are doomed to remain outside public life instead of coming to take their logical place in a cultural society.

2. WHAT MODERN ARCHITECTURE LACKS IS THE PLASTIC

The architect, having to deliver a structure, is becoming more rational and, will have neither the time nor the enthusiasm to acquire the plastic experience that plastic artists have. Yet, the spatial and plastic creation requires more than ever a profound study of aesthetic issues, without which no progress will be possible.
Architecture, if it hopes to rise to the level of art without being its derivative, will not be able to do so without the active participation of plastic artists. While the work of the architect must necessarily come closer to that of the engineer, given the complexity of new construction processes, the plastic artist, within the team of builders, will be able to take on responsibility for aesthetics.
This aesthetic part can never imply work of a decorative or ornamental nature, and we strongly oppose any tendency to decorate architecture with mural paintings or monumental sculptures, abstract or not.
Neoplasticist painting has put an end, once and for all, to decoration and has replaced it with basic aesthetic rules applicable to any plastic creation. Thanks to this, architecture has been able to free itself of the predominance of the facade and has purified its means, even down to the structure itself.
This is where we are today, and any tendency that aims for a synthesis of this architecture that has become more functional and the plastic arts that remain decorative would be a step backward.
By contrast, the identification of the aesthetic principles of architecture with the major arts has created the very condition for a coming together that goes so far as an absolute integration. Subject to the same rules of creation, the various plastic means, form, colour, construction, light, once strictly linked to a specific mode of expression, will now be able to be combined in order to complete one another within a new unity of space.
The painter interested in space, the sculptor in construction, the architect in colour – these are the first clear indications of the path towards a true integration of the arts.
Indeed, the place of painting is clearly where colour is called for, therefore in space, and thus its style will not be able to distance itself from architectural style and space without resulting in a dualism disastrous for both painting and architecture. Form and colour in the plastic and spatial arts will never be anything but one and the same, and the architect and the painter come together in the same quest to create space for this unity of means.*

3. THE HABITAT IS THE MOST COMPLETE WORK OF ART

Given that the aim of art is the aesthetic emotion evoked within man, one notes that this aim is most directly and to the greatest extent produced in the everyday human environment itself. The primary objective of creative man is the transformation of his habitat according to the evolution of his physical and psychological needs. When one includes among the latter his essential need for colour and form, one can easily imagine the task that can be achieved by the plastic arts in the creation of the human habitat.
CIAM has defined the habitat as the environment suited to satisfy material and emotional needs of man and to stimulate human spiritual development. This implies the direct contribution of art, from the very first steps taken toward building the habitat.
For too long, function has been seen as the satisfaction of material needs only. It seems the time has come to recognize psychological and emotional functions as at least as important as material functions, and inseparable from them. Only in this way will the habitat be able to become the perfect unity of all the aspects of life, which will be extended into the organizations of collective life. In this all plastic means will be able to flourish and reach their most complete achievement.
It is vital that the same aesthetic principles be maintained from the smallest housing unit to the whole of large cities, principles that must be dictated by function, in the new concept of the word. The opposition of the individual interior to the hostile and chaotic exterior is not conducive to rest and psychological equilibrium. And so urban designers have reached the point of studying the relationship between outside and inside, by relying on the thesis that the street and the common space are merely the extension of the family space inside dwellings. The most complete unity of both will be the logical

result of a functionalism that will have adopted the functions of spiritual life. One can therefore say that the style of the habitat is dictated by function, and by nothing else. Under these conditions, the need for beauty that, at present, remains unsatisfied for the majority of humanity will enter into a direct and permanent relationship with plastic creation. Art will cease to be the expression of the individual and, while serving a general purpose, will derive from it its universal character. Function, in the broader sense, will become essential to every plastic problem faced by the artist, to the point that a common style, social in the true sense of the word, will result. The birth of such a style is all the more pressing given the need to build entire cities within a short time frame, a need born of the acute housing crisis precipitated by the war and the urbanization of agrarian countries. In such circumstances, urbanization must take into account the multiplication of standardized forms, and the urban design aesthetics that must be developed will only have to be based on the rhythm of an unlimited number.

* The final paragraph of this section was added by hand to the typescript.

The typed manuscript 'Art et Habitat' (1955) is in the Constant archive at the Netherlands Institute for Art History (RKD).

From Collaboration to Absolute Unity Among the Plastic Arts, 1955

This text appeared in *Forum* in 1955 and is part of a widespread debate during the 1950s. In this debate about collaboration among architects and visual artists, Constant stakes his position by calling for a radical amalgamation of architecture and other plastic arts. Erasing the boundaries between the various disciplines must lead to an 'absolute unity of construction, function, form and colour'. This new art, according to Constant, will appeal to the imagination of the masses because it has an immediate function in everyday life.

From Collaboration to Absolute Unity Among the Plastic Arts

It is useless to talk about collaboration so long as we do not know what demands both architecture and the visual arts must satisfy in order for this collaboration to be of any benefit. In the visual arts domain alone, there already exist such unbridgeable differences that it is impossible to speak of visual art in terms of a single clear concept.
The idea of an amalgamation with architecture arose at a time when visual art had reached a point in its development when the concept of space acquired a more direct significance than it had enjoyed so far.
Even so, there would probably have been no question of collaboration had it not been for De Stijl. De Stijl resisted individualism in the visual arts and architecture. An individualism was held responsible for the decline of plastic form in favour of nebulous 'expression'. This *Geltungsdrang* of the individual, this expressionism, had and still has to be stopped. In architecture, direct support was found in the economic advantages of mechanization and, partly because of this, costly expressionism was short-lived there. But in the visual arts, which provided the initial impetus, the situation is rather different.
At the present moment, expressionism – abstract and figurative – is on the offensive and, paradoxically enough, is finding some support among architects: waverers who are not philosopher enough to refrain from this unnatural marriage with a visual arts phenomenon that stifles architecture under the pretext of collaboration. Today's architecture is apparently still too impoverished in terms of plasticity not to be afflicted by an inferiority complex when faced with this turbulent stream of artistic hocus-pocus. Salvation must come from the visual arts but not, of course, in this form.
There is only one possible route to collaboration between architecture and other plastic arts and it is signalled by mechanization, the same mechanization that previously protected architecture from dilution.
Mechanization is in command and the logical and indelible consequence of this is a new universal and objective aesthetic. The demands of this new aesthetic come down to absolute unity of construction, function, form and colour. This unity of all space-creating factors erases the boundaries between the various plastic arts, so rendering further discussion of 'collaboration' superfluous. Architecture has no need of plastic enrichment in the form of decoration or emblems, no need to deck itself in borrowed feathers. No, what architecture draws from the visual arts is a new lifeblood that rejuvenates and strengthens it and allows it to derive *artistic* benefit from mechanization.
Architecture must become a new plastic art whose universal nature enables it to take the place of painting and sculpture which are drowning in subjectivism. A new visual art sufficient in itself and incorporating everything that can objectively be realized in form, colour and three-dimensional effects. An art that with a single leap is able to bridge the gap with society because it has, by its very nature, an immediate function that allows it to be assimilated into daily life. An art that appeals to the imagination of the masses because it is able to exploit fully the inexhaustible potential of technology and is thus able to deliver what the modern human being expects of art: harmony, imagination and a sense of space.
Where does the architect, the visual artist, stand in all this?
The time when the community was a sounding board for the individual is over and done with, and the roles are now reversed.
The community sets the individual a task: to form the *habitat,* a fundamental form that encompasses all facets of life.
As soon as one rejects the merging of individual artworks in a more or less impaired whole, and starts to reflect on this new and gigantic task, the distinctive features of personality and profession lose their relevance.
The architect must become an artist and the artist a constructor in order to tackle the

creative work as part of a team, together with specialized technicians and engineers. But a lot will have to happen before individual artists are able to work as part of a group without imagining themselves lost. To reach this point is the first and necessary step, and perhaps this is also the point of all this talk about collaboration.

'Van samenwerking naar absolute eenheid van de plastische kunsten', *Forum. Maandblad voor architectuur en gebonden kunsten*, vol. 10, no. 6, July-August 1955, 207.

Technicism, 1956

This hitherto unpublished text by Constant dates from 1956. Thematically it has a strong affinity with 'Tomorrow Life Will Reside in Poetry' from the same year. Constant outlines the gap between the visual arts on the one hand and architecture and design on the other. He goes on to argue for a new kind of aesthetics – 'technicism'. This must be founded on the structural qualities of the materials that technological progress has produced and which were already being used extensively in industry and construction at the time. He proclaims technicism to be a new principle of plastic creation in the visual arts.

Technicism

The plastic consciousness of creators has barely been influenced, in spite of the progress technology has made in the past century, having determined our way of life and having given it a new face. This unfortunate situation has today produced a dualism that keeps us from progressing further in the realm of the plastic arts without coming into conflict with technological realities. While maintaining a pre-technological tradition that no longer has any value, today's plastic artists seek to present continuous forms, and consequently to camouflage construction.

The ugliness of (the designs of) cars, planes, houses testifies to the fear of adopting the technical requirements of the machine and its method of production.

Today's artists are in the process of returning to the level of the artisan, by placing greater and greater emphasis on individual signature rather than using the aesthetic potential inherent in machine labour.

Faced with this situation we realize that the plastic arts are on the verge of being surpassed by the science of the engineer, who, deprived of any tradition, bases his work on technical requirements from the start. We wish to follow this example, which can already pride itself on many remarkable works, and we declare technicism the new principle of plastic creation in the visual arts.

This implies that we adopt the realities of technological production as key to an aesthetic of form and that we reject any tendency to camouflage the appearance of construction by sacrificing what is most valid about current plastic arts consciousness for a renewal of form.

'Le Technicisme', unpublished text, July 1956, included in manuscript in the Constant archive at the Netherlands Institute for Art History (RKD).

Tomorrow Life Will Reside in Poetry, 1956

Former Cobra comrade Asger Jorn had invited Constant, as a specialist in architecture, to take part in the First World Congress of Free Artists, organized by the Mouvement International pour un Bauhaus Imaginiste contre un Bauhaus Imaginaire (M.I.B.I.) in Alba in September 1956. The text, intended as a lecture, demonstrates Constant's faith in progress during the second half of the 1950s. He emphasizes the artistic evocative power of construction and calls for an art as complete as possible, 'at once lyrical in its means and social in its very nature'.

Tomorrow Life Will Reside in Poetry

We are living in a time of fundamental transformation taking place in different domains, which cannot fail to have profound implications for contemporary architecture. We issue this appeal to architects in order to warn them against losing themselves between the science of the engineer and the imagination of the sculptor, thus making themselves superfluous, but instead to openly confront the new conditions.

Nowadays
AESTHETICS, following a period of experimentation in every possible direction, have managed to break with a limitation of form as a result of the transition from figuration to abstraction in the recent past. Experimental painting reacted against tendencies such as neoplasticism, and has succeeded in once again liberating human imagination from any taboo, and thus paving the way for a new phase in visual art.

TECHNICAL SCIENCE, during the same post-war period, has evolved to such an extent that construction methods present practically no obstacle at all to the realization of extremely free forms, in an unprecedented conception of space.
One need only refer to prestressed concrete and prestressing steel, thin sheets of reinforced concrete, stainless steel and their welds, in order to get an idea of the means currently available to a free and audacious imagination.
On the other hand, the rectangle – for a long time the basis of any architectural aesthetics – is gradually losing its significance, for various reasons. Which is why it is important in large-scale structures that the wind resistance of rounded forms is very favourable in comparison to flat planes. Moreover, concrete performs better in sheet-form than in the girder-form, as is usually used today. In order to develop fully, , technical science seems only to be awaiting an aesthetics with a broad vision.

CONTEMPORARY ARCHITECTURE, thanks to the happy coincidence of these two circumstances of an aesthetic and technical nature, has no further reason to remain confined in the severe doctrine of functionalism imposed, on the one hand, by an outdated imagination and on the other, by still primitive technique, forcing the architect to use methods of decoration to arrive at the aesthetic quality he was after. For a long time, architectural aesthetics, due to the lack of construction possibilities providing sufficient space for a free plastic expression, have only been able to scratch the surface of the form, without being able to get inside the skeleton, so that architecture remained a second-rate decorative art.
For the first time in history, architecture will be able to become a true art of construction. An art whose plastic expression will depend on the organization and assembly of its elements, the same way as a painter organizes his brushstrokes.
It is only logical that at the outset, this tendency, already present in functionalism, manifested itself through the use of materials such as steel and glass, which allow for a clear and obvious construction.
Today, however, architecture has at its disposal unlimited construction techniques, turning it into an art absolutely independent of pictorial or sculptural decoration, without falling into the sterility of functionalism. It will be able to make use of techniques as an artistic material with the same value as sound, colour, speech have for other arts. It will be able to integrate into its aesthetics the manipulation of volumes and voids by the sculptor and the spatial colorism of the painter, in order to create the most complete of arts, at once lyrical in its means and social in its very nature. It is in poetry that life will find a home.

'Demain la poésie logera la vie', dated Paris, 19 August 1956, written as a lecture to be given at the First World Congress of Free Artists, organized by Mouvement Internationale pour un Bauhaus Imaginiste contre un Bauhaus Imaginaire (M.I.B.I.), held in Alba (Italy), 2-8 September 1956.

The typed manuscript is in the Constant archive at the Netherlands Institute for Art History (RKD).

The Path to Unitary Urbanism, 1960

This is the only known text by Constant that establishes a link to the Situationist International. Constant was associated with this movement from 1958 to 1960.
The texts Constant wrote during the course of the 1950s are an outstanding record of how his conception of space developed into a notion of a complete urban habitat – 'unitary urbanism' – and the social space necessary for the development of human creativity. Constant derived the concept of unitary urbanism from Gilles Ivain, the pseudonym of Ivan Chtcheglov, who wrote about it in 1953. When Gil Wolman, a member of the Lettrist International, gave a lecture on this in Alba in 1956, Constant was instantly inspired. Constant elaborated on unitary urbanism with Guy Debord, the leader of the Situationist International, and later used it in his *New Babylon* project.

The Path to Unitary Urbanism

This does not involve art.
Our life is a game.
The world around us is constantly changing. Should we remain on the fringes and leave it to scientists, engineers and politicians to decide the shape of our lives and the world in which we live?
There are marvellous inventions with countless opportunities and yet what is lacking is playfulness; we cannot do anything with it.
All attempts this century to initiate cultural reforms have failed because they took the individual as their starting point. The collective imagination was not taken into account, was misunderstood or despised. Nevertheless, the face of our world today is largely the result of collective effort.
The artist thinks he has to choose between the lack of imagination of industrial functionalism and the impotent scream from the ivory tower. He has become a regressive element in society's development; the transformations around him occur without his participation.
Our new cities and districts are as boring as the life that unfolds inside them.
For the time being the problem can only be tackled at the macro level: completely new situations are required.
Automation will increasingly give rise to economic conditions and will, while restricting the workload of each individual, favour the playful side of our life. The cultural contribution of each of us will thus flourish. Culture does not exclusively mean the artificial; a strict distinction between the different fields of human action is not possible when we talk of culture. Boundaries dividing science, technology and art will be blurred constantly. The changes in the world align to the big picture, to a unitary attitude. The need for eternity as championed by mystic Absolutism has lost its appeal. We can identify the dynamic principle of our existence in the transient, in the mutable. There is no beauty independent of the influences of everyday life. The individual artwork relies on wrong premises; it no longer suffices. Our artistic activity should be related to life in its entirety.
To live is to act creatively.
We must incessantly recreate the world around us and change it, if only by our way of living.
Our goal is dynamic variation and thus the intensification of the social atmosphere.
There is no longer an audience, and it will no longer be possible to have a passive stance on art. Art arises solely from a general creative activity, once this ceases, art, too, disappears. Neither art nor the work of art, but the activity that produces the work of art, should be permanent. That is the essence of our life and its realization.
We will live at an ever greater distance from nature. I have proposed a new city that corresponds to a new and different way of life. It will consist of a single, huge building whose countless rooms merge. In here, light, colour, shape, sound and movement will combine to create a constantly changing interplay with the environment, moving from one room to the other and in harmony with the creative game of life that we seek to establish.
We leave behind us the old idea of a *Gesamtkunst* that simply called for the aggregation of the existing arts. A *Gesamtkunstwerk* today is bound up with life in its entirety.
In such a Unitary society, urban life in the current meaning of the term will no longer exist. Urbanism will mean life forms that are complex in all respects.
Solutions to practical issues such as traffic, housing, etc. can of course only be found in this collective spirit, compliant with the outlook of society in its entirety as described above.
What should such a city look like? Which artistic requirements can we expect to see? We should not limit ourselves to some aesthetic principles. We can only intuit what technological developments the future may bring.
Needless to say, the future will forgo the primitive spatial projects of current architecture. Space travel and chemistry will decisively influence the engineers of tomorrow.
Our present experimental work merely seeks to create sketchy outlines. We play with the opportunities and the fantastic proposals.
Our game creates the science fiction of social life and urban planning.
Realizing this will perhaps be the task of future generations.

'Der Weg zum unitären Urbanismus', published in: *Constant, Konstruktionen und Modelle*, exh. cat. Essen (Galerie van de Loo) 1960.

Text recorded for the Stedelijk Museum, Amsterdam, 1958

In this text Constant reflects on the current state of the arts. He defines his own position in the art world and looks back at 15 years of artistic practice, in which the pursuit of 'the experimental spirit' that emerged after the Second World War has led him through a variety of domains. This experimental period is marked by a certain destructivism. He defines his activity as a 'ceaseless building and tearing down again'. A quest for an unknown, an eternally variable form. This text is a demonstration of Constant's characteristic dialectic thinking.

Text recorded for the Stedelijk Museum, Amsterdam

The abstract artist, insofar as this obsolete word can still be applied to the creative person of today, finds himself in a dark place at the moment. For the public, the artistic playboy with his movie-star airs counterfeits the image of the cultural revolution he is participating in, while the emerging industrial culture uses his work without acknowledging him or recognizing him in it. So he has gone on with his experimental labours, for nearly half a century, in the silence of his workshop, and although his influence is significant, his activity is barely known, if at all.
Yet even as the last bit players of the individualistic era jostle each other in front of the footlights, the sets have been replaced. A new culture has already been born while the old still shows signs of life. In this chaotic phase it is difficult to distinguish what is usable and positive from what is negative and should be rejected. Surrealism, and Neoplasticism, Expressionism and Constructivism are on opposite sides and contest each other for a share in the new culture.
It was amid this uncertainty and doubt, after the war, that experimental thinking emerged, which allows the experience rather than the preconceived notion to decide, which places the experience of the act above the correctness of the idea. I have been guided in my work by this thinking for the last 15 years, and it has led me through the most varied domains.
Experimental thinking is a reaction to the premature proclamation of a style in the previous phase, and is irreconcilable with any style or art, especially with the contradiction that is occasionally labelled experimental art in Holland.
Those who believe in a new emerging culture, and many signs indicate this, I think, would do better not to speak about art at all. That word has already been too compromised, and what's more, art is something that more often presumes the absence of culture, since in an actual culture it is not unusual for a creative act to be called artificial.
This experimental period is characterized by a certain destructivism. Form can only be created in a process in which it is also demolished. Where one builds, one tears down. Every creation is simultaneously a destruction. Anything that comes about balances on the edge of the void. My milieu is the seamy side of art, where creation and destruction come in contact.
My truth consists of two parts, and they are each other's opposites. My activity is a ceaseless building and tearing down again. My ideal is not the absolute harmonious form, but the form in motion, the form that is born and dies, the relative form.
What I seek is *la forme informe*, the undetermined form, the form with a thousand faces, the form without beginning and without end, without boundaries, the formless, the invisible form, the eternally repeatable, eternally variable, yet never familiar form.

Unpublished typescript, originally written in Dutch for audio-documentation in the Stedelijk Museum Amsterdam, spring 1958. Held in typed manuscript form in the Constant archive at the Netherlands Institute for Art History (RKD) and as an audio file at the Stedelijk Museum Amsterdam.

Our Ambition Lies in Ambiance, c. 1958-1959

This is the most far-reaching of Constant's writings about urban design as an art form. There is a crisis at hand in urbanism: old neighbourhoods have become commercialized districts, new-build developments are sterile and offer no opportunities for creative, playful human beings. As a response to this crisis, Constant proposes a 'unitary urbanism', an adventurous architecture, constructed for the purpose of fun. In the cities of the future, 'distruptive' factors like nature, climate, light and sound will be regulated in inventive ways in the form of a covered city. This will achieve the maximum social space for *homo ludens* to move about in. The text shows the influence of developments in space travel and increased technological possibilities.

Our Ambition Lies in Ambiance

The crisis of urbanism is getting worse. There is an obvious discrepancy between the new modes of living we are aiming for, established modes of living, and the construction of old and new housing estates (note: the result is a dead and sterile ambiance in our surroundings). In the old districts, streets have degenerated into *autostrade*, leisure venues have been commercialized and deformed by tourism (note: social cohesion is declining). New large housing estates present only two themes, which predominate: automobile traffic and comfort in the home. They are but the meagre expression of bourgeois happiness, and they lack any possibility of fun and play.

The response to the need to rapidly build entire cities is to construct cemeteries of reinforced concrete in which great masses of the populace are condemned to be bored to death. What use are the amazing engineering inventions the world now has at its disposal, if the conditions for taking advantage of them are lacking, if they don't offer opportunities for recreation, if imagination fails?
We are looking for adventure. No longer finding it on earth, some are going to look for it on the moon. We, however, still aim for change here on earth.
We endeavour to create new and unprecedented situations. We intend to break the laws that impede the development of effective activities within culture. We are at the

dawn of a new era, and we are attempting, already, to sketch the picture of a happier life and of a unitary urbanism, made to be enjoyed.
Our domain is therefore the urban network, the natural expression of a collective creativity, able to conceive the creative forces that are liberated by the decline of the traditional arts, of a culture based on individualism.
We believe that the existing arts will not be able to play any role in the creation of the new and joyous ambiance in which we wish to live.
We are in the process of creating new techniques; we are examining the possibilities presented by existing cities; we build models and plans for future cities.
We are aware that we need to make use of every technological invention and we know that future constructions will need to be flexible enough to respond to a dynamic conception of life, which will create our environment in direct relation to constantly changing modes of behaviour.

Our concept of urbanism is therefore primarily social. We oppose the concept of a green city, where widely spaced and isolated skyscrapers necessarily limit direct contact between people and their daily interaction. In order for a close relationship between the environment and behaviour to come about, agglomeration is indispensable. Those who think that the speed of our travels and the possibility of telecommunication are going to dissolve the shared life in agglomerations are not well versed in the true needs of man.

Against the idea of a green city we propose the image of the covered city, where differentiation among buildings makes way for a seamless construction, which will contain groupings of dwellings as well as public spaces (allowing for changes in purpose according to the needs of the moment).
Far from a return to nature, from the idea of living in a park, like the secluded aristocrats of yesteryear, we foresee within such immense constructions the opportunity to conquer nature and to make the climate, the noise, the lighting of these agglomerations submit to our will. Do we mean by this a new functionalism that will emphasize idealized utilitarian living even more? Although such a functionalism is the basis of any social and cultural upheaval, one must not forget that once functions are established, what follows is play. Architecture long ago became a game with space and ambiance.

The future cities we envision offer an unprecedented variability of sensations in this area, and unexpected games will be made possible by the inventive use of material conditions, such as air conditioning, sound and lighting. Urban designers are already studying the possibilities of harmonizing the cacophony that reigns in current cities; it will not be long before this becomes a new creative field, as in many others that will emerge. The voyages into outer space that are being predicted may well influence this development, since the bases that will be established on other planets will immediately pose the problem of enclosed cities, which will serve as a model for our study of future urbanism. In the meantime, the reduction in labour required for production brought about by advancing automation will generate a lot of free time.

Our idea of a covered city is based on the concept of a collective habitat with maximum social space, in contrast to the idea of a green city where social space is limited to a minimum.
The future city must be conceived as a permanent structure, or else an extended system of different structures on structures, within which are rooms for housing, entertainment, etc., as well as rooms designed for production and distribution, keeping the ground free for traffic and public gatherings. The use of ultra-light and insulating materials, as are being experimented with today, will allow the construction of light structures, free-standing areas and supporting structures. In this way we will be able to construct a city in several layers: basement, ground floor, storeys, terraces, in sizes varying from that of a current neighbourhood to that of a metropolis. The terraces form an open-air area extending across the entire surface of the city and provide accommodation for playing sports, taking a stroll, platforms for airports, cultivating greenery; they will be accessible everywhere by stairs and lifts. The various storeys will be divided into adjoining and communicating spaces, with artificial heating and air conditioning in order to offer the option of creating an infinite variety of ambiances, allowing inhabitants a constant *dérive* as well as an increase in fortuitous encounters.

An in-depth study of the means for creating ambiances and of their psychological impact is one of the tasks currently undertaken by the Situationists.
Studies concerning the technical production of constructed structures and of their aesthetics are the specific task of plastic artists and of engineers.
The input of the latter, especially, is urgently needed in order to make progress in the preliminary work in which we are engaged.
Because there is a risk that the project we have just outlined in broad strokes, might be considered as the dream of fantasists, we insist upon the fact that it is achievable in technical terms, that it is desirable in human terms, that it is essential in social terms.
The growing dissatisfaction that dominates humanity will reach a point at which we will be forced to implement the projects for which we have the means and which will be able to contribute to bringing about a richer and more accomplished life.

Therefore, in such a city, the built surface area will be 100% and the open area 200% (ground floor and terrace), whereas in traditional cities these figures are something like 80% and 20%, and in a green city this ratio may, at best, be inverted.

'Notre ambition est dans l'ambiance', unpublished text, c. 1958-1959.
The typed manuscript is in the Constant archive at the Netherlands Institute for Art History (RKD).

The Dialectic of the Experiment, 1965

Constant looks back at the preceding period in his career and the radical transformation that took place in his artistic development during the 1950s. He declares that while he can visualize 'unitary urbanism', the present state of society is fundamentally different from the societal situation essential to the realization of such a revolutionary programme. Consequently, unitary urbanism remains limited to isolated experiments and a programme. The creative process is shifting from reality to a conception of reality. This 1965 text foreshadows the end of the *New Babylon* project, a process that began in 1969 and became definitive in 1974 with a retrospective exhibition at the Gemeentemuseum Den Haag in The Hague.

The Dialectic of the Experiment

'The problematic period in the history of modern art is over and is being followed by an experimental period. That is to say that from the experience (*expérience*) gained in this state of unfettered freedom will flow the rules by which the new creativity will abide. From what emerges, as yet more or less unconsciously, according to the dialectic method, a new consciousness will be shaped.'

This paragraph concludes the manifesto I wrote in 1948 for the Experimental Group in Holland, published in the group's organ, *Reflex*. Now, after 17 years, I feel it necessary to quote these words, not only because they form the best foundation for an explanation of my work since then, but also to put an end to the misunderstandings and misinterpretations that hinder a correct understanding of the cultural situation since the Second World War. When you see art historians and critics insisting on continuing to write about 'experimental art' as though it concerned a particular pictorial style, when you see a uniform mess of 'action-painting' displayed as 'experimental art' in some museums, you realize the extent of the confusion that surrounds this subject. It is high time to establish clearly that **there is no experimental art**, that an experimental art never existed.
The artists who designated themselves with the label 'experimentals' (*experimentelen*) shortly after the war did this in order to express their scepticism about any style, indeed about any stylistic innovation. The experiment is therefore primarily the negation of style. Adventure replaces logical development, ruthless abandon replaces complacent certainty, and the acceptance of the chaotic space replaces the clear line.
Two essential hallmarks of the experiment are named in the quoted text. First of all, the experiment is empirical; it derives its value from experience, the *expérience*. Elsewhere the same manifesto states: 'The act of bringing forth is more important than what is brought forth.' The experience the artist gains through the creative act enables him to elevate himself to a higher level and therefore achieve a clearer picture of himself and of the situation in which he finds himself. The relative nature of the 'work of art' itself, the result of the creative act, is entirely in line with the anti-stylistic character of the experiment. Those who have sought to circumscribe the experiment in order to exploit it – the cultural officials, the dealers and collectors, as well as certain artists – have an interest in denying the relative value of the result. Therefore, it cannot be emphasized enough how from the very beginning, any style, any aesthetic norm was rejected. In so doing the artists went an entirely new way, a way they continue, by and large, to follow to this day. The artist has refused to be bound any longer to any norm whatsoever; on the contrary, he is reacting violently to aesthetics, in whatever form they take; he focuses all his activity on the annihilation of aesthetic principles.
Indeed, the experimental phase that began after the war is essentially distinct from the episode of the pre-war 'avant-garde'. This distinction is clearly expressed in the second hallmark of the experiment: **the experiment is a dialectical method**. This means that the experiment unfolds along opposite lines and not in a straight line as is the case in the evolution of a style.
The pre-war avant-garde groups still based their activity on aesthetic theses that, though they may have differed from one another, were individually determinant for each group. The new element that the experimental artists brought within the culture was precisely the reassessment of aesthetics as relative through the introduction of the aesthetic antithesis.
The antithesis is of course dependent on the thesis that precedes it: the experiment is always based on that which is excluded by the prevailing aesthetics. The moment the existing culture takes possession of the experimental antithesis – the moment the antithesis is thus declared a norm, and people begin to speak of an official, recognized 'experimental art' – a new antithesis is needed in order to continue the experiment. As soon as the anti-style becomes a style, the anti-anti-style emerges, the negation of the negation. When you consider that in the period of cultural restoration following the war – the period in which the experimental group was formed – it was precisely the abstract-geometric tendencies – with De Stijl at the forefront – that set the tone, you can understand why expressionist tendencies predominated among the experimentals of the time. These are not to be seen as typical of experimental activity in any way. They are simply connected to an image of the time and in fact they now seem dated. Equally understandable, however, should be why at the moment when 'experimental art' became accepted as a new aesthetics, the experimental artists shifted the emphasis to anti-expressionist methods.
The experiment can only exist as an antithesis of the prevailing aesthetics; the experiment is therefore essentially dialectical. The moment the creative process is entirely liberated from aesthetic preoccupations, the experiment loses its point and its existence. As this moment approaches, the rhythm of successive antitheses accelerates. We can observe this easily through a cursory study of art history over the last ten years. We see that every 'new' artistic tendency is more short-lived than the last, that artists ultimately feel compelled – just like fashion designers – to bring out something new every year.
The experimental period in modern art – the last episode of the individualistic culture – therefore shows not a picture of an evolution, as in previous periods, but an accelerated series of antitheses. This series cannot be prolonged indefinitely, of course; this is an accelerated process that must sooner or later reach a climax. This climax will be reached when every style is deemed relative in advance and therefore no norm can be valid any longer, when the antitheses succeed one another at such a rapid pace that it becomes impossible for epigones to take possession of the results of the experiment. At that moment – which has already been reached – thesis and antithesis converge and become synthesis.

The experimental period is followed by a period of synthesis
During this period the individualistic culture will lose its foundation – 'genius' will have become inconceivable – individual arts will dissolve, 'teamwork' and other forms of collaboration will come to define the image of the culture.
The experimental period is an interim phase between waning individualism and emerging collectivism. So it is not just a period of destruction, of the annihilation of existing traditional art forms. Parallel to this annihilation, other, collective forms of creativity will be shaped, in conjunction with the forming of a new creative consciousness, which was already touched upon in the quoted excerpt above. We can see such forms – however insufficient and incomplete as yet – in the 'happening', the 'ambiance', the 'event'. At the same time, the increasing devaluation of aesthetic norms opens the way to all sorts of combinations of styles and artistic media into constructs of a more complex nature. A first step in this direction was the *détournements*, playing with products from previous stylistic periods ripped from their context, as practised by the Situationists. The most radical (hypothetical) synthesis of creative means is the conception of 'unitary urbanism'. This concept promoted by the Situationists was first clearly defined in an 'Amsterdam Declaration' composed by G.E. Debord and myself and published in issue no. 2 of the journal *Internationale Situationiste* in 1958. In it, unitary urbanism is described as 'the complex, ongoing activity that consciously recreates man's environment according to the most advanced conceptions in every domain'. This declaration also clearly states that the end of individual art forms is a fact and that the creative people have a new realm of activities to explore. This is no longer about 'art' or 'aesthetics' but about a much broader concept: the transformation of social life as a whole. The proposed Situationist programme envisions experimenting with the human environment as a whole as well as with new patterns of behaviour compatible with the new decors for life. The ultimate objective of these experiments is the creation of a unitary urbanism. Naturally, such a revolutionary programme can only be implemented in a social situation that is essentially different from the situation in which we live. As long as this new situation has not emerged, unitary urbanism remains limited to a programme and to isolated experiments. This programme, however, forms the only possible basis for the continued development of creative activity. The creative process shifts from reality to a conception of reality. Existing reality has gradually fallen so far behind the reality that is potentially possible that creativity within the context of current social reality is impossible. The culture is becoming 'utopian'; artists are focusing more and more on projects that for the moment are labelled 'unfeasible'. Today's creativity can only manifest itself as an invasion of, a conflict with, the reality of today. The *New Babylon* plan that concludes this exhibition should be seen from this perspective.

'De dialektiek van het experiment', published in *Constant*, exh. cat. The Hague (Haags Gemeentemuseum) 1 October - 21 November 1965, no page numbers.

Lenders to the Exhibition

The Cobra Museum of Modern Art would like to thank the following museums, institutions and individuals who have supported the exhibition 'Constant. Space+Colour' as lender

ArtBrokerDesign
Centraal Museum Utrecht
Collection the Bijenkorf
Collection Titus Darley and Monique Laenen
Collection G. Dreesmann, Amsterdam
Collection Gemeentemuseum Den Haag, The Hague
Collection de Heus-Zomer
Collection Meeuwissen, Oirschot
Collection Heirs of Carel Visser
Cultural Heritage Agency of the Netherlands, Amersfoort
Defares Collection
EYE Film Institute Netherlands
Fondation Constant, Utrecht
Galerie van de Loo, Munich
Groninger Museum
Kröller-Müller Museum, Otterlo
Kuhne Design, Alkmaar
Kunstmuseum Bochum
Lehmbruck Museum, Duisburg
Musée de Grenoble
Museu d'Art Contemporani de Barcelona
ProWinko Switzerland
Rabo Art Collection
Royal Museums of Fine Arts of Belgium, Brussels
Rijksmuseum, Amsterdam
Rijksmuseum Twenthe, Enschede
Sainsbury Collection, University of East Anglia
Stedelijk Museum Amsterdam
Stedelijk Museum Schiedam
Teylers Museum, Haarlem

And all those lenders who wish to remain anonymous.

Variations rythmiques, 1953 (p. 71)

Variations rythmiques was the first work by Constant to be acquired for the Netherlands State Art Collection, in 1958. The Dutch state would continue to acquire works by Constant on a regular basis until the late 1980s. Constant made *Variations rythmiques* in 1953; it can be linked to *Compositie met 158 blokjes* (Composition with 158 Blocks), which is now in the possession of the Gemeentemuseum Den Haag. *Variations rythmiques* consists of a hardboard surface glued and nailed onto a wooden cross. Brown paper tape was glued along the outer edges. A layer of black paint was applied with a broad brush directly onto the smooth side of the hardboard, and paper squares were then glued onto the paint. The whole was covered in a transparent layer of wax. In the black-and-white photograph taken after the acquisition of the artwork in 1958, a pattern of spots is clearly visible. These light, matte spots must therefore have appeared soon after its completion, between 1953 and 1958. Research into the spot pattern in 2006 failed to yield definitive answers as to how these spots developed or any possible treatment. Because of its condition, *Variations rythmiques* has scarcely been exhibited in the intervening years. The fact that Constant was aware of the piece's condition and in fact sold it as it was might suggest that the artist did not find the matte spots troublesome. The Netherlands Cultural Heritage Agency has therefore chosen to respect the piece's present condition and not treat the spot pattern. Any loose paper tape along the edges as well as any curling edges of the paper squares have been carefully glued down, however. Gaps in the paper tape were reconstructed using new brown tape, and where necessary small spots and scratches in the surface were retouched. *Variations rythmiques* will be shown for the first time in many years as part of the exhibition 'Constant. Space+Colour'.

Zeph Benders
Simone Vermaat
Art Collections Department
Cultural Heritage Agency of the Netherlands

Acknowledgments

This publication is published to coincide with the exhibition 'Constant. Space+Colour. From Cobra to New Babylon'
Cobra Museum of Modern Art, Amstelveen
28 May - 25 September 2016

The exhibition 'Constant – New Babylon. To Us, Liberty' was hosted concurrently by our Dutch partner the Gemeentemuseum Den Haag, The Hague.

Exhibition

Artistic Director
Katja Weitering
Executive Director
Els Ottenhof
Guest Curator
Ludo van Halem
Co-curator
Trudy Nieuwenhuys-van der Horst
Curator/Project Leader Cobra Museum
Hilde de Bruijn
in collaboration with Dawn Trompet
Fondation Constant
Trudy Nieuwenhuys-van der Horst
Kim van der Horst
Exhibition Design
Ben van Berkel / UNStudio
in collaboration with Machteld Kors, Philipp Meisse, Christian Veddeler and Lex Reitsma
Public Relations and Communication
Eric Wie
Business Development and Partnerships
Bert Mennings

The exhibition was made possible through the support of
Municipality of Amstelveen
BankGiro Loterij
Business Club Cobra Museum
Mondriaan Fonds
Prowinko Nederland BV
Forbo Flooring

With thanks to
Graham Birtwistle, Roby Boes, Charlotte Caspers, Jurjen Creman, Titus Darley, Tess van Eyck Wickham, Fondation Constant, Tom Haartsen, Het Nieuwe Instituut, Rotterdam, Marcel Hummelink, Els Kerremans, André Koch, Friso Kramer, Nederlandse Organisatie voor Wetenschappelijk Onderzoek (NWO), Michiel van Nieuwland (Forbo Atelier, Bunnik), Mariël Polman (Cultural Heritage Agency of the Netherlands), RKD Netherlands Institute for Art History, Rijksmuseum, Amsterdam, Hans van der Schaaf, Joop Schot (ArtBrokerDesign), Stichting auteursrechten G.Th. Rietveld, Laura Stamps (Gemeentemuseum Den Haag), Hans Vrijmoed (Sikkens Museum, Sassenheim)

cobra museum
voor moderne kunst
museum of modern art
amstelveen

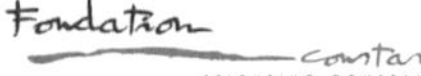

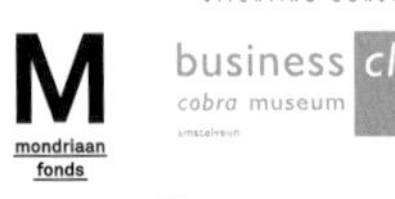

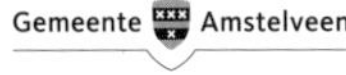

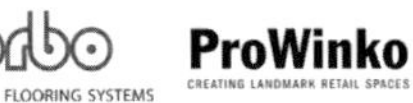

Publication

Editors
Ludo van Halem, Trudy Nieuwenhuys-van der Horst
Authors
Constant, Ludo van Halem, Trudy Nieuwenhuys-van der Horst, Laura Stamps, Katja Weitering
Translation
Dutch-English: Pierre Bouvier (Foreword, Constant. Space+Colour, Space and Colour in Practice, It Is Our Desire That Makes Revolution, Art and Habitat, Text recorded for the Stedelijk Museum, The Dialectic of the Experiment) Robyn Dalziel (Spatial Colorism, From Collaboration to Absolute Unity Among the Plastic Arts) French-English: Pierre Bouvier (Technism, Tomorrow Life will Reside in Poetry, Our Ambition Lies in Ambiance) German-English: Jeremy Gains (The Path to Unitary Urbanism)
Copy Editing
Robyn Dalziel, Trudy Nieuwenhuys-van der Horst
Image Editing
Hilde de Bruijn, Trudy Nieuwenhuys-van der Horst
Design and Lithography
Lex Reitsma
Printer and Binder
Wilco Art Books, Amersfoort
Paper
Profibulk, 150 gr.
Munken Polar, 400 gr.
Publisher
Cobra Museum of Modern Art, Amstelveen/
Barbera van Kooij, nai010 publishers, Rotterdam

Photography
All photographs of works by Constant are © Constant / Fondation Constant c/o Pictoright Amsterdam 2016
All photographs of works by Constant:
Tom Haartsen, unless stated otherwise
Unknown photographer, collection Fondation Constant (p.4, 17, 27, 63, 117, 134, 135, 136, 140, 142 (fig. 10, 11), 144)
Archivio Gallizio, Turin (p.14, 142 (fig.9))
Amsterdam Museum (p.18)
Henni van Beek (p.38-41, 110-115)
Courtesy of Christie's (p. 77)
Courtesy of Angeline Pike (p.16)
Peter Cox (p.107)
A. Frequin, The Hague (p.10)
Aart Klein, Nederlands Fotomuseum, Rotterdam (p.2)
R. Klein Gotink (p.80)
Tom Haartsen (p. 23b, 139, 141, 143b)
Kunstmuseum Bochum (p. 30, 95)
Jean-Luc Lacroix © Adagp, Paris (p.15r)
Jan Landau/Lighthouse, Deurne (p.11m)
Lehmbruck Museum, Duisburg (p.132)
Het Nieuwe Instituut, Rotterdam (p.25m)
Trudy Nieuwenhuys-van der Horst (p.138o)
Wendy Oakes (p.71)
Rijksmuseum, Amsterdam (p.37)
Rijksmuseum Twenthe, Enschede (p.97)
RKD Netherlands Institute for Art History, The Hague (p.25b)
Royal Museums of Fine Arts of Belgium, Brussels / photo J. Geleyns (p.13)
Sainsbury Centre for Visual Arts, University of East Anglia (p.12)
Joop Schot (p.86t)
Spectrum Design (p.86b)
Stedelijk Museum Amsterdam (p.11r, 15l)
John Stoel (p.42)
Bram Wisman (p.126)
Jan Versnel, Maria Austria Instituut, Amsterdam (p.22r, 23t, 24)
Martijn Zegel (p.34)
Cover
Front: *Vegetatie* (p.56) and *Constructie met gekleurde vlakken* (p.69). Back: Constant in his studio (p.117) and *een ruimte in kleur* (p.139, photo: Tom Haartsen)

About the Authors

Ludo van Halem is an art historian, specializing in twentieth-century Dutch art and design. He is currently curator of twentieth-century art at the Rijksmuseum in Amsterdam. He researched Constant's oeuvre as part of the 'Dutch Culture in a European Context' research programme of the Netherlands Organization for Scientific Research (1993-1995) and the Stedelijk Museum Schiedam's Cobra Collection Conservation Project, with the support of the European Commission's Raphaël Programme (1997-2002). He has published a number of writings on Constant.

Trudy van der Horst (Trudy Nieuwenhuys-van der Horst) is an art historian, author and exhibition consultant. She was married to Constant. In 2011, she established the Fondation Constant and is engaged in ongoing research for Constant's Catalogue Raisonné. The work, inventoried and investigated as to authenticity, is being made accessible on the foundation's extensive website, maintained by Kim van der Horst. She has contributed writings to various catalogues and books since 2000, including *Constant. Grafiek* (2004) and the monograph *Constant. De late periode* (2008).

Laura Stamps is an art historian and modern art curator at the Gemeentemuseum Den Haag. Stamps has a specific interest in the period spanning the 1950s to the 1970s. She curated, among others, the major exhibition 'Constant New Babylon' at the Gemeentemuseum Den Haag (2016), which was previously on show at the Museo Nacional Centro de Arte Reina Sofía in Madrid (2015-2016).

www.cobramuseum.nl
www.stichtingconstant.nl

nai010 publishers is an internationally orientated publisher specialized in developing, producing and distributing books on architecture, visual arts and related disciplines. www.nai010.com

nai010 books are available internationally at selected bookstores and from the following distribution partners:
North, Central and South America - Artbook | D.A.P., New York, USA, dap@dapinc.com
Rest of the world - Idea Books, Amsterdam, the Netherlands, idea@ideabooks.nl
For general questions, please contact nai010 publishers directly at sales@nai010.com or visit our website www.nai010.com for further information.

ISBN 978-94-6208-301-1
Printed and bound in the Netherlands